EAST ASIA, THE WEST AND
INTERNATIONAL SECURITY

International Institute for Strategic Studies conference papers published by Archon Books in association with the IISS

Christoph Bertram (*editor*):
    PROSPECTS OF SOVIET POWER IN THE 1980s
    THE FUTURE OF STRATEGIC DETERRENCE
    THIRD-WORLD CONFLICT AND INTERNATIONAL SECURITY

Robert O'Neill (*editor*):
    THE CONDUCT OF EAST–WEST RELATIONS IN THE 1980s
    NEW TECHNOLOGY AND WESTERN SECURITY POLICY
    DOCTRINE, THE ALLIANCE AND ARMS CONTROL
    EAST ASIA, THE WEST AND INTERNATIONAL SECURITY

EAST ASIA, THE WEST AND INTERNATIONAL SECURITY

Edited by

ROBERT O'NEILL

Archon Books
1987

© International Institute for Strategic Studies 1987

All rights reserved. No reproduction, copy or transmission of this publication may be made without written permission.

First published in 1987 in the United Kingdom by
THE MACMILLAN PRESS LTD
Houndmills, Basingstoke, Hampshire RG21 2XS
and London
and in the United States by
ARCHON BOOKS, an imprint of
The Shoe String Press, Inc.
925 Sherman Avenue
Hamden, CT 06514

Printed and bound in Great Britain

Library of Congress Cataloging-in-Publication Data
East Asia, the West, and international security.
   (International Institute for Strategic Studies
conference papers)
   Papers presented to the 28th IISS Annual Conference held in Kyoto, Japan, September 8–11, 1986.
   Includes bibliographies.
   1. East Asia—National security—Congresses.
2. Security, International—Congresses. I. O'Neill, Robert John. II. Conference of the IISS (28th:1986: Kyoto, Japan) III. Series.
DS518.1.E33   1987   355'.03305   87-19377
ISBN 0-208-02198-1

Contents

Preface viii

East Asia, the Pacific and the West: Strategic Trends and Implications: Part I 1
Dr Henry Kissinger
US Secretary of State 1973–7; Professor of International Relations, Georgetown University, Washington

East Asia, the Pacific and the West: Strategic Trends and Implications: Part II 9
Professor Masataka Kosaka
Professor of International Politics, Kyoto University

Convergence and Divergence in East Asian and Western Security Interests: Part I 19
Professor Seizaburo Sato
Professor of Political Science, University of Tokyo

Convergence and Divergence in East Asian and Western Security Interests: Part II 29
Brigadier Kenneth Hunt
IISS

US Military Power in the Pacific: Problems and Prospects: Part I 41
Dr Geoffrey Kemp
Senior Associate, Carnegie Endowment for International Peace, Washington

US Military Power in the Pacific: Problems and Prospects: Part II 50
Dr Coral Bell
Senior Research Fellow, Department of International Relations, Australian National University, Canberra

Korea to Kampuchea: The Changing Nature of Warfare in East Asia 1950–86: Part I 60
Brigadier-General Edwin Simmons
US Marine Corps Historical Center, Washington

Korea to Kampuchea: The Changing Nature of Warfare in East Asia 1950–86: Part II 73
Professor Zhang Jingyi
The Institute of North American Studies, Chinese Academy of Social Sciences, Beijing

The Soviet Union, East Asia and the West: The Kremlin's Calculus of Opportunities and Risks   83
Harry Gelman
Senior Staff Member, The Rand Corporation, Santa Monica, CA

Soviet Influence in East Asia and the Pacific in the Coming Decade: Part I   107
Professor Robert A. Scalapino
Director, Institute of East Asian Studies, University of California, Berkeley, CA

Soviet Influence in East Asia and the Pacific in the Coming Decade: Part II   123
Paul Dibb
Director, Joint Intelligence Organization, Department of Defence, Canberra; formerly Ministerial Consultant to Minister of Defence 1985–6

China's Relations with East Asia and the Pacific Region: Part I   136
Dr Jonathan Pollack
Senior Staff Member, The Rand Corporation, Santa Monica, CA

China's Relations with East Asia and the Pacific Region: Part II: 155
Yao Wenbin
Research Fellow, Institute for International Strategic Studies, Beijing

The Security of North-East Asia: Part I   161
Professor Masashi Nishihara
Professor of International Relations, National Defense Academy, Yokosuka

The Security of North-East Asia: Part II   172
Professor Kim Chongwhi
Director, Research Institute on National Security Affairs, National Defense College, Seoul

Trade, Technology and Security: Implications for East Asia and the West: Part I   181
Dr Hanns Maull
Lecturer, Department of Politics, University of Munich

Trade, Technology and Security: Implications for East Asia and the West: Part II   197
Professor Takashi Inoguchi
Institute of Oriental Culture, University of Tokyo

Prospects for Security Co-operation between East Asia and the West   214
Ambassador Yoshio Okawara

Adviser, Ministry of Foreign Affairs; Executive Adviser, KEIDANREN (Japan Federation of Economic Organizations), Tokyo

Comment on Ambassador Okawara's Speech   221
Professor Joseph S. Nye Jr.

Director of the Center for Science and International Affairs, Harvard University, Cambridge, MA

Comment on Ambassador Okawara's Speech   224
Dr Johan Jørgen Holst

Minister of Defence, Oslo

Concluding Remarks   227
Dr Robert O'Neill

Director, IISS, London

Index   237

Preface

The Papers contained in this volume were first presented to the 28th IISS Annual Conference held in Kyoto, Japan, from 8th to 11th September 1986. They have been amended and revised as appropriate in the light of discussion and comment at the Conference.

The four plenary sessions were concerned with strategic trends and implications; Soviet policies in Asia; convergence and divergence in East Asian and Western security interests; and prospects for security co-operation between East Asia and the West. There were six committees which discussed: US military power in the Pacific; Soviet influence in East Asia and the Pacific; China's relations with the region; the security of North-east Asia; the changing nature of warfare in East Asia; and the implications for East Asia and the West of trade, technology and security. The Conference was concluded with a review of the issues debated.

East Asia, the Pacific and the West: Strategic Trends and Implications: Part I

DR HENRY KISSINGER

Last week I had the privilege of meeting Prime Minister Nakasone, and he asked me what I would speak about at Kyoto. I gave him the topic. I said it was quite striking how different the perceptions of security were in Asia from Europe. And he said something to me which he authorized me to quote. He said, 'The difference is the difference between European paintings and Japanese paintings. In Europe, in a European painting every detail is filled in and very little is left to the imagination. In a Japanese painting it is the empty spaces which give meaning to the design and they leave a great deal therefore to the perception of the observer'. I think he states the issue very well. The Western debate on security has more or less run into the sand. The positions of the chief protagonists are quite fixed. The basic theories were developed thirty years ago on both strategy and arms control. They tend to be repeated almost by rote, in my view to the extraordinary detriment of creative policy. Asian security has been less systematically addressed, at least in these circles.

Therefore let me begin by pointing out some of the key differences. In Europe there is a clear dividing line between opposing blocs. There is a definition of a potential aggressor. There is some debate about the intentions of the aggressor, but no debate about where the threat will come from should it take place. There is a large American troop presence. There is an integrated command, an attempt at a co-ordinated diplomacy, an attempt to achieve common East–West negotiating positions, and lately an increasing necessity on the part of almost all governments to present to their publics the progress towards an amelioration of tensions. This progress is put forward domestically almost entirely in terms of arms-control issues, which in turn are largely defined in terms of theories which were developed thirty years ago and now seem to be quite unaffected by technological changes.

In Asia few of these conditions exist. Of course many countries, if not most, realize that the Soviet Union is, or can be, a threat to their security. But it is also true that many countries perceive other threats to their security. Some are afraid of China. Some are afraid of Japan. Some are afraid of Vietnam. In the circles in which I move nobody admits to being afraid of the United States. But at any rate security considerations are more complex than in Europe. There are some

1

alliances – the United States has an alliance with Japan – but not a common strategy, nor an integrated command, nor any of the machinery characteristic of Europe. The alliance with Japan has some of the aspects of a unilateral military guarantee, though it is buttressed by an extremely intensive system of political consultation. The United States has bases in the Philippines, but no common military policy; and indeed the Philippines in many respects, and especially now, is more like a member of the Non-Aligned grouping than a member of an alliance and it does not necessarily share the perception of the dangers against which the use of our bases may be directed. China, the country that has culturally and spiritually been the most important factor in this region, is historically independent and self-reliant. South-east Asia exhibits the combination of motivations which I have already sketched. Only Korea has the aspect with which we are familiar from Europe, of a clear dividing line protected by a present military force that is part of an alliance system in an integrated command. But the other side of that dividing line in Korea is a great deal more complex than it is in Europe, with a contest between China and the Soviet Union about major influence.

So the security situation in Asia, though it exhibits growing Soviet power, nevertheless has quite different aspects: no common threat; no attempt to combine forces; no common diplomacy. On the other hand, there is an almost total reliance on conventional defence, however that defence is constituted; and a much greater reliance than in Europe on the protection that may be inherent in and a mobilization of resources *after* the security problem appears. It is striking that when the SS-20 missiles appeared in Europe the Europeans asked for an equivalent weapon to be stationed in Europe as an answer. They later changed their mind, or at least retreated to the edge of doing so. But in Asia no such demand ever emerged. It would be interesting to reflect whose perception of security was more nearly correct: the Europeans of the late 1970s or the Asians of this whole period. And it is equally interesting that the response in the arms-control field is quite the opposite: some Europeans seem quite willing to have us have a zero-zero position in Europe and leave aside the SS-20 deployment in Asia, as if these missiles were not mobile. As I understand it, that appears to be a position *not* acceptable to Japan.

The result of all this seems to be that the security and foreign policies of the Asian nations, different though they are, are more similar to what European foreign policy used to be in the nineteenth century, more dependent on a perception of the balance of power, a greater emphasis than has been the case in Western Europe on the political and geopolitical element, less insistence on American reassurance – perhaps because Asians believe that nations either understand their interests or they do not and that legal formulae do not add to their understanding very much.

Of course this emphasis on the empty spaces, as Prime Minister Nakasone says, runs a risk of faulty analysis both by the defender as well as by the aggressor. The United States got itself involved in two wars in this area, and so did the Communist countries; indeed they were the only wars America has fought in the post-war period, to its enormous frustration, because it was very hard to reconcile the American perception of security with Asian realities. For the United States, the situation that I have described presents enormous intellectual problems. Asian nations assume that the national interest of states is more or less permanently fixed; therefore the basic interest of countries will be protected in part by the geopolitical understanding of other members of the system (which is one reason, incidentally, why the Soviet peace offensives seems to me to have less impact in Asia than in Europe). But for the United States this is a complicated issue. It raises the question: What will the United States not permit to happen – no matter how it happens, how apparently legally, by what apparent methods? In fact, what many Americans at least subconsciously believe, and much of our literature implies, is that whether the United States defends a country or a region depends on our legal obligation. And the impression is often created that the first thing a President does in case of aggression is to consult his lawyers to see what the legal documents say. In 1936, when the Germans reoccupied the Rhineland, President Roosevelt asked the Secretary of State for an analysis of the implications of that action; he received a two-page memorandum that went into all the treaties that were broken by that act and then explained that the United States was not party to any of them. Therefore, it maintained, no American action of any kind could be considered. The fact that that action changed the strategic realities of Europe, made the smaller East European states defenceless and destroyed the French system of alliances was not even mentioned in the memorandum. It was not rejected that we had an interest in what had transpired; that interest or even that reality was not even mentioned!

That is one of our problems today. At the precise moment that Soviet bases are spreading through South-east Asia, the United States abjures any military position in South-east Asia. Our position is that we will help economically, humanly, all the nice things that one enjoys doing when one has the financial resources. But the difficult work of defence has to be left to somebody else. It is an interesting attitude, which is heavily affected by the lessons of Vietnam, and by the old slogan that America must never be involved on the mainland of Asia, a slogan that to any analyst of strategy is almost inexplicable. Why must we not be involved on the mainland of Asia, if the mainland of Asia is important? It is difficult to argue that the centre of world attention is moving from the Atlantic to the Pacific and at the same time to maintain that America has no direct relationship to Asian security.

I am not arguing that the United States should have a military establishment on the mainland of Asia: the conditions that I have described make that unlikely, and indeed undesirable. I am trying to discuss the intellectual approach to the issue. Let me illustrate this with the problem with China.

I confess that I have a considerable sentimental interest in China. But I also understand that China did not survive for three thousand years by being itself sentimental. In my experience, the most sophisticated analysis of the requirements of survival is made in Beijing, based on a strong sense of cultural identity and a long experience in dealing with foreigners. In this sense China moved towards the United States not because it was unfulfilled by the absence of American visitors but because of the Brezhnev Doctrine, the clashes on its Soviet border and the need to establish a balance of power for its own protection. At the same time it is inconceivable that China will make a military alliance with any other country. And it is undesirable for the United States or any other nation to think in those terms in relation to China. One can co-operate with China by establishing through extensive dialogue a sense of common purposes in specific areas. It is absurd to think that China is a card that can be used for Western, Japanese or anybody else's purposes. One has to rely on a sophisticated understanding of those areas where objectives coincide or where objectives coincide even when methods differ. But it will never be expressed in a legal obligation which an American legal adviser can show a President in a crisis. China is also obviously preoccupied with a complex process of modernization. It is the only Communist country in which the role of the Communist party in economic management has been systematically reduced; a process which runs counter not only to classic Stalinist economics but also to Chinese historical tradition because, if it succeeds, it will make China like every other nation in its economic structure and make it part of a world economy, something it has always resisted. And therefore in China, foreign policy will be used by some of those opposed to these tendencies as part of a structural and ideological debate, a fact which the West must clearly understand. But our assignment here is not domestic politics; I want to return to the foreign policy issue.

In the wake of the Vladivostok speech by Mr Gorbachev the question is often asked whether a rapprochement between China and the Soviet Union is likely. In my view relations will improve. Equally, I believe that the Chinese did not survive for all these millennia by being prone to sentimental illusion. They know that the Sino-Soviet frontier will not get any shorter, no matter how much relations improve and that troops being withdrawn can always return. From this I conclude that precisely because there is no alliance and can be no alliance between the non-Communist countries and China, China will take great care not to diminish the interest of those countries in its own positions. Therefore, while I expect relations with the Soviet

Union to improve, and while we should show no nervousness and, what is more important, feel no nervousness, I believe that the Chinese, short of a tremendous upheaval in Beijing, will not permit the West's interest in a cohesive China to be eroded by a loss of overall confidence. No responsible Chinese leader, as no responsible Japanese or American leader, can ever exclude that relations with the Soviet Union may worsen again, no matter what detente achieves at any period. Above all in my view, the critical period in Sino-Soviet relations will come when the Chinese modernization is on the verge of succeeding. When it becomes apparent – if it becomes apparent – that in a foreseeable future the Chinese economy will be on the road of the South Korean or even the Japanese economy of the 1960s. At that point the Soviet Union will have to decide whether to prevent this, not wishing to have powerful countries on all its borders, or whether it will recoil before the magnitude of the task. I do not care to speculate what decision the Soviet leaders will make at that point, only that it cannot be deduced from their current statements.

Prudent Chinese leaders surely will not exclude the possibility of pressures and this will affect their actions in the immediate future. For those of us here interested in strategic issues the question arises, in the admittedly improbable event of a Soviet attack on China, what is going to be the Western response? When I say improbable we have to ask ourselves: Is it more or less improbable than an attack on Europe? On the face of it, it seems to me no less improbable; it may be both are improbable and I am not predicting either; I am talking about contingencies. What should the Western response be? Those who analyse legal commitments and those who affirm that we must not be involved on the mainland of Asia: we have no obligation; even the hint of any obligation is rejected in China. Those of us, like myself, who contribute to American unity by infuriating both liberals and conservatives have a different view. I believe the weight of China is as great as the weight of Europe. Therefore a military attack on China has, in terms of the geopolitical equilibrium, the same impact as an attack on Europe. In my view it has to be resisted by the United States. How? By what methods? In what manner? I have no answer. Nobody has studied the issue as far as I know. It is a forbidden subject. I can understand that governments do not want to study it; but I do not understand why the Institute cannot reflect on the problem. This doesn't mean the Chinese want such a study, but it would be interesting to know what one would do should such a contingency arise. I cannot but believe that were China to be attacked, and I repeat, we don't want this to happen, for the democratic world to do nothing would be an abdication of historic consequence. But what the nature of the response might be is not now something for me to say.

In the meantime, I think it is important to have a dialogue with China about the nature of international trends so that at least there is clarity about objectives and methods. It cannot be done only by economics. And it is not always eased by the excessively pragmatic approach of the West and the centre-of-the-universe approach of China that will not admit that it needs to discuss its own requirements.

Let me say a few words about US- or Western-Japanese relations. I have already said that Japan is an ally, legally like NATO allies, in practice different in the military field. Like China, I think its leaders have a greater confidence in our ability to assess the international environment than European leaders possess. They do not ask us for a formula of reassurance. The dialogue is complicated by many factors, including the fact that culturally dialogue may not be the Japanese method of communication, which seems to me to be geared more towards achieving a consensus than debating different points of view. And it is for each new wave of American policy-makers to learn that when a Japanese official says 'yes' it means he has understood you or that he will report what you have said – not that he will carry out what you have proposed. It is again an interesting fact that the greatest threat to our relationship is not, as in Europe, debate about East–West issues and foreign-policy issues, but rather how to construct a world economy in which American and Japanese interests can be made congruent. I must say the present method of dialogue – in which the weakest American industries, those that are suffering most from Japanese inroads, are asking the strongest Japanese industries to accept self-restraint – cannot solve the problem. Some kind of global solution must be found to put an end to these industry-by-industry battles which are endless and in time may undermine the possibility of consensus.

I want to address, however, one issue that is relevant to the International Institute for Strategic Studies and that is the issue of Japanese rearmament. Some Americans periodically press Japan to devote greater resources to defence as a means to equalize the relative competitiveness of the United States and Japan. I strongly disagree with that view. Japanese defence policy must be guided by Japanese national security. It has nothing to do with trade policy with the United States. A nation that next to China has the longest history of independence will not and should not consider its defence policy for American purposes. And it would be naïve to believe that if and when Japan builds up its own forces it will do so to carry out designs established in the Pentagon. For that reason, while the United States cannot prevent, or should not seek to prevent, Japanese rearmament, it should not press it as an American initiative. It should be left to Japanese decisions in which the Japanese will no doubt consider the impact of excessive levels of Japanese arms on historical memories and on the political relationships with neighbours that are important for long-term security. And this again seems an area in which the implications of a rearmament carried out for Japanese motives might well be a subject for scholarly attention.

If this were a speech at a European meeting of the Institute, I would have to begin with the Soviet Union. And I now end with it, because, strangely enough, to most of the considerations put forward here, the endless European debate whether Mr Gorbachev is a new man or not is not so relevant. I do not believe that in Asia people think foreign-policy problems will be ended by the conversion of Soviet leaders. I read the Vladivostok speech as all of you did. I notice that Mr Gorbachev protested his peaceful intentions in the South Pacific. But if one studies how the Soviet forces got to the borders of Afghanistan, as they advanced through the various principalities conquered in the nineteenth century the language was almost exactly the same as the Gorbachev speech. They had, they said, no intention of annexing countries. They sent fulsome messages, usually to London, explaining that the occupation was for the purpose of protecting some limited commercial interest. I am not saying that the analogy is perfect; analogies never are. The Vladivostok speech is illuminating because the first half of it, which deals with economic problems, shows in what economic difficulty the Soviet Union finds itself. The second half which applies various Soviet schemes to Asia has its interesting aspects, above all because it evoked so little of a public response from Asian leaders. Thus, we may find the ironical situation that the real audience for the Vladivostok speech is not Asia but Europe, where such schemes as unity conferences find a greater resonance. And the question in Asia is the same as in Europe: it is yes, the Soviet Union wants a period of relaxation; yes, the West and Asia should encourage a period of relaxation. But are we able to express this desire in a concrete policy that in fact improves the situation, or are we merely going to make agreements, simply because they have been declared attainable by the Soviet leadership and thereby sweep every other problem under the rug? In Asia the Chinese have said as far as they are concerned there are three conditions. That is at least a picture of the world that admits criteria. Nobody else has yet come up with something equivalent. I would suggest, having just come from Korea, that one relatively easy place to begin a process would be there, by adopting the German solution: a recognition of both Korean states; their admission to the United Nations; the recognition of South Korea by Communist countries; and North Korea by democratic countries. That is not a final solution, but it would remove one of the great sources of potential danger, especially in the next two years when South Korea will undergo serious domestic problems, coupled with the temptation for North Korea of causing the Olympic Games to fail. One must remember all the super-powers have fought wars in Korea at one time or another: the Soviet Union, the United States, China and Japan, and it would be reckless to believe that one can encourage crises in Korea which are easily contained.

All concerned with the Soviet Union should keep in mind that Gorbachev may not know what he wants, that he may face the reality that to change his economic structure he needs the military and the secret police, who are in competition with the outside world and understand some of it; but to change the foreign-policy direction he may need the Communist Party. And to walk through this minefield, Gorbachev may simply temporize and offer precisely those schemes that make no real difference. At the risk of being accused of excessively hard-line tendencies, I find the arms-control programmes of the West nearly incomprehensible. Their chief attribute is that they are attainable. I do not understand the difference between 6,000 warheads and 11,000 warheads in any sense other than a psychological one. I find it difficult to believe that we can at one and the same time argue that a great opportunity for arms control exists and then not be able to express that opportunity in a concrete programme which alleviates at least some dangers. I will leave open the possibility that Vladivostok may be an aspect of an opportunity; and it may be an aspect of a strategy of expansionism, depending on which proves easier to accomplish. Our task is to steer it in a direction that contributes to security. In Asia it may be easier to think clearly about this than in Europe and America, where we all run to familiar barricades espousing familiar slogans.

It would not be the first time in history that the impetus for fundamental change came from conditions in Asia and from people who have had to think about the problems of their independence and their security for thousands of years.

East Asia, the Pacific and the West: Strategic Trends and Implications: Part II

PROFESSOR MASATAKA KOSAKA

The decade after the fall of Saigon has turned out to be a peaceful and happy one for most East Asian countries, contrary to many forecasts. There was good reason for pessimism. The failure of the United States in Vietnam did great damage to US capability and will. American prestige was tarnished and the trust of Asian countries in the United States as their guarantor was severely diminished. The Soviet Union, on the other hand, was vigorously building up its forces in the Far East. The days of American dominance in the Pacific seemed to be coming to an end.

Such thinking was not entirely wrong. The United States did not recover its former strength. Its efforts at revitalization brought only limited success at considerable cost. The human rights diplomacy of the Carter Administration perplexed and annoyed allies and friends of the United States more than it reassured them. The efforts of President Reagan to reassert US leadership somehow lacked credibility, as they ran counter to the political and economic changes in the world.

Yet, despite these changes, international relations in East Asia and the Pacific remained peaceful, and even became more stable. Such an unexpected development was brought about because on the whole both the United States and Asian countries adapted themselves successfully to the altered circumstances, and a new structure of regional relations came into being. This Paper first looks at the reasons for this unanticipated peace and stability, which in turn throw light on the new structure. But any success is bound to be short-lived, and the problems that are emerging are then discussed.

Stability in East Asia
The basic reason for the stability was that the United States was militarily still far stronger in the region than the Soviet Union, though the overwhelming superiority of the 1950s and 1960s had been lost. The growth of Soviet military capability since 1965 has been real, and since 1978 striking. Ground force strength in the Far East, Siberia and Central Asia has risen in the last twenty years from about 17–20 divisions and 170,000 men to more than 50 divisions and nearly half a million men; new and more capable aircraft, such as MiG-27 *Flogger* and Su-24 *Fencer*, have been introduced; the Soviet

Pacific Fleet has grown from about 50 vessels to 90, with remarkable qualitative improvements, such as a *Kiev*-class carrier and guided-missile anti-submarine warfare (ASW) cruisers; it has also acquired significant amphibious capability. Recently the Soviet Union has deployed long-range strike forces in the form of SS-20 intermediate range ballistic missiles (IRBM) and the *Backfire* bomber.

It is not unreasonable to say that the change is from a negligible Soviet force in the region to one which is a possible challenger to that of the United States. Soviet air and naval power now control Siberia and the adjacent seas, though beyond the Kurile Islands they are overshadowed by US forces. However, it should be noted that the increase of Soviet strength on land has been due largely to Sino-Soviet tensions. As yet, the United States has not been really challenged in its sphere of influence – the Pacific Ocean.

The second important reason was a fundamental change in Sino-US relations. What can be called a diplomatic revolution took place when Henry Kissinger met Chou En-lai in Beijing in 1971 and the two countries began to move towards normalization of their relationship. It would be incorrect to say that the United States and China concluded a kind of alliance opposing Soviet 'social imperialism', but the US did cease to treat China as one of its main adversaries in league with the Soviet Union, and instead rather as a sovereign and great power with its own interests and own concerns about the growth of Soviet power. China, in the face of the confrontation with the Soviet Union and the growing Soviet threat, obviously wanted to improve its diplomatic position by normalizing its relations with the United States. The two countries clearly have a common interest in restraining the Soviet Union and this largely overshadowed the 'Taiwan problem'. This they agreed to shelve through the tactful formula of 'one China but not now'. As China was no longer an antagonist, the burden for the United States in the region became much lighter. These developments also relieved Asian countries, including Japan, of their psychological insecurities. To them, the Soviet threat was largely a military one, to counter which US forces were both necessary and effective. But China represented a more complex influence in East Asia, and to try to cope with it by military means alone did not seem either necessary or likely to be effective.

Perhaps more important was the dramatic change in the orientation of China, which jettisoned its revolutionary foreign policy and radical domestic policy and instead adopted modernization as its main objective. This change may have started before 1971, but was clearly encouraged by the Sino-US normalization and had taken clear shape by 1978. To achieve its new goal, China now needed a calm and quiet international environment and the foreign capital and technology which could be best provided by the West. China seemed prepared to enter the regional family of nations instead of trying to upset it.

The third factor was a new US policy of asking its Asian allies to help themselves, which led to a more balanced relationship. This policy was set out in President Nixon's first Foreign Policy Report to Congress on 18 February 1970:

> Its central thesis is that the United States will participate in the defense and development of allies and friends, but that America cannot – and will not – conceive all the plans, design all the programs, execute all the decisions and undertake all the defense of the free nations of the world. We will help where it makes a real difference and is considered in our interest.

President Nixon actually reduced the number of US troops in South Korea and asked Japan to play a more positive role in its own security and foreign policy. Such a move could easily be excessive – a pendulum can swing too far. In fact, President Carter committed himself during his election campaign to withdraw all US ground forces from South Korea, which, if it had been carried through, would have changed the structure of international relations in the region drastically and probably unfavourably. But South Korea and Japan made persistent efforts quietly to change the mind of President Carter and, with the help of a number of Americans, succeeded. The end result of the process was that one US division remains in South Korea and South Korea is stepping up its own security efforts.

Japan has been quite slow to do more in the field of security, but its achievements have not been negligible. More importantly, Japan and the United States have constructed a better working relationship since 1975, through better consultation on security policy, the conduct of joint exercises and the exchange of intelligence information, demonstrated on the occasion of the shooting down of the Korean Air Lines aircraft KAL 007 in September 1983. One scholar described this development as 're-Americanization', which followed a rather brief period of 'de-Americanization' in the early years of the 1970s. The Japanese were resentful of the abrupt change of US policy towards China in 1971 and of the fact that the change was made without any warning to Tokyo, but by 1975 they had re-discovered the importance of the US-Japan relationship.

The reasons for 're-Americanization' were multiple and are not dealt with at length here. It must be pointed out, however, that the change of US policy towards China was basically sound. After all, to have a normal relationship with China is better than being troubled by a hostile China. Moreover, 're-Americanization' had a solid foundation in that the image of the United States in the eyes of the average Japanese began to recover in 1976. Until about 1965, the United States had been the most popular country for Japanese, but friendly feelings began to decrease when the US intervened in Vietnam, reaching a low point in 1975.

Such changes in South Korea and Japan may not appear important if measured only by how much the security burden, previously shouldered by the US, was now shared by the two countries. The direct costs to the United States of ensuring the security of South Korea and Japan have never been very large – one division in South Korea does not cost all that much. And the United States does not deploy troops and aircraft in Japan, or send naval vessels there, exclusively to help Japan: it needs to control the North-west Pacific to ensure its own status as a super-power. To put it differently, the additional costs of helping Japan to maintain its own security are not high. Accepting Soviet control of the North-west Pacific would result in a completely different structure of international politics in the region. Similarly, the United States could not accept Soviet control over Western Europe. But the important difference is that the additional cost of containing the Soviet Union in Europe is high, whereas in the Pacific it is low.

Nevertheless, the defence effort being made by South Korea, even if not large enough to permit withdrawal of the US troops is important in political terms. Of course, the US troop presence is evidence of the American commitment to the security of South Korea. This is a powerful deterrent to the North and exercises a degree of control over the military activities of the South. Though US forces in Korea are not large in number, the US Air Force squadrons there provide significant backing to South Korean aircraft. Japan's willingness to increase security co-operation with the United States is also significant, even if its defence efforts are not large enough to provide for the security of Japan by themselves. It can be argued that Japan's support function is more important than its combat capability.

The fourth reason has been the impressive economic performance of many countries in Asia, South Korea being only the most spectacular example. Paradoxically, the US intervention in Vietnam, though a historic blunder in itself, can be considered to have played an important role in buying time for many Asian countries. In 1965, the situation in East Asia was bleak. Indonesia seemed on the verge of a Communist take-over; most of the South-east Asian countries were weak and lacked confidence; South Korea appeared in need of a permanent flow of aid from the United States to maintain its government in power. By 1975 economic growth had begun, under such authoritarian governments as that of President Park in South Korea, Prime Minister Lee Kuan Yew in Singapore and President Suharto in Indonesia. These countries managed to weather the two oil crises and the stagnation of the world economy that followed. The region has been developing more rapidly than anywhere else in the past fifteen years.

This economic development has been a fundamental cause of the region's relative domestic stability and has also made many countries militarily stronger, as witness South Korea. Without its economic miracle, South Korea could hardly have built up its military forces, and without this the US commitment to South Korea might have been difficult to maintain. With some 5–6% of GDP devoted to defence, South Korea has been able roughly to match the military forces of North Korea, which is believed to spend as much as 20% of its GDP on defence.

The impact on the global balance
The above trend, if it continues, will have a very strong impact on the global balance. First, the economic development of the past fifteen years will ensure that the region will have global importance. Of course, Europe and the Atlantic world have greater weight than the Asian-Pacific region and will continue to have in the foreseeable future, but the tempo of change in the Asian-Pacific region is faster. An area which changes more rapidly tends to influence things more. Although Europe constitutes the central and therefore important element of the East–West balance it is, by the same token, in something of a stalemate and seems unlikely to change much. In contrast, the Asian-Pacific region is changing rapidly and if an Asian-Pacific Community, in which the United States and Japan would occupy a central place, should come into being in some form or other, it could become a major creative force in the world.

Second, China is in transition and developments within the region are likely to exert considerable influence on its future. China should not be seen as merely providing a counterweight to Soviet military power, or treated simply as a 'China card'. What is important about China is its basic orientation: the way it develops will, inevitably, influence the shape of a future world. If China continues on its present course of modernization, maintaining close contact with the West, it is likely to provide a new model for growth – neither a Soviet-style command economy nor a free-enterprise system. This itself constitutes a fundamental challenge to the Soviet Union, especially as the Soviet economy has begun to show marked signs of stagnation. Moreover, if China is successful, the Soviet Union will have to deal with a more powerful neighbour. Taken together, China and an Asian-Pacific region of vigorous economic growth will contribute to the containment of the Soviet Union.

It has often been pointed out that the Soviet Union has been largely unsuccessful in its diplomacy in the Asian-Pacific region. An important reason for this has been its heavy-handed approach, but this cannot be the sole explanation for its failure: the Soviet Union has been heavy-handed outside Asia and yet has had some diplomatic successes. It is more likely that it has failed diplomatically in Asia because it has been working from a position of weakness. It is militarily in an inferior position and cannot offer much in the field of economics. A growing Asian-Pacific region will not be much attracted by the Soviet Union.

Looming clouds

Every path has its pitfalls, and there are signs of difficulty ahead. Tensions are rising between China and Japan. There are growing anti-government movements in South Korea, and there is continuing political instability in the Philippines. Moreover, the cumulative psychological effect of the Soviet military build-up must not be neglected.

As to the military equation, it can be argued that this has not changed much and will not change further. The United States will maintain control of the Pacific: though the Soviet Union may cause problems and be a nuisance, it will not present a military challenge that cannot be met. In addition to its geographical handicaps, there are clear limits to Soviet power. Its economy has not been performing well, for fundamental structural reasons. Though it may be simplistic to believe that the Soviet Union will curb its military spending in order to revitalize its economy, the relatively poor economic performance is bound to affect military strength in the longer run.

Moreover, Soviet military advances have been achieved only at considerable cost. Although the Vietnamese invasion of Kampuchea and the subsequent Chinese punitive attack forced Vietnam into dependence on the Soviet Union and to concede a Soviet military foothold in Indochina, Soviet policy in South-east Asia will be handicapped as long as the present situation continues in Kampuchea. Soviet support of Vietnam is an important reason for the cool relations between the Soviet Union and China, and the Soviet invasion of Afghanistan weakened its diplomatic position in the Muslim countries of the Middle East – and more widely.

Yet there may be danger in an excessive or unwise reaction by the US to Soviet military power. The confidence of East Asian countries can and must be strengthened by adequate US guarantees, but it is important to note that very few countries in the region feel a direct and imminent Soviet threat. A general guarantee by the United States will continue therefore to satisfy most of them. Indeed, some already regard the US reaction as excessive, contributing to a superpower arms race in the region. Recent troubles between the United States and New Zealand seem to confirm such feelings.

The Soviet deployment of modern intermediate-range nuclear forces (INF) in East Asia must be met with great caution. The arrival of the missiles did not seem to alarm East Asian and Pacific countries as much as it did the West Europeans perhaps because the geographical situations are different. Nuclear weapons must always be treated largely as political and psychological weapons, in East Asia and the Pacific in particular. The United States can match Soviet INF deployments with sea-borne systems, which are clearly more acceptable to its allies and friends. Furthermore, confidence in the United States can be strengthened by appropriate efforts towards arms control.

The most important cause of trouble and disturbances in the coming decade seems likely to lie in the process of economic modernization itself. This modernization has greatly benefited the region in the past decade, but is a very difficult process to direct and control and can so easily end in failure. Even if it goes smoothly on the whole, it can still require difficult societal adjustment, the failure of which may result in serious political crisis. Such internal developments can obviously influence the orientation of countries and lead to significant geopolitical changes.

The first of such concerns relates to China. China embarked on modernization in earnest in 1978, as collective farms were abandoned and a market mechanism introduced with spectacular results – a very rapid increase of agricultural output. Emboldened by this success, Deng Xiaoping went on to introduce reforms in industry in 1984 and to step up measures to open the Chinese economy to the outside world. Then several problems came to the surface: gaps between rich and poor appeared; there were undesirable traits, such as materialism and indiscipline; some Chinese seemed to have been charmed by foreign products and the hedonistic culture of the West to an undesirable degree; and the open trade with the outside world resulted in a sharp deterioration of China's trade balance, which went into serious deficit in 1985.

As a consequence, internal opposition to Deng began to appear in mid-1985, from those who are either convinced or moderate believers in a centrally-planned economy, or from bureaucrats and party members with vested interests. An important target and symbol of the opposition has been Japan, which invaded China militarily fifty years ago and is now only too eager to sell its products to China and make large profits through a kind of economic invasion. The official visit of Prime Minister Nakasone to the Yasukuni Shrine (where not only war dead but some war criminals are commemorated) and a textbook written by revisionist historians gave the opposition the opportunity to voice their dissatisfaction. Japan is in a natural position to provide China with goods, capital and technology, but can easily create enmity for well-known historical and psychological reasons. The attitude of China to Japan is bound to be ambivalent: the Chinese at once resent Japan and are attracted by it. Japan's recent economic behaviour makes things more difficult: exports to China increased by 72.9% in 1985, but imports from China went up by only 8.8%; the Japanese have been reluctant to invest in China. For these several reasons, it is not at all clear whether China will continue smoothly on the present course of modernization.

In addition, the Soviet Union may not repeat its past mistake of antagonizing China. It will learn from the errors of the past, or may judge that it can no longer afford bad relations with China, as Soviet power has ceased to grow so rapidly. There is thus some likelihood that Sino-Soviet relations will improve in the coming decade, which together with the difficulties of modernization or its failure, could change China's orientation, with serious geopolitical implications.

Another possibility is that South Korea, which since 1965 has recorded an high extraordinarily growth rate, will run into political instability. The standard of living has been greatly improved and the people have grown more sure of themselves. But every success brings its problems. An emerging middle class now wishes to have a greater say in the management of the country and greater political freedom to choose how it is governed. Economic growth has changed South Korea's social structure and value system. Moreover, the memories of the Korean War are now too distant to unify the country. The overall effect of these changes is that authoritarian rule, in force since President Syngman Rhee, is no longer an appropriate form of government for the country. But it is always difficult to change an authoritarian form of government. Change should be gradual, but there are many who regard gradual change as dangerous and who want only radical change. Whether South Korea can carry out the necessary political reforms and maintain political stability remains to be seen.

North Korea will, of course, be watching events. Aware that it is lagging seriously behind the South in the race for economic growth, it might try to use the opportunity provided by domestic turmoil there to act in some way against South Korea. Or Seoul might decide to pursue a populist but unwise foreign policy in the face of growing instability at home. As the structure in the Korean Peninsula is so delicate and subtle, and as it constitutes perhaps the most sensitive element for the stability of the whole region, such changes may have serious geopolitical repercussions.

China and South Korea are merely examples. Many other countries, such as the Philippines, Indonesia and Malaysia, are also in a difficult phase of modernization. In East Asia and the Pacific, change in the military balance itself may not be particularly significant but, when combined with political strains resulting from over-rapid modernization in countries which occupy important positions, geopolitical changes of great significance can result. That is what is of concern.

US-Japan relations
Another possible cause of turbulence lies in US-Japan relations, which have become a key factor in the region. They can be described as a 'special relationship', analogous to Anglo-US relations after the war.

Japan is now an important supporter of the United States, which is still a dominant power. A few facts reveal the story. Each has an important role in the management of the world economy. The US accounts for a little more than 20% of world output, and Japan for about 10%. Therefore jointly they produce one third of the world's wealth.

Though the industrial output of the European countries is twice that of Japan, the weight of the United States and Japan is plain. First, today Japan is the largest net creditor, with $100 billion of assets, making it a very important country in the financial world, as the meeting of the 'Group of Five' in the autumn of 1985 demonstrated. Second, the US and Japan enjoy a clear lead in the high-technology industries, at least in the field of microelectronics, seen by many as having a decisive influence on the total balance of forces in the world and to have considerable civilian implications as well. Though conducting different programmes, the United States and Japan happen to be developing similar technologies. Both the Strategic Defense Initiative (SDI) programme and the plan of MITI (Japan's Ministry of International Trade & Industry) emphasize fifth-generation computers, artificial intelligence, new materials, lasers and optical fibres as the technologies likely to be dominant in future. Third, the economies of the two countries are very closely linked, perhaps without precedent. The US market, which takes about 30% of Japanese exports, is clearly vital to the Japanese economy, and the Japanese market is also important to the United States, though it may not be indispensable. Japan has invested a large amount of money in the United States, which needs investments. It has also extended large loans. Japanese firms have stakes of 50% or higher in some hundreds of American manufacturing concerns. Moreover, Japanese industry supplies a large variety of components to US firms. The US has been and still is the most important source of new technology for Japan. Clearly the two economies are very closely interlocked and gain strength from each other. It can be argued therefore that the US-Japan relationship is the driving force for the modernization of the economies of many of the regional countries.

In the field of security, Japan has still not played a very large role, but geography makes the US-Japan relationship the centrepiece of the security arrangements of the region. Japan is situated where it can guard against Soviet naval expansion into the Pacific. The Soviet Union is not completely blocked by Japan, as it faces the Sea of Okhotsk and has bases on the Kamchatka Peninsula, but the Soya Strait lies between Vladivostok and the Sea of Okhotsk and the passage through that Strait is not free, regardless of Japan's publicized intentions.

The main difficulty with the US-Japan relationship is that the benefits and costs for the two countries are not well balanced, at least in the ordinary way. First, Japan has benefited greatly from the US-Japan Security Treaty, and at very low cost. American nuclear forces provide Japan with the basis for its security, and the dominant sea and air power of the US in the Pacific has given Japan a very reliable security shield. The strength of the United States alone has been almost enough to provide Japan with its security. For the past twenty years or so, Japan has spent less than 1% of GNP on defence, one of the lowest percentages in the world. (If NATO criteria are used the figure goes up to nearly 1.5%, but this is still much less than the 3–4% of most NATO countries.) In contrast, the United States spent nearly 10% of GNP on defence until the end of the 1960s. The security burden for the United States and that for Japan bear no comparison.

The balance sheet of economic relations is, however, more complex. Economists have argued incessantly about the meaning of the US-Japanese trade balance. Some hold that a big surplus is bad while others doubt it. The political fact remains, however, that many Americans have criticized the Japanese trade surplus. They argue that the Japanese are eager to sell their products in the US market but are reluctant to buy from the United States in return. Therefore US-Japanese economic relations are not truly reciprocal. Such an argument lacks precision, and those who argue in this way tend to overlook the problems and weaknesses of the US economy, including the fact that the United States has not, until recently at least, been eager to export and therefore does not have the experience or the system to promote exports. Nevertheless, American criticism is not groundless and it does have political force. Fundamentally, a large US deficit on current account, in which Japan's trade surplus is an important factor, if it continues may cause serious disturbances in the world economy.

Though such trade and security imbalances must not be left uncorrected, trying to correct them in a direct and rash way will be counterproductive. For example, Japanese defence expenditures cannot be increased much beyond 1.5–2.0% of GNP without a negative impact on international – and especially regional – relations. Indeed, there could be an impact before such levels were reached. It may be thought that there would be no great difference between spending 1% and spending 1.5% of GNP. But the additional money would go on doubling the procurement of weapons and on base construction, possibly changing the regional balance to the considerable concern of Japan's neighbours. The trade imbalance will continue, though it can and should be somewhat reduced. Protectionist measures are not a remedy. Imaginative measures and a long-term view are required, but neither is easy to find.

Convergence and Divergence in East Asian and Western Security Interests: Part I

PROFESSOR SEIZABURO SATO

East Asia and the West
The term 'West', as it was understood by Japan during the latter half of the nineteenth century and until World War II, meant Western Europe and the advanced nations of North America. 'East' was used to refer to North-east Asia, the sphere under the influence of Chinese civilization, sometimes also including all other areas of Asia that were under colonial rule or threatened by the encroachment of Western colonialism.

Since World War II the confrontation between the United States and the Soviet Union has become the basic framework of international relations, giving rise to new Asian Communist nations such as China, North Korea and North Vietnam, which maintained close relations with the Soviet Union as well as among themselves. Under these new circumstances, the 'East' became a generally accepted term for the Communist camp, thus making Japan a member of the 'West' by virtue of its alliance with the United States. As American dominance weakened during the 1970s, the necessity for burden-sharing by the advanced nations of the West grew, while Japan's economic interdependence and integration with the Western nations continued to increase. All this has produced a widespread awareness among the Japanese people that Japan was indeed 'a member of the Western alliance'. Therefore, in this Paper the term 'West' is used to imply not only Western Europe and the Atlantic Alliance, but also other advanced democracies, including, in particular, Japan.

By East Asia, it is customary to refer to nations (or regions) situated in North-east Asia, such as Japan, the two Koreas, China, Taiwan, Hong Kong and Outer Mongolia; and the nations of South-east Asia such as the six ASEAN nations, the three nations of Indochina, and Burma. However, since this Paper is concerned with comparing non-Communist East Asia and the West, the Communist countries and the cloistered socialist Burma will not be discussed, but other nations such as Australia, New Zealand and the Pacific Island states will be included.

Security interests
There are a number of important differences between the security interests of the nations of East Asia and those of Western Europe. First, while the West European nations have a most important common security interest of effectively countering the Soviet threat, the peceived threats and the felt security interests of the East Asian nations are multiple and diverse. Second, Europe has traditionally been seen by the Soviet Union as the theatre that is most important for its national security, while East Asia has had only secondary importance. For East Asia, therefore, the Soviet threat has not been as serious a problem as it was for Western Europe. Third, in Europe, NATO and Warsaw Pact forces confront each other on land, so that there are geostrategic and force posture symmetries. In Asia, however, the Soviet land-based forces in East Siberia are countered by the United States and Japan with island-based and maritime forces, so that there is marked geostrategic and force posture asymmetries.

Fourth, between the Soviet Union and Western Europe lie the East European nations, which are Soviet client states, albeit in varying degrees. In East Asia there is no such buffer, and the Communist nations are severely divided among themselves. Fifth, in Europe, the political border dividing East and West Germany was recognized as part of the Helsinki Accord of 1975. In East Asia there remains a fundamental dispute over recognition between North and South Korea, and between China and Taiwan, and there are a number of serious territorial disputes, such as those between Japan and the Soviet Union, and between China and Vietnam.

Despite all these differences, there is no denying that the security interests of Western Europe and East Asia have tended to converge in recent years. The principal reason for this lies in the fact that the Soviet Union has greatly enhanced its military strength, nuclear and conventional, in both regions, and improved its force mobility and long-distance power projection. Both the differences and the trend towards convergence are examined below, after which the possibility of security co-operation and the remaining areas of divergent interest are discussed.

The range of East Asian security interests
For virtually all Western European nations the Soviet Union presents the most likely and the most powerful threat.[1] Similarly, many East Asian nations have recently become more acutely aware of the Soviet military presence, but for most of them the Soviet Union remains nonetheless a secondary or indirect threat and not an immediate danger. North Korea is the direct threat for South Korea, as China is for Taiwan, and Vietnam for Thailand. For Malaysia and Indonesia it is Vietnam, China and their own domestic ethnic conflicts which pose a more direct threat. For the Philippines, political chaos and economic stagnation are the clearest danger. Japan, China, Australia

and New Zealand are the only regional nations which see the Soviet Union as the main threat, but even then for the latter two the Soviet Union is a distant presence and the threat an unlikely one. Indeed, Premier David Lange of New Zealand has said: 'New Zealand is a fortunate country. It faces no external threat'.[2]

The United States maintains an amicable and close relationship with most of the East Asian nations and has defence commitments with many of them. With Japan, South Korea and the Philippines it has bilateral security treaties. For Taiwan, the US still assumes the obligation to supply 'defensive' weapons though the security treaty was abrogated in 1979. It also maintains a security tie with Thailand, using the Manila Treaty as the legal framework. It has, however, suspended its security obligations towards New Zealand under the ANZUS Treaty but has maintained them towards Australia.[3] Both Australia and New Zealand have security ties with Malaysia and Singapore through the Five-Power Defence Arrangement (FPDA).

There is no real likelihood that in the foreseeable future these various security ties will be integrated into a region-wide, formal multilateral alliance similar to the Atlantic Alliance. Instead, what might emerge by way of multilateral co-operation encompassing the East Asian region is a non-military, loose, economic co-operative relationship such as that being promoted by international bodies such as the Pacific Economic Co-operation Conference (PECC) and the Pacific Basin Economic Council (PBEC).

The Soviet military build-up

The Soviet Union has deployed in the European theatre larger and stronger forces than those in East Asia. Some 80% of the Soviet population lives west of the Ural Mountains, and by far the majority of its economic activities are concentrated there. Though Siberia is rich in underground resources they are extremely difficult to exploit because much of the land-mass (especially the eastern part of it) is permafrost and the poulation of the area is scanty. It should also be recalled that attacks on Russian territory have historically come from the west, notably that of Napoleon in the nineteenth century and the two German invasions in the twentieth century. In contrast, the eastern front has never been seriously violated except for the thirteenth century conquest by the Yuan Empire.

Since the latter half of the 1960s, however, and particularly from the late 1970s, there has been a marked strengthening and modernization of both conventional and nuclear Soviet forces, in East Siberia and East Asia.[4] In 1977, for instance, SS-20 deployment began, and in 1978 an independent theatre command for Soviet Far East forces was established. In 1979, Soviet forces began operating from the Cam Ranh Bay and Da Nang military facilities in Vietnam and *Backfire* bombers were stationed in eastern Siberia in 1980. In the last ten years the Soviet Pacific Fleet has grown by some 600,000 tons, becoming the largest of the four Soviet fleets. The Soviet Union has thus constructed military forces not only adequate for the defence of the Soviet Far East territories, but also with capabilities for power projection in all parts of East Asia.

Despite the spectacular military build-up, the Soviet Union has not yet established military superiority in the region and the East–West military balance in East Asia still favours the West, at least as far as conventional forces are concerned. The Soviet ground forces stationed principally along the Chinese border are adequate to deter possible Chinese attacks, but not powerful enough to be able to subjugate China's huge territories and population. Though the Soviet land-based air force is powerful, its reach remains limited except for the *Backfire* bomber.

As to maritime power projection, most of the Soviet Pacific Fleet must pass through the three choke points of the Japanese archipelago before reaching the outer ocean. Also, the two *Kiev*-class carriers in the Fleet have only vertical, short take-off and landing (VSTOL) aircraft and are thus much inferior to the US *Nimitz*-class carriers with their heavier and longer-range fighters. It is true that Cam Ranh Bay is the largest Soviet naval forward-deployment base outside the USSR, and as many as 25–30 Soviet vessels (including six to eight combatants and nuclear-propelled attack submarines (SSN)) now operate from there throughout the South China Sea. Long-range reconnaissance and ASW aircraft, *Badger* bombers and a squadron of MiG-23 fighters are also deployed at Cam Ranh Bay. However, the bases in Vietnam are far away from the Soviet Union, and while useful in peacetime for maintaining a military presence and for surveillance are in no way capable of withstanding US attack in time of war.

In contrast with its practice in Western Europe, the United States has never adopted a formal strategy that includes a possible first-use of nuclear weapons in East Asia. The reason why there is such a high nuclear threshold in East Asia is partly because the United States has been able to maintain a favourable conventional balance, especially in relation to the defence of the island nations such as Japan and the Philippines, but also because the regional nuclear threat other than from the Soviet Union is limited (in the case of China) or non-existent (North Korea). And though the Soviet regional nuclear forces have been considerably strengthened by the deployment of the SS-20 IRBM and the *Backfire*, in East Asia this has not produced the same kind of popular fear of nuclear war seen in Western Europe. Nor has the Soviet Union fostered a strong anti-nuclear, anti-American movement – primarily as a result of the balance of conventional forces. This balance also partly explains why, even after the United States lost overall nuclear superiority, there has been no increased concern in East Asia over the reliability of the US military commitment. Similarly, no conflict between 'deterrence' (the effective discouragement of war) and 'reassurance' (the maintenance of self-confidence among allies) has emerged in East Asia as it has in Western Europe.[5]

Geostrategic and force asymmetries
Barring some almost unthinkable realignments of international relations (such as China joining the Western alliance, or Japan linking forces with the Soviet Union) little is likely to change the present asymmetry in which the Soviet Union uses Eastern Siberia as its base, and the West (especially the US and Japan) use the islands and the seas. This is very different from the symmetrical land confrontation of NATO and the Warsaw Pact in Europe. In recent years, as a result of the longer range of Soviet submarine-launched ballistic missiles (SLBM), the Sea of Okhotsk has increased in strategic value as the operating area for Soviet missile submarines. Nonetheless, both the submarines deployed there and the naval and air forces defending them are still based in Eastern Siberia.

The East Asian allies of the United States (Japan is typical) take a negative view towards stationing US nuclear weapons on their soil. While such non-nuclear policies tend to weaken the credibility of US nuclear deterrence to some extent, they are wise for the alliance because they avoid a conflict in the region between deterrence and reassurance by not arousing latent anti-nuclear sentiment. However, US port visits by vessels which may be nuclear-armed can give rise to serious problems, as the case of New Zealand vividly demonstrates. (This issue is dealt with more fully in Dr Coral Bell's Paper.) But as long as US nuclear weapons are adequately deployed at sea as well as at US-owned bases (Guam), there is little possibility that the Soviet Union could threaten US allies with nuclear blackmail. The low visibility of US nuclear arms in East Asia accounts, to a considerable extent, for the limited success of anti-US and anti-nuclear movements there, despite the recent rapid strengthening of Soviet nuclear forces.

Another type of geostrategic asymmetry in the region is that of the vulnerability of principal targets. Among the nations of the West in the region (such as Japan and South Korea) the economic, social and military infrastructures are concentrated within small geographical areas with extremely high population densities. On the other hand, most areas of the wide expanse of Eastern Siberia remain undeveloped and thinly populated. While in Western Europe and the Soviet Union west of the Urals there is general symmetry of attack targets, any nuclear exchange, even a limited one, in East Asia would cause massive damage to Western allies. For this reason 'the primary defence tasks for the United States and its Asian security partners are to deter Soviet first use of its nuclear forces and to counter Moscow's efforts at political and military intimidation'.[6] A first-use nuclear strategy is not only unsuitable for East Asia, but also lacks persuasiveness and would even be self-defeating.

The third type of geostrategic asymmetry is that while the Soviet Union bases its forces almost entirely on its own territory, US forces are forward-deployed in allied countries. In Europe, NATO could inflict severe damage upon the Warsaw Pact by attacking the East European nations, without striking the Soviet Union itself. However, in East Asia, and especially in North-east Asia, any counter-attack or retaliation in response to a Soviet invasion must be directed against the Soviet Union. In such circumstances there would be a dangerously high probability of escalation to the use of nuclear weapons. The implications of this asymmetry are rather complex. In times of mounting tension, it might restrain Soviet action or it might erode and weaken the credibility of the American commitment. Which of these alternatives would become the reality would depend largely upon the balance of nuclear and conventional forces in the region.

Buffer states and divisions among Communists
The fact that there are buffer states between the Soviet Union and the Western European nations has a beneficial aspect because of the reduced likelihood of direct Western attack on the Soviet mainland at the outset of any hostilities.

In Eastern Europe, however, there is increasing anti-Soviet feeling and a growing desire for freedom and for the material wealth of the Western world. If economic and cultural intercourse between East and West develop, the present tendency of the East European nations to disengage from their Soviet ties will also be accelerated. However, as the Brezhnev Doctrine has demonstrated, the Soviet Union is unlikely to tolerate too much loosening of East European ties to Moscow. As Christoph Bertram points out, 'the very uncertainty of political stability in the East European empire of the Soviet Union is perhaps the most serious security threat for (Western) Europe in the foreseeable future'.[7]

In East Asia there are no client states between the Western nations and the Soviet Union. None of the East Asian Communist states belongs to the Soviet empire in this sense. Proud and independent China refuses to side with either of the two super-powers. Outer Mongolia provides a buffer between the Soviet Union and China; and North Korea will continue a cautious policy of keeping an equal distance from the two Communist giants. The relationship between Vietnam and the Soviet Union cannot be anything more than a marriage of convenience (and for the Soviet Union a rather expensive marriage at that). Even if these nations should become 'polluted' by Western civilization and drawn away from Soviet influence, this would not constitute a serious threat to the Soviet Union. In this respect, it can be said that there is in the region less danger of a Soviet confrontation with the West. The 'Imperial Order' of the Soviet Union does not exist in East Asia, and what is non-existent cannot break down.

The divisions among the Communist nations in East Asia are not at all unwelcome to the West so long as they do not escalate into a major war, because such divisions tend to restrict what the Soviet Union can do militarily in Europe or in East Asia. As long as the Soviet military superiority over other Communist nations remains evident, and China possesses, small as it is, its own nuclear force it is improbable that the Sino-Soviet confrontation will flare into a large-scale war. In recent years, there have been some attempts between China and the Soviet Union, as well as between China and Vietnam, to ease tensions. If there should be tangible progress in this direction, the Soviet military burden on its Chinese borders might be lessened to some extent, but it is highly unlikely that there would be a revival of the old military alliance between the Soviet Union and China, or that a new imperial order would emerge among the East Asian Communist states.

Divided states and territorial issues
There are some unresolved issues, however, in East Asia, of the kind which in Europe have long since been settled. They are the problems of achieving mutual recognition between divided states and the resolution of territorial disputes. Of the three types of divided states which arose in East Asia after World War II, one, Vietnam, was unified militarily by the North. In the case of the two Koreas and Taiwan, any attempt at unification by direct military means would certainly run a high risk of igniting a major war, and all concerned, Pyongyang, Seoul, Taipei and Beijing, of necessity must remain extremely cautious about launching any such attempt in the foreseeable future. However, it is also very difficult for them to bring about the conditions for peaceful unification, or for mutual recognition as independent states accepting the divided status. From a long-term viewpoint, China can perhaps become unified by means of a special framework of 'One State, Two Regimes' with Taiwan retaining its *de facto* independence. The two Koreas can possibly achieve a stable relationship similar to that between East and West Germany. But even if events should follow this optimistic scenario, the whole process will still take a very long time. The tensions between the two Koreas and between China and Taiwan will surely remain high for many years to come.

There are also a number of unresolved territorial problems. The territorial issue between Japan and the Soviet Union in North-east Asia; the disputed title to the islands in the South China Sea; and the continental shelf rights being contested by China, Vietnam, the Philippines and Malaysia, only add to the instability in the region.

In Europe, several confidence-building measures (CBM) have been proposed and in some cases implemented, as a step towards relaxing East–West tensions. These CBM are predicated upon the mutual recognition of nations as independent states and their acceptance of clearly-defined territorial borders. In East Asia, where these preconditions have not been fully realized, there is therefore much less likelihood of the European-type CBM being adopted. As Masashi

Nishihara points out, the kind of CBM practicable in East Asia would primarily be the 'unilateral but reciprocal restraints of arms deployment and military actions' on the part of the nations concerned.[8]

Problems of security co-operation

In recent years, there has been a growing need for global security co-operation among the Western nations for several reasons. First, the Soviet Union has markedly expanded its nuclear and conventional capabilities in Europe and East Asia. The erosion of US strategic nuclear superiority has brought about a condition of 'rough parity', or 'ambiguous equilibrium', with the result that the most pressing defence task for the West is to seek a more secure deterrent against Soviet attack. Second, now that missile mobility has been vastly improved and ranges considerably increased, arms-control negotiations limited to a specific theatre have lost their effectiveness. Third, so long as the Soviet Union considers that it can keep the Western camp divided, it will not become seriously involved in arms-control negotiations. Since the second and third reasons are self-evident, only the first reason will be examined here.

Three types of proposals have typically been advanced as a means of strengthening the West's ability to deter the Soviet Union. The first is to strengthen conventional deterrence and to raise the nuclear threshold. This approach assumes that the existing nuclear balance is to be maintained intact, both regionally and globally. As already discussed, this approach is desirable in that it would enhance the credibility of deterrence and, at the same time, provide allies with needed reassurance. The real problem with this proposal is that it is very costly, so making it difficult to secure the support of Western publics at a time of economic hardship. This is less of a constraint in East Asia however, where the conventional balance favours the West, but is a real difficulty in Western Europe where the balance is tipped the other way.

The second proposal is to establish a link between theatres – the concept of horizontal escalation. As long as the deterrent in each theatre is well organized there is no denying that such inter-theatre linkage would enhance the credibility of the overall deterrent. As Henry Rowen points out: 'Even though Soviet planners may rate as low the probability that widely separated and non-allied countries may act jointly against the USSR if it undertakes to attack any single country – and they may even have some doubts about the response of those that are members of alliances – with so many hostile states around it, even the modest probability of a grand inter-theatre coalition may weigh heavily on their minds'.[9] However, this inter-theatre linkage is likely to be criticized by those nations considered to be in an area relatively safe from the first Soviet nuclear attack (such as in East Asia) and who would prefer, therefore, to avoid risking possible Soviet attack as a result of involvement in conflicts in distant areas. In other words, this approach suffers from the conflict between deterrence and reassurance. Since the West depends in Western Europe upon nuclear first use or early use, any horizontal escalation could mean the spread of nuclear war, and invite all the more negative response from East Asia, where the nuclear threshold is relatively high. For an inter-theatre linkage strategy to be successful, it is important to improve the conventional balance in each theatre.

The third proposal for the enhancement of deterrence is to develop an extended air defence system. The Strategic Defense Initiative (SDI) forms part of this approach, but in addition to defence against long-range ballistic missiles, serious research efforts would have to be made for more effective defence against short-range missiles and cruise missiles. The various new technologies, especially for surveillance, that may be developed by such research will make a major contribution towards enhancing the credibility of Western deterrence. Despite serious East–West confrontations after the end of World War II, a direct military engagement by the United States and the Soviet Union has been avoided, thanks to the spectacular increase in sheer destructive capability achieved by the 'nuclear revolution' on the one hand, and the unheard-of advances in the surveillance of enemy military capabilities and operations on the other, made possible by the 'reconnaissance revolution'.[10]

However, clashes about the research and development of such an extended air defence system (as has already been seen in the case of SDI) will be inevitable among the participating states and commercial enterprises. Vital questions, such as who will provide the funding, where the trained personnel are to come from, and who will have the rights to the fruits of the research, must all be resolved. Also the heavy demands in funding and human resources are bound to conflict with the currently more important task of strengthening the nuclear and conventional means of deterrence.

In order to achieve feasible security co-operation, given the inherent problems discussed above, certain minimum preconditions must be met. First, the leaders of the Western nations must possess a clear understanding that their nations indeed have common security interests and that it is important for them that there should be such co-operation. Second, the West as a whole needs a framework within which to discuss and co-ordinate security co-operation. Third, each nation ought to have full consultations with others before formulating its own security policy. Fourth, the economies of the Western nations must maintain their health. Finally, the economic conflicts between Western nations must be kept under reasonable, common control. None of these tasks is easily attained. In order to create a safer world to live in, all of us must still prepare to walk a long way.

Notes

[1] Christoph Bertram, 'Japan's Security from the Perspective of a European' in *Japan and Europe: Toward Closer Cooperation* (Tokyo, JCIE Papers, 1984) p. 36.
[2] Speech at the UN Conference on Disarmament, in Geneva, May 1985.
[3] See Dr Coral Bell's Paper, p. 52–61
[4] See Harry Gelman, 'The Soviet Union, East Asia and the West: The Kremlin's Calculus of Opportunities and Risks', in *East Asia, The West and International Security: Prospects for Peace* Part II, Adelphi Paper 217, pp. 3–26.
[5] Michael Howard, 'Reassurance and Deterrence: Western Defense in the 1980's' in *The Causes of Wars* 2nd and enlarged edition (Cambridge, MA: Harvard University Press, 1984) pp. 246–64.
[6] Richard Solomon and Masataka Kosaka (eds), *The Soviet Far East Military Buildup: Nuclear Dilemmas and Asian Security* (Dover, MA: Auburn House, 1986) p. 16.
[7] Christoph Bertram, (*op. cit.*, in note 1), p. 35.
[8] Masashi Nishihara, *East Asian Security and the Trilateral Countries* (New York: New York University Press, 1985) pp. 67–8.
[9] Henry Rowen, 'Distant Relations: Links between Asian and European Security' in Solomon and Kosaka (*op. cit.* in note 6), p. 223.
[10] John Gaddis, 'The Long Peace: Elements of Stability in the Postwar International System', *International Security*, Vol. 10, No. 4 (Spring 1986) pp. 123–5.

Convergence and Divergence in East Asian and Western Security Interests: Part II

BRIGADIER KENNETH HUNT

Since World War II there has been a political and strategic confrontation between East and West. The Western states forming the Atlantic Alliance and those East Asian states with which this Paper is concerned have been caught up in this confrontation to one degree or another, to the point that it forms for most of them the context for their foreign and security policies. It has to a considerable extent also governed the pattern of their economic relationships, which are set within the Western community.

There has thus long been a broad identity of interest between East Asia and the West. However, both geography and history bring differences of perspective and emphasis. In East Asia in particular, stages of political and economic development vary widely, bringing their own priorities and vulnerabilities. Then there are regional tensions which, even if they may have East–West overtones or roots, are of much more direct concern to some nations than to others who may indeed endeavour to remain uninvolved in them.

Before embarking on a closer comparison of the interests of the two regions it is as well, however, to be clear that like is not being compared with like. East Asia does not have the cohesion of a Western Europe which is culturally and historically homogeneous and which contains a number of states of broadly similar size and capacity and with similar aspirations. Western Europe is organized and able generally to act collectively on political and economic issues; East Asia is not. Indeed East Asia is the only large regional grouping that lacks any kind of regional institution such as the European Community (EC), the Atlantic Alliance or the Organization of African Unity (OAU). There is no shared threat compelling enough to bring the region together in a security framework and no common thread of broad mutual interest to overcome the inherent diversity of security perceptions, cultures, religions and ethnic compositions. Japan dominates the region with its economic strength but has not been notably ready to act in concert with others, except to some extent in South-east Asia. Relations in East Asia have therefore tended to be bilateral, with the United States as a common point.

ASEAN has been something of a success but it is a sub-regional organization. The closest approach to any wider grouping is the annual meeting of ASEAN Foreign Ministers with their counterparts from the developed countries of the region – the United States, Japan, Australia, New Zealand and Canada.[1] It seems clear that co-operation in East Asia on security matters must generally be between individual states, while in the West it can be within a group.

Security policies
Nonetheless East Asia and the West have in common the wish to live in peace, freedom and safety, which in practice is reflected in a concern that major war should be deterred by the maintenance of an East–West strategic balance, nuclear and conventional, and that such deterrence should extend to protect the region and, of course, the nation. Since an East–West strategic balance essentially means one between the United States and the Soviet Union, security for both Western and East Asian states is either built around links with the United States or rests on an effective dependence on the stability that is underpinned by the US.

The Western nations have translated their security concerns in Europe into policies that identify the United States with European security through the Atlantic Alliance and its integrated military organization, NATO. As a result the Atlantic partners have reached general agreement on the military strategy to be adopted towards the Soviet Union and on the central part that nuclear weapons play, though not without some disputes about how the forces are to be found, nor, latterly, about nuclear strategy and doctrine. They are not quite agreed on a political strategy on how to live with the Soviet Union, so that there are differences between the United States and Western Europe from time to time over detente and arms control. There are differences, too, over the Middle East, where Europeans – notwithstanding their heavy dependence on Gulf oil – have generally been reluctant to be involved militarily, either judging political action to be more appropriate or preferring to deploy their limited defence resources nearer home. The result is that military deterrence in the Gulf and Indian Ocean region has really been left to the US, with some help from Britain and France.

In the Pacific, the West is also now represented militarily almost entirely by the United States, with the only remaining European defence commitments there being such links as Britain's responsibility for Hong Kong and its membership (along with Malaysia, Singapore, Australia and New Zealand) in the Five-Power Defence Arrangements; and the small residual security responsibilities that France has in the Pacific. Australia, and until recently New Zealand, also plays a part in ANZUS, an alliance at present somewhat troubled, but it is US power which is essentially relied upon not only to safeguard Western strategic interests but to contribute to regional stability and to maintain the freedom of the seas on which access to trade by the Western community as a whole ultimately depends.

East Asian nations benefit from all this but are not engaged in any collective security arrangements themselves; political and, in the case of Japan, constitutional impediments stand in the way of them. Bilateral treaties with the US are the basis of the security policies of Japan, South Korea and the Philippines and, in turn, for US security policy in the Pacific. For South Korea the threat is from the North; for Thailand and other South-east Asian nations it is from Vietnamese actions in Kampuchea; for Taiwan it is from China. No East Asian country sees a Soviet threat in quite the same way that the United States does, despite the Soviet military build-up in the region. As in Europe there is an awareness of the need to live with the Soviet Union and, although there is widespread support for the Asian policies of the present US Administration, this rarely extends to the confrontational aspects of US Soviet policy. For some, China remains an overhanging weight in the region, over the long term of more concern than the Soviet Union. Nuclear matters and arms control do not play the central part in security policies in East Asia that they do in the West, the Pacific being widely (if maybe mistakenly) regarded as primarily a conventional theatre. There are, of course, well-known frictions between Japan and the United States over defence burden-sharing.

Economics are an important element in security in Asia. For the developing countries, prosperity is a key to domestic and regional stability and to the health of regimes, even political systems. The loss of markets through protectionism in the West is therefore an immediate and serious threat. There is protectionism in East Asia too (and of course within the West), but it is the fear of losing outside markets, particularly in the United States, on which there is a heavy dependence, that looms largest. There is here a worrying divergence of view, since both Western and East Asian countries feel threatened by the actions of others, notably by Japan, whose huge trade surpluses are a source of friction both within and outside the region. But the threat to stability is much greater in East Asia, as will be argued later.

Key issues

If the foregoing is a very broad sketch of the security interests and concerns of the West and of East Asia, these need to be looked at more closely in relation to the practical problems in the Pacific now.

A number of key issues face the region. An overriding one is the maintenance of a military balance there which will deter war and underwrite stability. There are immediate security problems in Indochina and the Korean Peninsula, and there is a need to do whatever is required to help the Philippines back to health. The improvement of economic relationships, both with the West and within the region, is an urgent task and the division of labour in the security field, not unconnected politically, is another. Then there is the context in which much of this is situated, the harmonizing of policies towards the Soviet Union, now pursuing a much more active policy in Asia, and towards China.

The West shares an interest in all of the above, though usually – apart from the United States – with a less direct role to play. Western nations have their own parallel tasks in Europe. China has its own overriding issues: modernization and the economic and political reforms that are part of it. But it also shares many of the concerns which have been listed, albeit sometimes from a different perspective – notably stability in Indochina and the Korean Peninsula, and economic and trade relationships. China also wants a military balance to be maintained in East Asia so as to ensure a peaceful environment in which to continue modernization, and is working out its own relationships with the Soviet Union and the United States.

As far as the West and East Asia are concerned, the two most immediate security issues are Kampuchea and the Korean Peninsula. Neither seems likely to call for policies much different from those being followed now, which are based on convergent interests.

KAMPUCHEA

South-east Asian policy on Kampuchea has so far been hammered out in ASEAN and then given support by other regional states, such as Japan, by the US and by the West in general. It is true there have been some differences of view within ASEAN itself, as indicated by Indonesian initiatives towards Vietnam but, so long as Vietnam remains intransigent, agreement on a common policy acceptable to the most exposed state, Thailand, seems sustainable.

The principal Western country involved is the United States, through its military agreement with Thailand and its adversarial relationship with the Soviet Union, Vietnam's principal backer. There is no reason to suppose that American and Thai interests will diverge, certainly while Vietnamese actions are hostile and Soviet-supported. Similarly, there seems no reason why Western interests or those of Japan should diverge from those of ASEAN. If Vietnam does decide to seek a settlement in Kampuchea on terms acceptable to ASEAN, one motive could be to obtain badly-needed economic aid from the West, in particular from the United States and Japan. It is likely that this would be forthcoming under such circumstances, denoting a clear convergence of interests between the West and East Asia in support of ASEAN. If, on the other hand, the conflict should drag on, it would remain a Western and Japanese interest to continue to support ASEAN and Thailand.

THE KOREAN PENINSULA

Though there have been some signs of an easing of tension in the Korean Peninsula, including indeed talk of a North–South summit, the basic cleavage and heavily-armed confrontation remains.[2] Military support for South Korea is given by treaty by the United States through the presence of US forces there and through military and technological assistance, with emergency reinforcement being made possible by US bases in Japan. This US military aid is complemented by Japanese economic aid to South Korea.

There is thus convergence on the security aspect, with a division of labour which fits quite well within Japanese political constraints. There is also convergence on political support for South Korea in its attempts to carry on direct talks with the North, both the US – and the West in general – and Japan being willing to consider discussions or links with the North only if something substantial first comes out of talks between North and South. Dialogue with the South is thus North Korea's only real avenue towards a more positive relationship with Japan and the United States, and thereby to Japanese and American assistance for its economy, and towards the negotiations on the withdrawal of US forces from the Peninsula which have been its long-standing goal.

There seems no reason to suppose that the general support for the present position of South Korea will change unless the policies of the North warrant it. Stability in the Peninsula and the avoidance of war there are vastly important not only to the United States, which would be embroiled, and to Japan, which would find it hard not to be caught up in some way, but also to the West, since there would be a risk of hostilities spreading. China would surely not welcome such an upheaval, into which it could be drawn; it needs both a stable environment and Western and Japanese help for modernization and certainly does not want a clash with the United States. This should not be taken to mean that the way in which the United States meets its security commitment to the South will remain unchanged for all time; as South Korea slowly becomes militarily stronger, circumstances might allow the withdrawal of some US forces. Japan, however, is likely to remain in its present arms-length position, militarily linked to the United States and providing bases from which the South can be supported, but with no military links with South Korea itself.

If there is likely to be unanimity on the need to underpin South Korea's security, this may not extend to unqualified support of its domestic policies. Student and other unrest has highlighted political pressures for greater democracy and constitutional change. A National Assembly Committee has been formed to recommend change, focusing at least in part on the method of electing the President. It is by no means certain to reach agreement. President Chun Doo Hwan is due to step down when his term ends in March 1988, but there is no history of peaceful change of leadership in Korea, no politically accepted formula for it as yet and no guarantee of it in 1988. The US, most closely involved, will be concerned to see democratic reform introduced without upset, not least because domestic stability in the South is an essential component of security; instability would offer a field for exploitation by the North. The West in general will share this view and Japan, where there is a background of prickly relations with the South, could be particularly sensitive if it appeared that a popular wish for democracy was being flouted. It is President Chun and those who support him who must chart the course and decide whether and how to compromise. There is hope for a peaceful transition in March 1988, given the wish for calm conditions in which to hold the Olympic Games the following summer and the consequent importance of maintaining good international relations. Mishandling, however, could produce instability.

THE PHILIPPINES
The Philippines need little comment here but much attention. The Aquino Government has been universally welcomed but faces a multitude of problems, not least economic, but including Communist insurgency. Again, it is America which, for historical reasons and because of the all-important strategic bases, is most closely concerned and which, together with Japan, has provided timely economic aid in the past. But the West as a whole and other East Asian countries have a stake in the health of the Philippines. Interests here are completely identical.

ECONOMICS AND SECURITY
Regional economic relationships, on the other hand, are divisive, pitting many of the developing countries of East Asia against the United States and the EC and, it seems, pitting Japan against almost everyone. Trading imbalances have led to burgeoning protectionism, notably in the US Congress, and to widespread trade frictions within and between regions, as for example between Japan and China, between Japan and South Korea, and between the United States and the EC.

The economic causes of the imbalances and the remedies for them are outside the scope of this particular Paper, which is concerned only with their security implications. One obvious such implication is the strain that trade frictions put on the relationships between the US and those countries dependent on it for security: Japan, South Korea and the NATO allies. It is often said that there should not be a linkage between economic activities and security, but the plain fact is that there is: Congress makes one, as Japan well knows. Security links may suffer over time if economic frictions, including those of burden-sharing, touched on later, continually sour the atmosphere.

But this particular aspect principally concerns the developed countries of Europe and Japan. In East Asia there is another quite different economic dimension to security – the part that economic prosperity plays in promoting and maintaining stability. In East Asia there is a variety of social systems but in common there has been a remarkable degree of prosperity, save only in the Philippines, mishandled by the Marcos regime. The economies have been largely export-led, resting heavily on the American market, especially in recent years when the dollar has been high, but also on markets in Europe. Japan has followed the same path of export growth and in the US and Europe the result has been a protectionist reaction to a flood of Far Eastern imports. Asian countries have been finding markets closed to them, and economic problems have been compounded by the low prices now being obtained for primary products, such as tin, palm oil and crude oil. The Soviet Union has seized the opportunity to offer to take goods being shut out by the West.

Clearly the trade problem is not an easy one to resolve. The White House has tried to head off protectionist legislation, for example with a Presidential veto on the Jenkins Bill to restrict textile imports.[3] But real damage is being done to industries in the US and Europe; jobs have been lost and feelings therefore run high. If, however, Asian economies, which have been such a success story, are hit hard, internal stability is likely to suffer. In January 1985, in an address to the US Congress, Prime Minister Lee Kuan Yew of Singapore asked: 'Is the United States going to nullify the forty-year peaceful and constructive development it has endeavoured to realize? Does the United States desire to abandon the contest between democracy and the free market on the one hand and Communism ... on the other, at this very time when the United States has nearly won this contest for the hearts and minds of the Third World?' He suggested that erecting barriers to Japanese products instead of trying to eliminate Japan's own trade barriers would hit other Asian countries twice: they would suffer from the reduced trade, first with the United States and secondly with Japan, which would suffer from a decline in its own sales on the US market. The Prime Minister on this occasion was directing his criticism towards the United States but, of course, it has wider application. The interests of the West and East Asia should converge here, even if they have not seemed to so far, to prevent lasting damage being done. Having said this, it should be admitted that Japanese economic aid has had as one of its aims the promotion and maintenance of political stability in South-east Asia. This is a wise policy, but the trading patterns and low primary commodity prices described above have tended to work against it.[4]

A MILITARY BALANCE

Left until last here, for convenience of discussion, is the issue noted earlier as the overriding one: the common interest in the maintenance of a military balance in East Asia that will deter war and underpin regional stability. It is linked with burden-sharing and with the relations with the Soviet Union and China.

There is no doubt that both East Asia and the West want a military balance to be kept, but inevitably the lion's share of the effort needed falls to the United States, as a major maritime power and the only Western nuclear one in East Asia. A very important contribution is made by the Philippines through the provision of the strategic bases there, and the defence efforts of Australia, New Zealand and ASEAN states play a significant part in regional security. However, the only conventional assistance of any real size that the US can look for in East Asia must come from Japan and South Korea, though Korean resources are inevitably directed towards the Peninsula. It has been suggested by the US Defense Secretary, Caspar Weinberger, in June 1986, that NATO should be willing to project naval force far beyond its accepted area of concern, into the Gulf, Indian Ocean and the Pacific. Whatever the merits of sending ships of NATO countries into the Gulf area – and there are many – to deploy them in the Pacific would surely be an expensive misuse of scarce resources. To maintain European vessels many thousands of miles from home would be complicated and costly, involving much wasteful sailing time each way. There are in any case far too few ships in the Eastern Atlantic, let alone the Gulf area, as it is. The United States has a right to expect its allies to give it help, to share the defence burden equitably, but to send European forces to the Pacific does not seem the right way to go about it.

Japan is obviously the country which has been asked to do more in Asia. Its present forces are not inconsiderable and its defence expenditure has been growing incrementally for some years at a faster real rate than is the rule in Europe. But the Self-Defense Forces (SDF) are only around half the size of those of West Germany or France, from a population almost exactly double. Defence expenditure is well below that of West Germany from a GDP around twice as large. In manpower terms, therefore, the Japanese defence burden is about one-quarter that of the Federal Republic, in economic terms little more than a third. The constraints are thus not imposed by a lack of resources but are political, as is well known. There are currently difficulties in increasing Japanese defence efforts. The security consensus in Japan has to be carefully nurtured; opinion has moved a long way in the last few years (especially under the guidance of Prime Minister Nakasone) but time is still needed, in the absence of any urgent threat or perception of it. Neither in Japan nor in East Asian countries is there any appeal in building up Japanese strength in order that the admittedly stretched US forces could leave the region to take on necessary tasks elsewhere, even in the Gulf on which almost everyone relies for oil. Japan does, it must be noted, give economic aid to certain countries with security problems, such as Pakistan and Egypt, to complement US military aid to them. While not by any description defence expenditure, it is commonly considered to be in the nature of strategic aid, as shouldering part of a burden that might otherwise fall on the United States.

If Western and East Asian interests converge on the need for a military balance in East Asia, views diverge over the way in which the necessary forces should be found, leaving things all too typically to the United States. There is recognition in Japan that attention should be given to some weaknesses, such as securing the sea-lanes, but there is no real discontent with the present state of the balance.

One reason may be that US forces are still generally seen as stronger than those of the Soviet Union in the region. (This point is dealt with in Professor Kosaka's Paper) Another is that the Soviet threat does not loom so large to most East Asian states as it does to the US. Despite the Soviet military activity in North-east Asia – which has helped to keep the Japanese defence budget growing – the man in the street does not appear to feel unduly threatened. Furthermore there is, as in West Germany and elsewhere in Western Europe, an awareness of having to live with this large and often overbearing neighbour and therefore of the need to hammer out a policy which is not just based on confrontation.

THE SOVIET UNION

It is important, though, that East Asian attitudes towards the USSR be co-ordinated, in particular with the United States, in the face of the more active Asian policy now being conducted by the Soviet Union. The earlier Soviet Asian policy was crude and abrasive and might almost have been designed to fail, which it largely did. The new one shows a softer face and is probing for opportunities to improve the Soviet position. There have been the trade proposals to South-east Asia to take advantage of Western protectionism; troop withdrawals have been announced from Afghanistan and vaguely suggested from Mongolia, which are of a piece with a number of overtures to China; and a new approach to Japan, signalled initially by the agreement of Foreign Minister Shevardnadze to go to Tokyo in January 1986, the first such visit for ten years. There has also been the proposal for an All-Asia Forum – something of an updated version of the Asian Collective Security plan put forward by Brezhnev in 1969 – to find solutions to common problems and advocating *inter alia* the ending of all nuclear testing in Asia, other arms-control measures and opposition to SDI. The All-Asia Forum may have no more appeal than did the Brezhnev plan, not least while the Soviet Union is backing Vietnam's unwelcome actions in Kampuchea. China will set its own policy towards the Soviet Union and the Sino-Soviet relations which develop from this will do much to provide a context for the policies of other states in Asia. Nevertheless, it is a Western and East Asian security interest to consult on the way in which the current Soviet approaches are met.[5]

CHINA

There does seem to be a broad convergence of interest on the need for friendly and constructive relations with China, though Taiwan is obviously a special case (of particular importance to the United States) and there are the concerns about China's long-term role felt by states such as Indonesia. The need to help China to modernize is widely accepted. China's immediate aims in Indochina roughly match those of ASEAN and thus those of the West. While China's policy directions remain as they are, they seem to pose no particular problems for Western countries, though the same is hardly true for East Asia: the future of Hong Kong and Macau could be affected by Chinese domestic political considerations; China's bulk and its aims overshadow Taiwan; its relations with Vietnam over time – good or bad – affect South-east Asia; and its exports compete. Put another way, China is a regional power which must always figure largely in regional calculations.

ARMS CONTROL AND NUCLEAR WEAPONS
As noted above, the Soviet proposal for an All-Asia Forum highlights arms control, though with a distinct anti-American slant. Arms control is not a major preoccupation in most of East Asia, and there is not generally the public constituency for it that there is in the United States and Europe. Nuclear matters do not figure largely either, outside the South Pacific where French nuclear testing and the non-nuclear policies of New Zealand have kept them in the forefront, though they do represent an important political strand in Japan. The Soviet deployment of SS-20 missiles in Asia, however, has been universally opposed and has led Japan in particular to support the Western position in the INF negotiations – that Asian missiles should be covered in any agreement. Here there is an identity of interest, though one might speculate on what would be the position if the inclusion of Asian missiles were the *only* impediment to an INF agreement that was otherwise acceptable to Western Europe: there might then be the feeling there that an agreement should be concluded that would cover missiles in Europe, leaving those in Asia to be dealt with in an Asian context. But the discussions in Reykjavik suggest that the Asian SS-20 are likely to be included in any INF agreement reached.[6]

The concept of SDI has no great support in East Asia any more than it has in Europe, but Japan has followed the European pattern of supporting US research and also indicated a willingness to participate in this. To the extent that SDI is discussed, it is its impact on deterrence and arms control (apart from concerns about commercial applications) which seems uppermost. There is more convergence here with West European opinion than with that in Washington, a similar readiness to see SDI as a bargaining chip, but also the same determination not to let the Soviet Union profit from any gap with the United States that there may be. East Asia is effectively sheltered by US nuclear strength and, although this is of less immediate concern than that of conventional protection, it is likely to prompt general support for the US arms-control position – except perhaps on SDI – even if there is a general disposition not to be closely involved or to be vocal on the subject.

New Zealand's non-nuclear policy has led to US naval vessels being denied access to New Zealand's ports unless declared not to be carrying nuclear weapons or propelled by nuclear reactors. The United States has not accepted such a condition, not wanting to make any concession to non-nuclear feeling that might later be demanded by other allies as well. Ironically, only China, a nuclear power, followed New Zealand's example, for the time being anyway, perhaps merely to emphasize its independence of US strategic policy. The US has refused to separate the conventional and nuclear aspects of its protection and it is in the interests of both Western and East European states to respect this. Washington might do well, though, to adopt a low-key approach to what is potentially an awkward problem, one which the Soviet Union will do what it can to exploit. In relation to Japan's non-nuclear policy, a certain studied ambiguity has served the United States – and Japan – well enough so far.

Some conclusions
It is not difficult to find shared concerns between East Asia and the West; there is a natural broad convergence of interest. It is harder to find ways of securing greater security co-operation than there is now in a region where no framework for it exists or looks likely to be built. In the economic field there are pressing reasons for harmonizing policies but, except within ASEAN, there is no organization in the region such as the EC that might foster this. Indeed, there is probably more convergence of interest between the West and East Asia than within East Asia, where inherent diversities tend even to separate South-east Asia from North-east Asia – in particular where security is concerned – with the United States as the nexus between them.

This Paper has explored directions in which the West might co-operate with East Asia over security but has not looked at the reverse application, taking it as axiomatic that East Asian nations have no wish to be involved in European security problems. Nor has it looked at responses to terrorism, which largely has its seat outside the region.

By reason of its size and economic strength, it is inevitably Japan that is looked to in East Asia for any significantly greater security efforts that should be made. The political obstacles to this, some of which have been touched on, are well understood, though they are hardly bigger than those in the way of European nations giving any important help in Asia. All this tends, as is so often the case, to leave the US shouldering the main burden, helped, it must be said, by the national defence efforts of regional countries which have been noted earlier.

So divergence there is too, not only where detailed security and economic policies are concerned but also between East Asian states. Taiwan and South Korea are alone with their security problems as far as other regional countries are concerned. But, in sum, convergence of interest is the main theme of this Paper. It is increased co-operation that needs to be addressed.

Notes

[1] I am indebted here to the late Richard L. Sneider and to his Paper *Regionalism in East Asia*, prepared for a SeCAP (Security Conference, Asia and the Pacific) Workshop in Tokyo on 19–21 August 1985 and to be included in a SeCAP book to be published.
[2] See *Asian Security 1986* for a discussion of developments in the Korean Peninsula and in South Korea (London and Oxford: Brassey's Defence Publishers, 1986).
[3] For remarks on US protectionism, see the Paper by Professor Inoguchi, Adelphi Paper 218.
[4] See *Asian Security 1986* for an analysis of economic problems in East Asia.
[5] For a fuller discussion of Soviet Asian policy, see the Paper by Harry Gelman, Adelphi 217, pp. 3–26.
[6] *Ibid.*.

US Military Power in the Pacific: Problems and Prospects: Part I

DR GEOFFREY KEMP

Introduction
Over the past 45 years the most traumatic military events involving the United States have been in the Pacific theatre. Pearl Harbor and the war with Japan; Korea, in which 54,000 American military lives were lost; and Vietnam where 57,000 Americans died. Vietnam remains a central factor in American thinking about military power, especially concerning the protracted use of ground forces.[1]

Yet, for the near term, two of the most likely US military contingencies which could result in major operations are in the Pacific or Indo-Pacific region. These are a new war in Korea and physical threats to oil supplies in the Persian Gulf. Furthermore, it is in the Pacific that the Soviet Union has made its most impressive expansion of power in recent years. The United States, far from tiring of its Pacific commitments has expanded them. This has not been at the expense of the NATO commitment. In fact, the most significant addition has been in the Indian Ocean, which directly serves European, as well as Asian and American interests.

Direct comparisons between the NATO and Pacific theatres are misleading. NATO is made up of like-minded Western democracies which, for the large part, are located in a small area of Europe and which face a well-established, common threat. To be sure, some members of the Alliance have other security problems which may, on occasion, take precedence over the Soviet threat. But, by and large, consensus within the Alliance on the strategic agenda presently outweighs the differences, and most members of it pay a large amount of money for national defence.

In the Indo-Pacific region things are not so orderly. Aside from the vast geographical distances stretching from Egypt to San Diego, countries in the region have very different cultural, political, ethnic and economic backgrounds. There are widely different views on the threat posed by the Soviet Union because the nature and intensity of the strategic environment varies dramatically; South Korea and New Zealand may be part of the Pacific theatre but they have little in common except to be considered part of the Western political-economic system. Similarly, the military threats from Iran to the small Arab states along the Persian Gulf littoral are real; military 'threats' to Indonesia or the small islands in the South Pacific exist in scenarios of future, not present, conflict.

The use of US military power in the Pacific theatre is linked to broader political and economic factors that defy easy analysis. How best to serve the interests of the United States and its allies and friends poses major conceptual, as well as operational, problems. It comes at a time when the American role in the world is undergoing significant changes and when concerns at home about budget and trade deficits are leading to calls for new and – from a foreign-policy perspective – often insensitive and potentially very damaging legislation to redress them. How the US juggles its domestic and foreign-policy priorities will have a profound impact on the countries in the region, as will the behaviour of key allies like Japan. Mismanaged or misconceived policies could unleash strong, but unpredictable, regional forces which in turn could alter the Pacific equilibrium of power as the next century is approached.

Since the region under discussion covers over 60% of the earth's surface and the littoral states comprise the bulk of the world's population, it is not possible to cover all the factors which influence US political-military policy. Instead, this Paper will focus on five issues which are judged important in the context of an emerging debate about American global strategy. They are: *1)* interests and threats; *2)* commitments and presence; *3)* key strategic factors; *4)* access and bases; and *5)* the South Pacific problem.

Interests and threats

Those who expect to find a coherent relationship between American interests in the region, the commitments to uphold those interests, and the military forces deployed to protect them will be disappointed. Instead, what is seen is a wide range of very different interests and highly diversified threats, and a force structure that would never have been designed for the task at hand if a more rational process had been at work.

The major American interest in the region is to prevent direct military threats to the United States similar to those posed by Japan in World War II. Only the Soviet Union poses such a threat. A second key interest is to ensure the security of, and to develop close economic ties with, countries who share basic American values. Most important here is the security of Japan. A third set of important interests is directly related to the security of oil supplies from the Arabian Peninsula. The threats to this wide range of interests are numerous, varied and, in some cases, controversial. They range from the Soviet Union's conventional build-up in the Far East, its military presence in Afghanistan and its growing maritime capability in South-east Asia, to the continued military confrontation between North and South Korea and a low level, but still unresolved and potentially destabilizing insurgency in the Philippines. The continuing Vietnamese occupation of Kampuchea poses a threat to Thailand; India and Pakistan could adopt explicit nuclear weapons strategies, and any one of thousands of small islands could become an Indo-Pacific 'Grenada'. And a wide variety of threat scenarios can be imagined in the Persian Gulf region.

The problem is that while like-minded people might agree with this range of contingencies, their ordering of priorities as to what deserves highest attention and therefore resources will vary. There are also respectable differences of opinion over the role of long-term structural trends, as opposed to the Soviet threat and short-term political trends, on propensities for conflict. Population dynamics, economic deprivation, religious animosities and fundamentalism; these are major sources of Asian conflicts and cannot be explained away by Soviet behaviour even if they are exploited by it.

The American commitment and military presence
This diffuse threat environment is reflected in the nature of American commitments and military presence in the Pacific region.

DEFENCE AGREEMENTS
The formal commitments which tie the United States to the defence of allies in the region only involve five countries, all of which are located in the Pacific. They are the Philippine Treaty signed in August 1951; the ANZUS Treaty signed between the US, Australia and New Zealand in September 1951; the Republic of Korea Treaty signed in October 1953; and the US-Japan Security Treaty signed in January 1960.

The United States has military co-operation agreements with Australia, Thailand and Taiwan and an agreement with Britain over the use of Diego Garcia. It also has bilateral agreements with Egypt, Somalia, Oman and Bahrain which have primarily to do with access rights to local bases in the Middle East Gulf region.

However, these commitments do not tell the whole story. One of the most important developments in the region since 1981 has been the growing military supply relationship between the US and China. Its significance is not yet reflected in either the quantity or quality of the technology transferred, but rather in a process which could eventually lead to high level military co-operation. This would have far-reaching implications for the Soviet Union and other regional powers.

THE US MILITARY PRESENCE
The United States maintains a military presence in the Indo-Pacific region, deployed from Hawaii to Egypt. The major deployments are in Japan, South Korea and the Philippines. There is a minor but nevertheless very important presence in Diego Garcia, Egypt and Saudi Arabia. In addition, there is a small US Air Force contingent in Australia. The primary US-controlled territories in the region include Guam and Kwajalein.

With the exception of the 30,000 US Army personnel in South Korea, the bulk of the US forces in the Indo-Pacific are air and maritime. The US Air Force, for instance, has over 16,000 personnel assigned to Japan, 11,000 to Korea and nearly 10,000 at Clark Air Force base in the Philippines. The Air Force also has nearly 400 people in Saudi Arabia, maintaining the E-3 AWACS (Airborne Warning and Control System) aircraft and the KC-135 and KC-10 aerial tankers that support them. The Air Force's Pacific presence is backed up by a wide variety of combat aircraft, including a squadron of B-52 stationed at Guam. The US Navy presence is equally impressive, with large facilities in the Philippines, over 1,300 personnel on Diego Garcia and a permanent presence in Bahrain. The US Navy in Japan includes 7,800 Navy and 26,000 Marine personnel. There are no major Navy units in Korea.

The strong emphasis on air and sea capabilities reflects the geography and the nature of the threats and commitments to the various countries of the region. Thus, the US Army presence in Korea is designed to support the much larger South Korean forces which, in turn, face a highly-mobilized and large standing force in North Korea. With the possible exception of the Gulf, none of the other US commitments are likely to involve direct attacks from ground forces. The threat to the Philippines is primarily internal and to the extent to which there is an external threat, it is maritime. The same applies to Japan unless massive airborne Soviet assault on the Northern Islands is envisaged. Similarly, Australia and New Zealand face no ground force threats and as a consequence the ANZUS Treaty revolves primarily around air and sea capabilities. A maritime strategy provides great flexibility for the deployment and use of US military power.

In Europe the allies have very clear-cut lines of demarcation on the ground for defence against a Soviet/Warsaw Pact attack; the most likely avenues of Soviet advance have been well studied. With the exception of Korea, Pacific threats are far less clearly defined.

The uses to which American power have been put in the region over the past forty years show a wide range of encounters, most of which were never anticipated. The same thing could be said for the future. The volatility of the various regional conflicts and the uncertainty about the Soviet–Chinese relationship provide for an almost unlimited number of permutations as to what might happen. If this is the case, is current American military power in the region well suited to its task? On a case-by-case basis, the answer is no: US forces are not ideally configured or deployed for, say, another Korean war or a major confrontation in the Persian Gulf. In the foreseeable future they are not likely to be either: it costs too much money. Hence it is 'flexibility' which continues to be the hallmark of US military power in the Pacific. Good logistics are the prerequisite for flexibility. When the United States became involved in Korea and Vietnam, it did so at a time when the surrounding region was 'permissive'; that is to say it was able to fight in Korea and Vietnam without any serious threat of interdiction of the long lines of communication (LOC) back to Hawaii and the continental United States. The ability to project power forward with secure LOC was perhaps the single most telling indicator of the predominance of US military forces in the post-war era. Threats to the US logistic capabilities which enable forces in the forward areas to be sustained are an important indicator of the military balance throughout the region.

US strategy

Very few persons, even in senior positions in Washington, can define in any precise manner just what the overall US strategy for the Pacific involves. To be sure, there are some specific commitments: defence of Korea and Japan; protection of the sea-lanes; security of the Persian Gulf oil-fields and so forth, but this does not add up to a coherent and readily understood strategy. Admiral S. R. Foley, former Commander-in-Chief of the US Pacific Fleet, has made an attempt to bring some logic to the subject. American Pacific strategy is a maritime one and has two basic components: deterrence, and, if it fails, the ability to win a war at sea. In the context of war-fighting he has argued that there are four strategic factors which would need to be taken into account. First, the human factor: how to respond to less than clear-cut events. This, indeed, is the essence of good leadership; a firm response to ambiguous evidence rarely pleases everybody, yet it is often the most cost-free option if exercised. Second, the anticipated role of Japan, the Philippines and China. If any combination of these key players were to opt out of co-operation with the United States in the event of serious crisis or war, the consequences would be great, given the US dependence on the first two for logistic support and operational bases and, in the last case, the impact on the Soviet Union, which could be of crucial importance in determining the outcome of the maritime battle. Third, in view of the long-term importance of access to and control of Middle East oil, preventing the region from falling under the domination of the Soviet Union would be a vital task, even if there were not dependency on the oil itself for short-term need. Fourth, the defence of the Aleutian Archipelago would be a high priority, given its geography and the vulnerability of the Pacific west coast of the US.[2]

Clearly the most difficult issue concerns the nature and content of the Soviet military threat. Although the Soviet Union is an Asian power, it is only recently that its power projection capability has enabled it to undertake an active presence in regions not adjacent to, or in close proximity to, its land mass. Three factors account for this: the US defeat in Vietnam and the replacement of American by Soviet maritime power at bases on the Vietnamese coast, especially Cam Ranh Bay; the growth in size and quality of the Soviet navy; and the continuing economic development of the Soviet Far East and the concomitant expansion in economic activity. Of these three phenomena, the last two were inevitable. To this extent the growing Pacific role of the Soviet Union has its own momentum which will be difficult, if not impossible, to stop.

Geography and access
Understanding logistics and strategy without reference to geography is not possible. The distances between the various sub-theatres in the Indo-Pacific region pose such fundamental constraints on any country's operational capabilities that a review of some of the distances is useful. It is 3,300 nautical miles (nm) from Hawaii to the big US facilities in Guam – already the equivalent of crossing the North Atlantic. From Guam it is 1,500 nm to the Philippines and over 5,300 nm to Western Australia. From the Philippines to Diego Garcia, via the Indonesian Straits, is 3,500 nm; and once at Diego Garcia, it is still another transatlantic equivalent to the mouth of the Persian Gulf. Western Australia is slightly closer to Diego Garcia and the Gulf (2,800 nm to Diego Garcia) but not that much. Even in the age of long-range in-flight refuelling and nuclear-powered surface ships the distances are still awesome and point to one very basic fact:

without access to forward bases and other facilities, the US cannot maintain a presence of any stature.[3]

This raises the very vexing question of the Philippines bases and what would happen if they could not be used. Although it is assumed that Mrs Aquino's government will not close the bases down, their existence remains a cause for controversy. This is enough reason to ask what would happen if a successor government said 'no' or limited their use. There is little reason to be complacent about the situation in the Philippines: the Communist insurgency continues, the army is weak, and the economy is a shambles. Things could get much worse in the years ahead.

The advantages of the US military facilities at Clark Field and Subic Bay, which are the largest outside North America, are both strategic and economic. From a strategic standpoint the bases provide the capability to monitor, on a real-time basis, activities in the South China Sea, including the increased Soviet presence in Vietnam, as well as events further to the west in the Indonesian Straits. Without these forward facilities the United States would be less able to influence events in the South China Sea and, if necessary, confront the Soviet maritime presence in time of war. The bases also provide an extremely important halfway house between major Pacific facilities in Japan and the Indian Ocean. Of special relevance in this context is Clark Field.

The economic advantages of the bases stem from the concentration of facilities which have been developed over time and the excellent labour force which is available at wages far lower than those found in many other parts of Asia. Thus, even if the equivalent facilities could be found elsewhere, the labour costs over time would be much higher.

While many studies have suggested alternatives to the bases in the Philippines, all of them have drawbacks. These can be looked at in three categories: strategic, political and economic. From a *strategic* standpoint each alternative, such as the island of Palau, or relocating major facilities in Japan, Guam or Western Australia would detract from the overall mission in the South China Sea. While new facilities in these places would enable the US to maintain a very powerful presence in the region, military efficiency would be lost; in the case of the South China Sea and South-east Asia this might be critical, dependent upon the status of the Philippines and its role in any major conflict. If major facilities were established in Western Australia, the Indian Ocean contingency might be easier to undertake. However, what would be gained for the Indian Ocean contingency would be lost for South-east Asia. Hence going to Western Australia alone would not meet the need unless the other facilities in the Western Pacific were expanded.

Each alternative poses different *political* problems. To start with the most obvious, a move to Taiwan would clearly jeopardize the delicate relationship between the United States and China, which is of such strategic importance that it overrides the value of Taiwan as a base. To move to Japan would add to already extensive American facilities and would concentrate US military presence in a country where political attitudes regarding the use of American military power are ambivalent. The small Pacific islands pose fewer political problems but these are not completely absent. Western Australia used to be considered a 'safe' alternative but now could pose formidable obstacles in view of US trade policy and the political winds running through the South Pacific.

Finally, there are the *economic* factors. It would cost billions of dollars to relocate and to duplicate completely the Philippines bases, and the missions they support would require not only additional facilities but additional maritime forces and, in particular, at least one or two extra aircraft carrier battle groups. Hence, over time the total cost would be very significant. The question is, in times of budgetary restraint, whether it is in the interest of the US to assume an even greater burden when fundamental questions are being asked about the very purpose of the mission.

The South Pacific
In no area is the confusion about threat, roles and missions more apparent than in the South Pacific region, including Australia and New Zealand. From an American perspective, the argument with the New Zealand government of David Lange raises some very basic questions about the future of the ANZUS Treaty and the relationship between deterrence, which has both nuclear and non-nuclear components, and likely scenarios which could involve the use of force.

Regarding the specific issue of access for US naval vessels which may be carrying nuclear weapons, the United States will not change its long-standing policy of 'neither confirming nor denying' the presence of nuclear weapons on its ships. To do so would make a mockery of a strategy of deterrence which depends for its success on maintaining a global posture with the capability to go anywhere with whatever weapons are deemed necessary for the mission. If ships are now to be denied access to the ports of an ally because they 'might' be carrying nuclear weapons, it becomes much easier for other countries to deny access or transit rights to warships that are nuclear-powered or suspected of carrying nuclear weapons. Since the US Navy does not maintain separate nuclear and non-nuclear fleets, and since any use of naval power is likely to involve some nuclear components of the fleet, there is no way members of a US alliance can be defended by only non-nuclear navies.

The irony in the case of New Zealand is that the most likely physical use of US military power that would be important would be the use of naval forces to secure the sea-lanes from the Persian Gulf and Southeast Asia which carry much of the Southern Hemisphere's oil. American plans to keep the sea-lanes open must involve the use of nuclear-powered and nuclear-armed vessels. True, such operations would probably take place many thousands of miles from New Zealand's pristine shores, but that, of course, is why many in the US government, while accepting New Zealand's right to choose its own policies for national security, cannot accept its strategic logic. After all, the Tanker War in the Gulf in 1984 and the mining of the Red Sea the same year required an active Western maritime presence to limit the dangers. This type of contingency affects all US allies who import oil.

A second issue concerns the future of the South Pacific and, in particular, economic problems and the efforts to establish a nuclear-free zone. On these scores the local countries do have some grievances against the US for not being sensitive enough to their needs. Take, for instance, the case of Kiribati. Kiribati needs money to develop its fledgling economy; the Soviet Union has been prepared to pay for fishing rights offshore. The sums of money are minuscule but, from the perspective of Kiribati, significant. In return, the Soviet Union not only gained access to much-needed fish, but built up political credit. But can or should the United States and ANZUS countries attempt to deny the Soviet Union such capabilities? Unless the US or its rich Pacific allies are prepared to offer equally good deals, they will find it difficult to stop small, poor countries from seizing the chance to better themselves financially. Thus, efforts to increase economic assistance to the South Pacific community and to take seriously the nuclear weapons testing issue should be a priority for US strategy.

The direction of US policy
What are current attitudes in the United States to the relationship between the Indo-Pacific and America's global role? First, one must not exaggerate; at this time talk of an American 'debate' about Asia similar to that conducted on TV talk shows and in the press about terrorism does not exist.[4] Nor is there presently a strong caucus on Capitol Hill for reassessing commitments. Rather what there are today are rumblings: a combination of budgetary realities and a consensus within the foreign-policy 'community' that a crunch is coming and that, sooner than later, the international implications of budgetary legislation will begin to be felt. The first and most vulnerable casualty will be the foreign aid account. Even if there were a willingness on the part of the Department of Defense to give up some of its own money for foreign assistance, there is a very good chance that the funds would not be appropriated by the Congress unless they were for Egypt and Israel or possibly the Philippines. The reason is simple: foreign aid is not popular on Capitol Hill.

Nevertheless, in the absence of a traumatic event such as the forced closure of the US bases in the Philippines or a spread to Australia or Japan of the New Zealand 'allergy', the substance of the US commitments towards the Pacific will not change radically. The focus will be upon strengthening the maritime capabilities of the US forces; trying to persuade Japan and others to assume an even larger share of the overall security burden, including more untied foreign aid; and efforts to resolve the very thorny economic problems which are beginning to haunt US relations with friends as diversified as Bangladesh and Australia. Military relationships will remain a cornerstone of the strategy, and arms sales to China could assume more military importance than is now the case.

Beyond these trends there are new political attitudes in the United States which have implications no one can foresee. There is loose talk, albeit muted, of a unilateral US reduction of forces from NATO and the Pacific as part of a retrenchment from an increasingly hostile and ungrateful world. Justification for such attitudes can be camouflaged under the guise of fiscal constraint and pressing strategic problems in Latin America. However, underneath it all is the prickly attitude of many Americans who feel their country has been made a scapegoat for every conceivable ill in the world. Terrorist attacks that single out Americans for vengeance are the ultimate symbol of this condition. In terms of domestic politics it is now the Democrats who head the charge against the anti-Americans. The 'blame America first' syndrome may have been a legitimate criticism of liberal Democrats in 1984; but the lesson was learned. No serious Democratic contender for the 1988 election will ignore the strong appeal of patriotism which has been the hallmark of Ronald Reagan. But this does not mean that high defence budgets will be back in vogue; quite the contrary. Cutting spending and blaming foreigners go hand in hand.

Unless the regional allies, especially Japan, show an even greater willingness to spend money on 'national security' and, at the same time, open up their markets to fair competition for American goods, 'Asia bashing' in Congress will grow and with it the argument that the United States pays more than its fair share for alliance security. No one believes that the US is going to withdraw from Asia. So long as the US presence can be maintained with maritime forces operating out of friendly bases, the foundation of the commitment will remain. However, if some traumatic event occurs, such as the closing of the Philippines bases, the American attitude could well change from 'what should we do next?' to 'what are we doing this for anyway?'.

Notes

[1] For the purposes of this Paper 'the Pacific theatre' is taken to include the area of responsibility assigned to the Commander-in-Chief Pacific Fleet, which covers the Indian Ocean and Persian Gulf, as well as the Pacific.
[2] S. R. Foley 'Strategic Factors in the Pacific', US Naval Institute Proceedings, August 1985, p. 34.
[3] The important exception to this emphasis on distance is the relative proximity of the Western seaboard of the US to the USSR, especially Alaska and the Aleutians.
[4] There is, however, a sophisticated debate going on among strategists concerning the role of the 600-ship navy and Secretary Lehman's call for a 'forward offensive strategy' which would have the US Navy attack Soviet warships and bases before they could reach the high seas.

US Military Power in the Pacific: Problems and Prospects: Part II

DR CORAL BELL

The American alliance system in the Pacific
America's alliance structure in the Pacific is rather like the city of San Francisco: widespread and impressive, but built over some diplomatic equivalents of the San Andreas Fault and therefore liable to be severely shaken from time to time. Nor can the possibility be dismissed that the subterranean movements which produce these periodic tremors may some day result in a serious swathe of destruction.

Between America's allies eastward across the Atlantic and those westward and southward across the Pacific there has always been one salient difference. The Europeans managed to organize themselves early into a single alliance, NATO, sufficiently coherent to maintain a coalition army. Moreover, the European members of NATO have always been assertive enough, and diplomatically or militarily powerful enough, to maintain a relatively equal dialogue with Washington.

None of that has been true in Asia and the Pacific. The essential alliance structure is a set of bilateral relationships between Washington and the other capitals concerned. (Even the one formerly trilateral arrangement (ANZUS) is now replaced by a sort of double-bilateral arrangement.) The original difference from NATO was undoubtedly inevitable, since in 1951, when the Pacific alliance structure was put together (in a period dominated by the Korean War and the Japan Peace Treaty), nothing else would have been possible. The countries concerned did not have enough in common, either in the way of shared culture and institutions or in the way of assumed joint strategic interests to make a multilateral arrangement feasible. So in effect the US extended its security umbrella to Japan, to South Korea, to the Philippines, to Australia and New Zealand, and to assorted Pacific islands, severally and on varying terms rather than jointly and on the same terms, as had been the case in Europe. A shaky multilateral annex was added to this essentially bilateral set of structures by SEATO in 1954, covering Thailand and the Indochina states. But that organization came to a bruising end in the upheavals of 1975, and the only effective remaining element of the theoretically still-valid Manila Treaty is the US bilateral connection with Thailand. So even now, thirty-five years from its origins, after two major wars on the Pacific rim (Korea and Vietnam) and after remarkably rapid growth in economic standing by many countries in the area, the security structure remains essentially a set of bilateral connections between Washington and various Asian and Pacific capitals.

This has had its convenient aspects for American policy-makers over the years, though it probably increases the air of fragility and prospective susceptibility to serious damage which hangs over the region at present. However, ten years ago (in 1975–6, after the final collapse of South Vietnam) or seventeen years ago (after the enunciation of the Guam Doctrine in 1969) the portents seemed still more ominous, yet the system held together. So the inherent resilience of its basic elements should not be underrated. That resilience springs from the conviction among the policy-making elites of the area that the connection with Washington helps to safeguard their respective countries against threats to their particular national interests, or sometimes against threats to regime security. While that conviction lasts, the governments concerned are unlikely to want to discard the Washington connection. Even New Zealand, which has now to be classed as an ex-ally from Washington's point of view, did not want that. (The Lange Government wanted, one might say, to have its anti-nuclear cake and eat it within the security of the alliance; Washington, for reasons to be sketched presently, signalled loudly the diplomatic equivalent of 'no way').[1]

The troubles with New Zealand offer a minor but illuminating example of the central problem of the alliance structure as a whole: the tension between global and regional (or domestic) preoccupations. For Washington the meaning of the treaty structure is and must remain spelled out in terms of America's central diplomatic and strategic task, the balancing and containing of Soviet power. The US faces no regional threat in Asia or the Pacific, now that China is a diplomatic 'co-belligerent' (at least for the foreseeable future). Vietnam and Korea are painful nagging memories, and Japan a vital and sedulously cherished ally. If Soviet power did not reach as far as the Pacific, it would be difficult to think of any contemporary reason (as against historic reasons) for Washington to maintain an alliance structure there at all, let alone so elaborate a one. But of course Soviet power is there, is not going to go away, and has become more substantial each year since 1975. So American policy in the Pacific is, and will remain, geared to the overall US strategic stance *vis-à-vis* the Soviet Union. That is, it will remain geared to nuclear deterrence. Because of the nature of the area and the vast Pacific distances, American naval capacity and naval strategic doctrine are even more important in the Pacific and Asian arena than in the Atlantic and European arena. That point will be further examined later.

By contrast, among the minor members of the alliance structure, the dangers that chiefly preoccupy policy-makers are regional and domestic. There is political and diplomatic logic in that, but it means that American policy-makers have an uphill battle in convincing even the more sophisticated of the political elites concerned that they should turn their minds towards Soviet capacities and intentions.

That is not the problem, however, with the major ally, Japan, which shares almost equally in Washington's preoccupation with Soviet power as the one visible, proximate and immediate threat. Japan's apparent insouciance about any foreseeable Chinese capacities in that respect is rather surprising to those intellectually nurtured on European balance-of-power assumptions, but it is convenient for American policy-makers. There are other tensions, however, in the US-Japan connection and, though the dangers are not immediate, they stem from powerful political forces on both sides of the Pacific. On the Japanese side, the basic factor is the 'nuclear allergy' enshrined in the well-known 'Three Non-Nuclear Principles', to which every Japanese government must pay at least plausible lip-service: 'Not possessing nuclear weapons'; 'Not producing nuclear weapons'; 'Not permitting their introduction into the country'. It is the third of these which creates problems for US strategists, especially naval ones. The US Navy has an obvious need to visit Japanese ports, and, of course, a substantial proportion of US naval ships are nuclear-armed or nuclear-capable. Any US naval ship, except those of the smallest classes, must be assumed therefore to be possibly carrying nuclear weapons. And one cannot see where or how these weapons could be off-loaded before the ship enters a Japanese port. To date, the apparent incompatibility between US and Japanese requirements has been simply enough resolved, by what one might call a Nelson-like policy (on the part of successive Japanese governments) of clapping the telescope to a blind eye when contemplating a US naval ship in a Japanese port, and failing to see any signals that it is nuclear-equipped. That is, in effect, refusing to construe the presence of such weapons on US ships in Japanese ports or home waters as constituting 'introduction' of such weapons to Japan, in terms of the Three Principles.

This has proved a workable enough solution so far, and may continue so long as the Liberal Democratic Party (LDP) can maintain a consensus in its favour. But the delicacy of restraint required to keep it in being was indicated by the furore in May 1981, when the former US Ambassador to Japan, Edwin Reischauer, mentioned out loud that there had been an unwritten consultative understanding on this matter. A similar brouhaha erupted when the communiqué issued after the Reagan–Suzuki meeting of early May 1981 used the word 'alliance' to describe the US relationship with Japan, that word being held to contain too clear an overtone of potential or actual military commitment to fit comfortably into the Japanese system of euphemisms. (The Japanese Foreign Minister found himself obliged to resign.) Sensibilities so delicate that they do not permit an alliance to be called an alliance, or allow mention of universally-known strategic arrangements, may constitute no more than a matter of semantic inconvenience, provided the actual US-Japan relationship remains solidly grounded in as much diplomatic mutual interest as exists at present. But obviously the relationship is also plagued by a real and rising level of economic tension, which might one day find political expression in the US, probably through Congress rather than the Administration. At present, there seems to be a delicate asymmetrical balance between Washington's tolerance of a level of Japanese imports many Americans resent, and Tokyo's acquiescence in nuclear ship-visits that some Japanese resent. Any disturbance of that balance would be catastrophically inconvenient to US strategic arrangements in the Pacific. Japan is in every way crucial to the overall US stance *vis-à-vis* the Soviet Union.

American strategic hopes concerning Japan over the longer term envisage Japanese naval or air forces taking over surveillance and control of the sea-lanes out of Japanese ports, for a thousand nautical miles south towards the Philippines and east towards Guam. A more effective air-defence screen over the Japanese islands and the Sea of Japan would be useful, one adequate to cope with Soviet long-range bombers and tactical fighters. And if agreement could be reached for the Tsushima, Tsugaru and Soya Straits to be mined in time of war or very severe crisis, Soviet naval access to the Pacific would be much impeded. But acquisition of such extra capabilities by Japan might mean breaching the symbolic 'one percent' limit on defence spending. (Actually by the NATO method of accounting the real level is almost 1.5%.) Since Japanese politics work through consensus rather than majority decision, movement in the desired direction may not be fast. From the point of view of the alliance structure as a whole, the main advantage would be to reduce the strain on US resources in naval and air power, permitting them to be deployed elsewhere. Against gains in that direction one must balance some offsetting costs among allies and presently friendly bystanders.

Only two of the ASEAN countries are US allies (the Philippines and Thailand), but ambiguities of feeling in ASEAN as a whole about the US stance in the Pacific offer considerable illumination of the general strategic complexities of alliances in the area. The tension previously noted between global and regional preoccupations is particularly visible here. The US as a global power must cherish as assets both its close relationship with Japan and its increasing strategic rapprochement with China. But the historic records in South-east Asia of those two powers make it inevitable that the ASEAN capitals should be, in differing degrees, wary of both, and therefore inherently distrustful (and sometimes resentful) of the United States as the super-power which is promoting increased armament for Japan (along with wider responsibilities, especially of a naval sort) and the long-term development and modernization of China. They remember that what is now the ASEAN area was the theatre of swift and efficient Japanese invasion and conquest, and long years of occupation, within the memory of those still in political office in the area. The memory carries differing levels of bitterness in the ASEAN capitals: perhaps most in the Philippines and least in Malaysia. More remotely, for many centuries before the imperial takeover by the West, China had claimed the status of suzerain power over much of the same area, and the notion that it may eventually reassert an equivalent level of long-term paramountcy there is quite widespread among the local political elites. Chinese remembrance of past tribute is assumed to be at least as enduring as the memories of those societies which once sent tribute to Beijing. So contemporary American attitudes to China are often regarded in South-east Asia as short-sighted or even naïve, because of what is construed as their apparent determination to recreate the power of China, regardless of what the ASEAN countries fear as possible longer-term consequences. Again, however, there are differences between the capitals concerned, with the strongest anti-Chinese feeling in Indonesia (which remembers in particular the allegedly Chinese-sponsored attempted coup in 1965) and Malaysia (the once strong and still extant Malaysian Communist Party having been almost entirely Chinese, and allegedly supplied from China as late as Cultural Revolution days). Singapore (for ethnic reasons and because Lee Kuan Yew gets along well with Americans and with Deng Xiaoping) directs its anti-Communism rather against the Soviet Union than China. So does Thailand, since it construes Vietnam as the main source of danger to its own society, and Vietnam is the protégé of the Soviet Union. But actually all the ASEAN countries, even Indonesia, have reasons for a basic wariness of Vietnam, seen as possessing one of the largest and most experienced armies in the world and a super-power ally to supply it with advanced weapons and diplomatic backing. So, despite the longer-term worries about American encouragement of revived Chinese and Japanese power, the necessity of American backing for Thailand and ASEAN in general against potential Vietnamese ascendancy in the area is widely agreed, at least among governing elites.

American power, not in the region itself, but just over the horizon, is thus seen as a source of balance and reassurance against quite an assortment of dangers. The recent disarray in ANZUS has therefore been viewed with some concern beyond the actual member countries. To the ASEAN capitals, and to most of the tiny polities of the Pacific, the alliance has been a way of tying American power to the security of South-east Asia and Oceania, without requiring these societies themselves to be identified as American 'fellow travellers'.

There is an obvious element of what must be called alliance symbolism in what otherwise would seem an unreasonably strong US reaction to the New Zealand decision to exclude nuclear-armed ships. The ban was a matter of no strategic importance to speak of in the case of New Zealand itself, but as an official of the Reagan

Administration put it, 'unless we hold our allies' feet to the fire over ship visits and nuclear deployments, one will run away and then the next ... We will not be put in a position where they want our protection but without the necessary weapons in place to do the job'.

Between the New Zealand decision and the American reaction, ANZUS had by 1986 become an example of how a long-standing alliance can be unexpectedly reduced to disarray by a movement of political feeling in portions of a democratic electorate. The motives for which David Lange, the Prime Minister of New Zealand (elected in July 1984 and facing elections again by late 1987), was induced to enact a ban on nuclear-armed ships did not include rejection of alliances as such, or of the American connection. But anti-nuclear sentiment in the New Zealand Labour Party was of long standing (at least since 1966), and had been exacerbated by assorted factors, including friction with France over testing at Mururoa, during the term of office of the previous Nationalist government. The US reaction in 1985–6 gave the issue a prominence it would not otherwise have enjoyed, and produced a sufficient backlash of New Zealand nationalism to increase distinctly the number of Lange supporters, even in the opposition party. American policy-makers (perhaps especially those in the office of CINCPAC, the Navy and the Defense Department rather than those in the State Department) felt the issue of principle too important, however, merely to shrug off the ban as a matter of no real operational significance, and hoped the example would not be noticed.

The upshot of it all is that ANZUS is for the time being reduced from a trilateral to a bilateral alliance, with New Zealand being cut off from its earlier access to US-originated intelligence, excluded from exercises involving US ships and demoted from the status of 'ally' to that of 'friend'. Presumably this 'making-an-example-of' may have had a useful warning impact elsewhere in the US alliance system: that obviously was the intention of the Washington policy-makers who decided on it, and on the evidence thus far in Europe one might conclude it had worked as was hoped. The change does not, however, mean that New Zealand is now outside the Western alliance system. It remains a member of the old ANZAC Pact of 1944 with Australia, much resented by Washington policy-makers at the time but now useful in a number of ways. So ANZUS as a trilateral arrangement has thus been in effect replaced by what was described earlier as a double-bilateral arrangement – US-Australia in ANZUS and Australia-New Zealand in the ANZAC Agreement. Though Australian policy-makers still grumble at New Zealand's decision, Australia's diplomatic leverage has probably been rather enhanced by its consequences. New Zealand also remains a member of the Five-Power Defence Arrangements (Britain, Australia, New Zealand, Singapore and Malaysia) originally brought into being in 1971 to provide some transitional security for Malaysia and Singapore as newly-sovereign states. Perhaps its potential functions should now be re-thought.

Australia is not at all likely to follow the New Zealand example, despite some similarities in the political pressures on the two Prime Ministers. The Australian Labor Party and the New Zealand Labour Party differ in more than the chosen spelling of their names. The doctrinal background in Australia is Catholic (Irish, Italian or Polish) and the right wing is inclined to ardent anti-Communism. The left of the party does have tendencies to neutralism (like the New Zealand party), but the Prime Minister and his three potential successors are firmly based on the right and centre of the Party, and well able to keep the left in line. Even more important, Australia's strategic situation is less like New Zealand's than outsiders usually assume. Australia (but not New Zealand) has a substantial Asian neighbour (Indonesia) of uncertain future ambitions. Australia (but not New Zealand) has a moral commitment (to Papua New Guinea) which might bring it into conflict with that Asian neighbour. Australia (but not New Zealand) has a long coastline facing the Indian Ocean and a couple of island territories there (Cocos and Christmas Islands) which seem as seizable as the Falklands. Australia (but not New Zealand) has a traumatic memory of bombs on its soil in World War II, and six months when Australia feared invasion. Australia (but not New Zealand) has for more than twenty years now played a role of some significance in the central balance of power, through the importance of the US installations at Pine Gap, Nurrungar and North-west Cape. Short of a complete revolution of feeling in the Australian Labor Party, no change from the present adhesion to the American connection appears likely. Some American naval opinion seems to have interpreted the recent Dibb Report on the future structure of Australia's Armed Forces as a sort of prelude to Australian isolationism, but that is a misunderstanding. It is actually a very belated but logical response to the Guam Doctrine of President Nixon's day (July 1969), suggesting more capacity to deal with local threats. It is in no way incompatible with a firm attachment to the American alliance: in fact the importance of that alliance is cogently defended by the author of the Report.

But even assuming this part of the alliance structure remains firm, there are other potential worries. Freedom of movement for US naval forces might conceivably be threatened over the long term by the growing popularity of declaring nuclear-free zones. The present Australian-sponsored one in the South-west Pacific is carefully toothless, but some local powers are likely to work to equip it with teeth. A few of the small governments of the Pacific Islands, specifically Kiribati and Vanuatu, are sometimes inclined to lend an ear to siren songs from the Soviet Union, Cuba and even Libya. Mostly this is because for some years they felt that almost their only economic resource, the fish in their very large ocean zones, was being plundered by members of the American Tunaboat Association. That did more than the Soviet Union to alienate Pacific Island governments from Washington. With economies as tiny as those, even two or three million dollars or roubles for fishing rights can provide a quarter of the government's budget. The problem has now been redressed by State Department action, but it will be some time before the bitterness wears off. And there are of course other issues: bases, weapons-testing, and some political aspects of various independence or autonomy agreements. Moreover, the US has refused to quarrel with France over atomic testing at Mururoa. Reproaches from the US to France on that matter would have seemed too flagrant a case of the pot calling the kettle black. Besides, France is an important but touchy ally in the global balance and, as in other matters, global considerations have priority over regional ones.

The threats to which Washington's alliance managers for the Pacific must respond within the foreseeable future are basically political or diplomatic, though many of them might have major strategic consequences. The clearest recent example has been the Philippines. In the years of President Marcos' decline, the US was faced with a situation dismayingly analogous to that which it faced in South Vietnam in 1962: a protégé (once deemed promising) in serious trouble, facing two insurgencies (one Communist-led, one Muslim-regionalist) which appeared to be making major military inroads into his control of the outlying districts, plus a rival leadership within the system with apparently a better claim to voice the real feelings of the people. Like Ngo Dinh Diem by 1962, Marcos by 1985 appeared less and less able to cope with either the internal wars or the opposition challenge. Nor could he be credited any longer with the ability to reform what had come to be judged an excessively corrupt, irresponsible and self-interested political elite. By some accounts, especially that of ex-President Marcos himself,[2] the hand of Washington was as active in the dramatic events of early 1986 in Manila as it was in those of 1962 in Saigon. And the subsequent problems were again parallel: whether the successor leadership would prove more able to turn the situation round, halt the decay in governmental control and institute the necessary reforms in the armed forces and elsewhere. If the sanguine original expectations of the new leadership in Manila prove justified, it may still not wholly remove the possibility of a future threat to US bases at Clark Field and Subic Bay, but it would ease some of the political and diplomatic embarrassments for Washington. The defence installations themselves might be found substitutes elsewhere (Guam, Tinian, Saipan or Palau) though only at heavy cost.

There are enough similarities (though also some clear differences) between the situation of the former regime in Manila and the present regime in Seoul, to make inevitable wide speculation as to whether what Mrs Aquino, 'people power' and elements of the Army did in the Philippines could conceivably be paralleled by a similar conjunction of forces in South Korea. And as to whether, in the event of such a development, there might be the far more dangerous possibility of an attack from the North across the border and a new version of the Korean War. If events move in that direction, even more careful crisis-management would be necessary from Washington than was the case in the Philippines, including perhaps seeking the aid of Beijing and Moscow, since neither of those two capitals appears likely to want a new version of the Korean War in the foreseeable future, and only they are likely to be able to exert adequate restraint on the decision-makers in Pyongyang, who have reason to believe that their military chances will decline by the end of this decade. Reportedly a good deal of American diplomatic effort is already going into a process of persuasion aimed at securing in Korea a smooth transition by 1988 to a more democratic South Korean regime, likely to remain stable and to be able in time to cope militarily with any threat from the North. It is probably inevitable that the South Korean opposition should feel that these efforts are not enough.

The recent activism of the Reagan Administration in hastening the exit of faltering autocratic governments of the right as well as left has had its successes, but has naturally disconcerted those who see their own regimes as possible targets, perhaps for some ambitious Congressman out to make a name for himself before election year comes round. There are some vulnerable regimes in the area which, though not allies, control assets essential to America's strategic purposes. Convenient ship and submarine transit from the Pacific to the Indian Ocean, for instance, depends on straits mostly under the control of Indonesia (the Sunda, Malacca, Lombok, Ombai-Wetar, and Makassar Straits). In the event of these being denied, there is the alternative 'south about' route round Australia, but that adds greatly to sailing times. If, for some reason, that route had to be resorted to, the importance of facilities like those at Cockburn Sound on the west coast of Australia would increase. But that is unlikely unless for some reason the present relationship between Washington and Djakarta ceases to be cordial.

Finally, there is one ominous doctrinal cloud on the horizon of the Pacific alliance. It arises from the so-called 'Lehman Doctrine', which US Navy sources insist should more properly be attributed to past and present US Chiefs of Naval Operations. With a 600-ship, 15-carrier US Navy now in prospect, and rather more than half of it, especially the most modern vessels, likely to be deployed in the Pacific, there is bound to be speculation among Pacific allies of the United States as to what the strategic mission of that formidable force would be, in for instance the case of a substantial outbreak of conventional hostilities on the Korean border. Assuming that the aggressor is judged to be North Korea, and that the Soviet Union remains (as now) North Korea's most important ally and supplier of advanced armaments, would there be excessive danger of 'horizontal escalation'? The general picture derived by outsiders from statements by Mr Lehman and Admiral Watkins (US Chief of Naval Operations) is of US submarines and surface combatants being 'surged' towards the Sea of Okhotsk and the Sea of Japan in order to 'bottle up' or destroy Soviet combatants, including submarines. Presumably if Soviet submarines are housed in the submarine-pens reported to be under construction at Cam Ranh Bay, the same would apply there. Such a process seems to contain a worrying potential that diplomatic efforts at crisis-management might be undercut by rapid naval escalation. There are already some murmurings of unease at what might be implied in such an operational policy in political quarters, for instance in Australia. A parliamentary question in February 1986 about whether North-west Cape would be involved in a US strategy of attacking Soviet nuclear-armed submarines during a major conventional war, evoked the official answer that the base would be closed if used in a nuclear first-strike strategy.[3] Perhaps question and answer ought to be construed as a conscious diplomatic warning shot. In reality the 'Lehman Doctrine' may be no more than a declaratory signal (perhaps a parallel to 'first use' doctrine in NATO) or even just a bogey-man inflated by critics of current US policies. Yet the Pacific alliance, like most alliances, lives by the political consent of its members, and the maintenance of consent depends on the credibility of Washington's reputation for prudence and good judgment during crises.

Notes

[1] The New Zealand electorate clearly believed it could have things both ways: a poll taken at the time showed 59% in favour of the ban, but 71% wanting continued membership of ANZUS. Washington policy-makers, including the Secretary of State himself, were apparently irked by what they saw as bad faith on the Prime Minister's part. They believed they had a deal on a visit by the USS *Buchanan*, which was nuclear-capable but (according to independent intelligence monitoring) not actually nuclear-armed. But it was still refused.

[2] See an interview in *Time*, 28 April 1986.

[3] Senate Debate, 11 February 1986 (Senator Evans answering for the Minister of Defence).

Korea to Kampuchea: the Changing Nature of Warfare in East Asia 1950-86: Part I

BRIGADIER-GENERAL EDWIN SIMMONS, USMC (RETIRED)

An American viewpoint

The war in Korea began in a clear, unequivocal, incontrovertible way: on 25 June l950 the North Koreans invaded South Korea.[1] The war in Vietnam, on the other hand, did not have such a sharp-edged beginning. Instead there were the ambiguous Tonkin Gulf attacks of August 1964 and the subsequent, equally ambiguous, Tonkin Gulf Resolution.[2]

It is impossible to deal with a 36-year continuum of armed struggle in one brief Paper. This essay will therefore be limited to a comparison of the American military experience at the operational level in the Korean War, 1950–53, with that in the Vietnam War, 1965–75.

The United States, caught by surprise by the North Korean invasion, was unprepared militarily to counter it. As had happened after every one of America's wars, peace in 1945 had brought immediate demobilization, a process accelerated by the attitudes of the new President, Harry S. Truman.[3] The peace of the world, or at least the prevention of larger conflicts, it was thought, was guaranteed by the American monopoly of atomic weapons. The forces the United States maintained as an occupying authority in such places as Japan and Germany were made deliberately unwarlike.

Korea received scant American attention in these years. The closest ground troops were the four US divisions making up the Eighth US Army in Japan. These divisions were in no way ready for active operations. At the time of the North Korean invasion, the South Korean army numbered about 98,000 men. Only four of its eight divisions were at anything like full strength. They had neither tanks nor heavy artillery. Both the Navy and Air Force of the South were inconsequential.

By comparison the condition of the South Vietnamese armed forces in late 1964 and early 1965 was much more substantial. Their strength was an imposing 514,000 and there were already 23,000 American military personnel in the country.

The division of the Republic of South Vietnam into four corps areas was most significant.[4] The corps commanders exercised both political and military control over their respective 'tactical zones'. The assignment of infantry divisions to the corps tended to be constant and unchanging.[5] Less tied to terrain were the elitist Airborne and Marine brigades, which together constituted the strategic reserve of the Joint General Staff, and the lightly armed but highly mobile Ranger battalions, which were most often used as corps reserves. In the political chain, immediately subordinate to the corps commanders were the province chiefs, who at least in the critical, most threatened areas were almost always military officers. Beneath the province chiefs were the district chiefs, again, most frequently military officers. And then, beneath the district chiefs, were the village chiefs and, finally, at the bottom of this pyramid, were the hamlet chiefs.[6] In this rigid, hierarchical system political and military purposes were inextricably entwined and nearly all troops of nearly all categories had fixed and mostly unchanging geographical areas of responsibility.

Geography
The military geographies of the two theatres of operations, Korea and Vietnam, have some rough similarities and some critical differences. The most obvious similarity is that both are peninsular appendages to the East Asian mainland. This suggests that as theatres of operations they might be readily isolated from the mainland, which in both cases was China. To the east of Korea is the Sea of Japan. To the west is the Yellow Sea. These can be readily controlled by a dominant naval power.[7] The boundary with China was something like 450 miles long. Could this very wide mouth to the funnel be sealed off by air operations? This would be one of the big questions of the war. The isolation of Vietnam posed a much more difficult military problem than the isolation of Korea.[8] Although the Indochina Peninsula was bounded by the Gulf of Tonkin, the South China Sea and the Gulf of Siam,[9] Laos and Cambodia lay to the west of Vietnam and here the land boundaries were not at all well-defined.[10]

Leadership and command
Next to be compared are the command structures and American military leadership in both wars.

First comes that towering figure, General of the Army, Douglas MacArthur. In 1950 he was CINCFE – Commander-in-Chief, Far East. His military authority within his assigned geographical area – which included Korea – was virtually identical to that enjoyed by the Allied theatre commanders of World War II. His mantle of authority was soon embroidered with another title, CINCUNC – Commander-in-Chief, United Nations Command. His operations in Korea and surrounding waters would be fought under the light blue and white flag of the United Nations. Subject to political constraints, geographic limits, and major strategic decisions, he was quite free to conduct military operations as he saw fit. Or so he thought. Eventually there would be his cataclysmic conflict with President Truman over their respective powers to control or direct military operations.

General MacArthur's counterpart in the Vietnam War was General William Westmoreland. General Westmoreland arrived in South Vietnam in 1964 and departed in 1968, not a very long time in a war that perhaps began in 1954 and which ended in 1975, but his stamp on American operations is indelible. His title was COMUSMACV (Commander, United States Military Assistance Command, Vietnam). He was not a 'commander-in-chief' but a 'commander'. It was not a theatre command, but a 'military assistance command' – a name which carries with it connotations of limited authority. Technically, Westmoreland's command was a subordinate unified command of Pacific Command, itself a theatre command under CINCPAC (Commander-in-Chief, Pacific) in the person of Admiral Ulysses S. Grant Sharp.[11]

Geographically, Westmoreland's authority was tightly limited to the boundaries of South Vietnam and even within these boundaries he had to negotiate with the Joint General Staff of the Republic of South Vietnam for tactical areas of responsibility in which American troops could operate. He exerted no authority other than persuasion over the Armed Forces of South Vietnam. He would argue valiantly then and later that 'co-operation and co-ordination' were an adequate substitute for unity of command but operations were not truly combined. There was obviously no United Nations Command in South Vietnam. The bits and pieces of third-country forces – the contributions of South Korea and Australia were the most significant in this respect – were loosely grouped into something called FWMF (Free World Military Forces). Westmoreland did not command these third-country forces; he exerted something called 'operational guidance'.

The government of South Korea (Republic of Korea – ROK) had one great and enduring asset in President Syngman Rhee. Through it all, Rhee projected an image of iron-like constancy. Also, most significantly, the North Koreans had no base of popular support in South Korea. There was nothing comparable to the Viet Cong. Compare this favourable political condition with that pertaining in South Vietnam. Ngo Dinh Diem had nine years, from 1954 until 1963, in which to unify South Vietnam and he was in a decline – an apparently irreversible decline – when he was assassinated. What followed was a bewildering kaleidoscope of changing governments made up of various combinations of generals. In 1965 the two strongest of these emerged, the mordant General Nguyen Van Thieu, who would be President, and the flamboyant Air Marshal Nguyen Cao Ky, who would be at times Premier and at times Vice-President. Thieu and Ky were bitter rivals, not partners. The most serious challenge to the Saigon government was the Buddhist Revolt of the first half of 1966, a virtual civil war.[12] The Buddhist Revolt should have made it painfully obvious that the Army of South Vietnam was not only deeply divided into factions but also regionalized, and that the hierarchical political and military organization was actually a pyramid of warlords, large and small.

War in Korea

The North Korean invasion of South Korea, a veritable blitzkrieg, began with the crossing of the 38th Parallel on 25 June 1950 by the North Korean People's Army (NKPA), some 165,000 men organized into seven infantry divisions and an armoured brigade. By 28 June, just three days later, Seoul, the capital of South Korea had fallen. It soon became apparent, however, that the loss of the capital did not mean the end of the war.

Two days after the North Korean invasion, the Security Council of the United Nations called upon all member nations to assist the Republic of Korea. Truman ordered a naval blockade on 30 June. The instrument for this was the US Seventh Fleet with subsequent substantial help by Britain's Royal Navy.

On 29 June, MacArthur flew to Korea to make his own reconnaissance. He came back to Tokyo with two ideas fixed firmly in his mind. First, American troops had to be committed immediately to the land battle. He gained President Truman's approval for this during the early hours of 30 June, and immediately the US 24th Division, the best of his under-strength, under-trained divisions, began moving piecemeal from Japan to Korea.[13] Second, that to seize the initiative the US must use its amphibious capability to land behind the North Koreans. Seoul would be the target of the operation. On 13 July, Lieutenant General Walton Walker arrived as commander of the Eighth US Army in Korea (EUSAK) and was given command of all ground forces, including South Korean. At the end of July, Walker ordered all of his troops to fall behind the Naktong River.[14] Walker enjoyed the one great advantage of air power.[15] Beginning in August, the fighter-bomber squadrons of the Fifth Air Force and the aircraft carriers of Task Force 77 were heavily committed to the defence of the Pusan Perimeter.

The amphibious assault on Korea's west coast was made on 15 September with X Corps, spearheaded by the US 1st Marine Division, landing at Inchon in the face of almost overwhelming technical problems. MacArthur's masterstroke turned the war around. By 28 September, Seoul had been retaken and Walker's troops had come bursting out of the Pusan Perimeter. MacArthur, in a grand gesture, reinstated Rhee in Seoul on 29 September.[16] The collapse of the NKPA was at hand. To ensure its destruction, MacArthur asked for authority to go north of the 38th Parallel. This authority was given to him with the caveats that he must halt if there was an entry into North Korea by major Soviet or Chinese Communist forces and that under no circumstances was he to cross the Chinese or Soviet borders.[17]

The Eighth Army was given the mission of seizing the North Korean capital, Pyongyang, and the still independent X Corps moved in amphibious ships to land at Wonsan on the east coast. On 10 October MacArthur had his famous Wake Island meeting with President Truman at which he confidently predicted that the Chinese would not intervene. Pyongyang was taken on 19 October. The landing of X Corps at Wonsan was made on 26 October. On the same day, the ROK Sixth Division ran into the Chinese 39th Army. By the end of October, Lin Piao's Fourth Field Army was south of the Yalu, and was about to be joined by Chen Yi's Third Field Army.[18] Walker began a cautious withdrawal, but MacArthur, still confident of complete victory, ordered him to regain the offensive.[19]

Walker's offensive began on 24 November.[20] Two days later Lin Piao launched his own attack and the two forces collided. Chen Yi moved similarly against X Corps. X Corps was extricated by an amphibious withdrawal from Hungnam, completed on Christmas Eve. The evacuation of Hungnam was the last significant use of the US Navy's amphibious capability. From time to time further amphibious assaults on the Inchon pattern would be proposed, but would not be implemented. Meanwhile, the Eighth Army, which had broken into large fragments, fell back to a line north of Seoul where, on 23 December, General Walker was killed in a vehicle accident. Lieutenant General Matthew B. Ridgway was flown out from Washington to replace him, arriving in Korea the day after Christmas.

China resumed the offensive on 1 January 1951, and by 4 January Seoul was again under Communist control. The UN line fell back but did not shatter, and by 24 January the Chinese offensive had stalled.[21] On 25 January, Ridgway, who must be considered one of America's finest operational commanders of the twentieth century, began his counter-attack which would continue until mid-April, rolling unrelentingly forward until the UN lines were just north of the 38th Parallel. MacArthur, who initially had not been confident of Ridgway's chances of success, once again began arguing for complete victory. This put him at cross-purposes with Truman who sought to limit the conflict and to maintain strict control of the military. An increasingly exasperated Truman, with the endorsement of the Joint Chiefs of Staff (JCS), dismissed MacArthur on 11 April.

Ridgway moved up to MacArthur's position as CINCFE and CINCUNC, and General James Van Fleet came out to take command in Korea. The full fury of the Chinese spring offensive came down on the UN lines on 21 April.[22] Van Fleet launched a general counter-offensive on 22 May. The Chinese appeared to be at the point of complete defeat when orders reached Van Fleet forbidding a further advance to the north.[23]

Truce talks began in July 1951. The lines were at the narrow waist of the Peninsula and here both sides settled down to entrenched positions. The fighting would go on for two more bloody years, but essentially the war was stalemated.[24] The UN navies had been overwhelmingly successful in the blockading of the two coasts of North Korea. Efforts to seal off the northern border by air power were much less rewarding.[25] The stalemated war continued until the armistice was signed on 27 July 1953. By then Eisenhower had succeeded Truman as President and the American military investment in what was still French Indochina was already considerable.

South Vietnam
In September 1950 the United States established a Military Assistance Advisory Group (MAAG) in Saigon to furnish aid through the French to Laos, Vietnam and Cambodia.[26] In February 1962 a new echelon, Military Assistance Command, Vietnam, or MACV, was superimposed over the Military Assistance Advisory Group.

The South Vietnamese Army had had nearly nine years of direct American advice and support when it suffered its first major defeats by the Viet Cong in 1963. Diem was assassinated in November of that year.[27] General William Westmoreland arrived in Saigon in January 1964 and in June became COMUSMACV.

On 7 February 1965 the Viet Cong attacked two US Army installations near Pleiku in the Central Highlands.[28] In a 'tit-for-tat' response, President Johnson ordered air attacks against two North Vietnamese barracks at Dong Hoi. The Viet Cong, undeterred, blew up a hotel housing US personnel at Qui Nhon on 10 February. This set off more retaliatory air attacks, followed in March by *Rolling Thunder*, a continuing aerial campaign against North Vietnam designed to interdict the flow of supplies to the south.

On 8 March, the 9th Marine Expeditionary Brigade landed at Da Nang, the first commitment of US ground troops to South Vietnam.[29] In July 1965 Westmoreland estimated that, with the help of 44 battalions, South Vietnam could stop losing the war, and with 24 more battalions in 1966 they could start winning it.[30] US Army units fought their first big battle of the war in Iadrang River valley in November. MACV's order of battle now showed the enemy as having 110 battalions, of which 27 were North Vietnamese. Westmoreland raised his troop requirements: by the end of 1966 he wished to have 74 US and 23 FWMF battalions and support for 162 battalions of the ARVN (Army, Republic of Vietnam).[31]

The year 1965 had seen the transition of the American role from an essentially advisory effort to what was in reality the US direction and prosecution of the war.[32] Simply stated, the operational goals were:

(a) to destroy the Viet Cong main force units and force the North Vietnamese to withdraw;
(b) to establish a militarily secure environment by the eradication of Viet Cong local forces and infrastructure; and
(c) to support the Republic of South Vietnam in nation-building.

Priority was given to the first of these objectives.

In December 1965, as a companion piece to *Rolling Thunder*, the US Air Force began Operation *Tiger Hound*, the bombing of targets in Laos to interdict troop and supply movements down what had come to be called the Ho Chi Minh Trail. The Navy's share of the aerial interdiction of North Vietnam and Laos and of close air support in South Vietnam was carried out by aircraft carriers operating in the South China Sea.[33]

In mid-summer 1966 the North Vietnamese began infiltrating regular divisions across the demilitarized zone (DMZ). Westmoreland, constrained by the American self-imposed rules for the conduct of the war, which gave the North Vietnamese sanctuary against ground action until they actually emerged from the DMZ, ruled out a Korean-style trench line defence as being impossibly expensive in manpower. He decided instead on a string of strong points linked by a high-technology obstacle system. One of the strong points was the Special Forces camp (later a US Marine combat base) at Khe Sanh. Westmoreland hoped someday to mount a major thrust into Laos to cut the Ho Chi Minh trail and he saw Khe Sanh as being the jumping-off place.

On the ground there were many named operations – as, for example, *Hastings, Prairie* and *Cedar Falls*. Most lacked enough form, shape or tangible results other than the questionable and ubiquitous 'body count', to be called battles. The named operations multiplied in 1967, but, for the most part, they came to be a book-keeping device by which the number of units assigned to a prescribed region could be monitored and controlled, with results measured more and more in terms of body count. While the battles against the North Vietnamese regulars went on, the 'paddy war' against the Viet Cong continued.[34] High-mobility helicopter operations, which whisked American troops and their allies back and forth across their 'tactical areas of responsibility', gave an illusion of control that did not really exist on the ground. Areas which were 'pacified' refused to stay pacified. 'Reaction force' became part of the jargon of the war and, ironically, its very use reflected the fact that much of the rushing back and forth was in response to attacks or other actions initiated by the Viet Cong.

The US Navy also had its operations: Operation *Market Time* was a generally successful effort to cut off infiltration from the sea by the detection and interception of enemy traffic in South Vietnamese coastal waters. Operation *Game Warden* was the interdiction of enemy bases and lines of communication in inland waterways in III and IV Corps areas, the beginning of what came to be called riverine operations. Operation *Sea Dragon* was the interdiction of enemy supply vessels in coastal waters off North Vietnam. *Sea Dragon* could not be called a blockade as third-country shipping steamed in and out of North Vietnam's ports with impunity.

In November 1967, Johnson called Westmoreland to Washington, ostensibly for consultations but really to rally support for the war. Westmoreland told his television audience that withdrawal of US troops could begin in two years.

January 1968 began with rumours of an impending major attack against the Marine regiment at Khe Sanh, a kind of re-play of Dien Bien Phu.[35] Westmoreland planned to meet it with a massive aerial counter-offensive that he called Operation *Niagara*. The enemy attack began on 21 January, and it seemed that three North Vietnamese divisions were converging on the base. Vietnam's celebration of the lunar New Year (Tet) was supposed to be observed with a country-wide truce from 27 January until 3 February. Instead the enemy celebrated Tet with a general offensive. Saigon, Da Nang, and most particularly Hué, were penetrated. The so-called 'siege of Khe Sanh' – it never really even approached being a Dien Bien Phu – lasted until 6 April. As a consequence of Tet the enemy abandoned, for a lengthy time, large-scale operations. One of the American casualties of the Tet offensive was President Johnson. On 31 March he announced to the nation that he was de-escalating the war and had decided not to seek re-election.

General Creighton Abrams, Westmoreland's deputy, replaced Westmoreland as COMUSMACV on 1 July.[36] In September, Abrams articulated the 'one war' concept which recognized that the war of the big battalions was not separate from the war of pacification and population security. Richard Nixon, in his campaigning for the Presidency, promised a 'secret' plan for ending the war. This turned out to be Vietnamization,[37] and the phased withdrawal of American troops. As a prod to Vietnamization, President Nixon authorized a limited incursion into Cambodia. The incursion lasted until 30 June 1970 and 10,000 enemy casualties were claimed. As a companion piece, Westmoreland's long-cherished plan for an incursion into Laos began on 30 January 1971, only it was the ARVN I Corps that marched out along Route 9. No American ground troops, not even advisers, went with them. Even with heavy US support, particularly by helicopters and air strikes, the operation turned into a disaster.[38]

Nearly all US combat troops were out of South Vietnam when the North Vietnamese launched their Easter Offensive in 1972.[39] With American advisers providing a communications link and with massive US air and naval support, the South Vietnamese, after considerable loss, turned back the invasion.[40] Such would not be the case in 1975. The Peace Accords, for what they were worth, were signed in Paris on 27 January 1973. The uneasy 'peace' continued for almost two years. After initial probes in December 1974, the North Vietnamese began their full-scale invasion in March 1975 with three major thrusts not unlike the operational pattern of Easter 1972. General Thieu attempted to withdraw his I and II Corps from the north and the Central Highlands so as to concentrate his forces around Saigon and the vital coastal areas. This time there were no American advisers, no American helicopters or fighter-bombers, no massive influx of logistic support. On 29 April 1975 there was a well-executed helicopter evacuation of American citizens and a good number of other foreign nationals and South Vietnamese from Saigon. That was the end of it.

An operational comparison
In summary, what can be said about the operational patterns of these two wars?

Korea was a conventional war fought with conventional uniformed forces using conventional weapons in a conventional way. It became, from the end of 1950 at least, a war of east–west lines moving up and down a north–south axis until equilibrium was reached. The pattern of operations was roughly analogous to the pattern of World War I as fought on the Western Front. The first year was a war of movement characterized by sudden and dramatic successes and reverses as new elements of force were introduced. After the truce talks began, the fighting settled down to a stalemated war of position, during which neither side risked a general offensive, until the armistice was signed.

A clear operational pattern in the Vietnam War is much less discernible. Following a long ten-year period of US advice and support to the changing Saigon governments – a period of applied 'counter-insurgency' theory, which was filled with circumlocutions and circumventions – American ground forces were introduced into the war in gradual numbers and at first in a semi-garrison way. The enemy was largely invisible and at the same time seemed to be everywhere. The enemy troops fought unconventionally and artfully countered American efforts to force them to fight on conventional terms. Even so, each time enemy forces risked a battle of any size they lost. This was true in the opening rounds of 1965 and 1966, most certainly true of their attempts at a general offensive in 1968, and again true in 1972, even after most of the US forces had departed. Not until 1975, when all American troops were gone, did the enemy win on the battlefield.

In both wars, the enemy had guaranteed sanctuaries, both geographic boundaries and thresholds of military action that they knew the Americans would not cross. After the first year in Korea, the enemy knew almost with certainty that the war would not be carried into the Chinese homeland. The guarantees in the Vietnam War were even more constraining. The Chinese homeland was never threatened. The Soviet Union was even more immune. High-technology efforts to seal off the borders of South Vietnam from North Vietnam, Laos and Cambodia were expensive and ineffective. Clandestine efforts to penetrate these areas were, in general, a failure. The brief incursions into Cambodia and Laos in 1970 and 1971 were, in the first case, a transitory success and, in the second case, a disastrous failure. 'Strategic' weapons such as B-52 bombers and aircraft carriers were used as tactical weapons at great expense and with limited results.

America's supremacy in tactical air power over the battlefield in both wars was offset by the enemy's passive and active defences. In the case of Vietnam, these defences grew out of experience of wars against Japan and France. Strategically, North Vietnam was bombed at a level of intensity that steeled North Vietnamese resolve but did not threaten the homeland with physical destruction, which was quite within US capability.

America's naval near-monopoly was used most effectively during the first year of the Korean War. After that there were virtual guarantees that there would be no further amphibious operations against the North Korean coasts. During the Vietnam War, amphibious operations against North Vietnam were much discussed (Vinh was seen as a target comparable to Inchon), but never seriously contemplated. The North Vietnamese were secure in their knowledge that their homeland would not be invaded.

In the Korean War, Seoul was twice taken by the enemy and twice re-captured. Similarly, Pyongyang was taken by the UN forces and retaken by the Communists. Loss of these respective capitals did not end the war for either side. The loss of Saigon in 1975, however, was the death knell of the Republic of South Vietnam.

Conclusion

This brief comparative analysis has suggested some of the underlying reasons why the American military experience in Korea, viewed in operational terms, was a qualified success, and why the experience in Vietnam was a qualified failure. In Korea, the territorial *status quo ante* was achieved, but not all military objectives were attained. Vietnam, despite the ultimate collapse of the South Vietnamese government, was not, in operational terms, a complete military failure. From 1965 until 1972, American military might, at great cost and not always with admirable efficiency, dominated the battlefield. This was not of itself sufficient to bring about an acceptable outcome to the war. Of all the lessons of the Vietnam War, perhaps the greatest lesson is that force alone does not translate into power.[41]

What does all this portend for the future? Both wars demonstrated that the United States is in truth a Pacific power, not an Asian power. In projecting force across the Pacific its greatest strengths are its air and naval capabilities. These capabilities were somewhat under-used in the Korean War and grossly misused in the Vietnam War. Certainly this is a lesson that has been learned, just as it has most certainly been learned that the United States is at grave risk whenever it essays a ground war in East Asia.

Notes

[1] Most of America's wars – most particularly the successful ones – have begun with an immediate *casus belli* so compelling that it brought a coalescing of American public opinion. The best example of this, of course, is the Japanese attack on Pearl Harbor in December 1941.

[2] President Johnson saw the Tonkin Gulf Resolution as a kind of *de facto* declaration of war, or at least a legitimization of the expansion of US military effort in South Vietnam beyond the artificial 'counter-insurgency' level into one of overt US military operations.

[3] Truman, a National Guard officer, in World War I, had a visceral distrust of large standing armies.

[4] These corps areas were designated as 'tactical zones'. Later they would be re-designated as 'military regions'.

[5] The ARVN (Army, Republic of Vietnam) divisions occupied 'tactical zones' whose boundaries tended to be coincident with the political boundaries of the provinces encompassed by the tactical zone. There were also a number of 'special defence sectors', usually garrisoned by a separate regiment.

[6] The province chiefs did have a limited military capability in the form of the Regional Forces assigned to them. These Regional Forces were locally raised militia which theoretically could not be used outside their home provinces. Even more constrained was the use of the very local Popular Forces which were essentially district, village and hamlet garrisons.

[7] Korea is about 650 straight-line miles from its northernmost to southernmost extremities and is shaped like a funnel, a funnel that opens out into a very wide top. This northern boundary is very clearly delineated for almost all of its length by the Yalu and Tumen Rivers. All of it borders China except for a tiny land link with the Soviet Union at its extreme eastern end.

[8] The problem areas in both cases were the land borders and where those land borders were poorly defined the task was made just that much more difficult.

[9] North and South Vietnam together formed a shallow letter 'S' fronting on the South China Sea to the east. The widest part of this long, narrow country – it is about 1,200 miles from top to bottom – is its boundary at the top with China. This, again, is rather funnel-shaped, and the top of the funnel is something like 450 miles long, about the same length as the Korean–Chinese border, but lacking the convenient rivers to give it clear definition.

[10] The boundaries of Vietnam with Laos and Cambodia run for the most part along the tops of the Annamite mountain chain and they are shrouded with rain forest. To the west of Laos and Cambodia is Thailand, with a good part of its boundary marked clearly by the Mekong River.

[11] Westmoreland's Military Assistance Command, Vietnam, had Army, Navy and Air Force components each with its own commander. He had operational control of these components only for operations within the boundaries of South Vietnam. Naval operations, up to the very water's edge of the South China Sea, were the province of the Seventh Fleet whose commander reported to Commander-in-Chief, Pacific Fleet, who in turn was a component commander of the Pacific Command. When aircraft of the Seventh Air Force took off from fields in South Vietnam for air strikes against targets in North Vietnam and Laos they were not under Westmoreland's command. Instead, the chain of command ran back from Seventh Air Force to Pacific Air Force, another component of Pacific Command.

[12] The Buddhist Revolt was led by the militant monk Thich Tri Quang who had as his military ally General Nguyen Chanh Thi, the commanding general of I Corps Tactical Zone.

[13] The 24th Division was followed in mid-July by the 25th Division and the 1st Cavalry Division.

[14] The defensive line, manned by about 47,000 US troops and some 45,000 South Koreans, was called the Pusan Perimeter.

[15] At the war's outbreak, the only immediate combat support that could be given to the retreating ROK army was that which could be provided by the US Far East Air Forces (FEAF). This command had at its disposal the Fifth

Air Force based in Japan, and, at a greater distance, the 20th Air Force on Okinawa and the 13th Air Force in the Philippines.

16 Seoul was lost again in December 1950, regained in February 1951, and held for the remainder of the war.

17 By this time the UN Command had grown to 315,000, of whom 200,000 were ground combat troops, half American and half South Korean. The British 27th Brigade and a Philippine battalion combat team had also arrived.

18 The Fourth Field Army, considered China's best, consisted of the 38th, 39th, 40th and 42nd Armies. The Third Field Army consisted of the 20th, 26th and 27th Armies. Each numbered Chinese army had about 30,000 men and was roughly the equivalent of a US corps.

19 Substantial reinforcements had arrived, including the British 29th Brigade, the Turkish Brigade and battalions from Thailand, the Netherlands and Canada. Ultimately, 14 members of the UN other than the United States sent troops to South Korea.

20 China's entry into the war brought MiG-15 interceptors into the equation, imperilling the US bombers, particularly the B-29 *Superfortress* that were pounding North Korea in what was essentially an interdiction campaign. The threat posed by the MiG-15s, however, was quickly countered by the introduction of the superior F-86 *Sabre* jets.

21 Intelligence reported that Lin Piao had been wounded and replaced by Peng Teh-huai.

22 As would be repeatedly the case, the Chinese could not sustain a fully-fledged offensive. By the end of April it was clear that Peng's attack had lost its momentum. He paused for two weeks and then on 15 May attacked again. By US estimates, the spring offensive cost Peng 90,000 men.

23 Less dramatic than the aerial combats being fought by jets in the North Korean skies was the introduction by the US of helicopters into combat. Casualty evacuation had been a first use, but, as the lines began to harden, Army and Marine helicopters were increasingly used for frontline troop movement and re-supply.

24 A No Man's Land 155 miles long stretched across the waist of Korea. The Communist forces now numbered 850,000, but lacking in air power and lighter in fire support than the 700,000 UN troops, they dug in more deeply.

25 A great air interdiction effort, Operation *Strangle*, was launched to cut Communist lines of communication from the Yalu south to the front. This massive effort, ultimately failed, as was demonstrated by the capability of the Communists to maintain an army of one million men in a war of position and to launch limited attacks in the last year of the war.

26 The 1950 MAAG was the nucleus for direct US military assistance to Vietnam after the French departure following their defeat at Dien Bien Phu in May 1954 and the subsequent Geneva Accords. The agreement reached at Geneva on 20 July 1954 divided Vietnam at the Ben Hai River and superimposed a DMZ over the partition line.

27 By the end of 1963 there were 16,300 US military personnel in South Vietnam supporting and advising South Vietnamese armed forces numbering 243,000.

28 Nine Americans were killed and 128 wounded at Pleiku. Twenty-two aircraft were damaged or destroyed. On 30 October the Viet Cong had attacked Bien Hoa air base, destroying six US B-57 bombers and killing five US servicemen, and on 24 December had bombed US billets in Saigon, killing two US servicemen.

29 The US Marines' initial mission was to defend the Da Nang air base. In the next few weeks rules of engagement evolved: the Marines could shoot back if shot at, they could go to the aid of the ARVN under certain circumstances, and, finally, they were authorized to undertake limited offensive operations.

30 B-52 bombers were used against targets in South Vietnam for the first time in August. In that same month the US Marines fought their first regimental-size action of the war against the Viet Cong 1st Regiment south of Chu Lai in Quang Nam province.

31 Secretary of Defense McNamara accepted Westmoreland's estimates and told President Johnson to be prepared for 1,000 Americans killed-in-action each month.

32 By the end of 1966 there were 385,300 US and 52,500 FWMF personnel in South Vietnam, and the size of the South Vietnamese armed forces had climbed to 735,900. These numbers exceeded the peak figures reached by the UN Command in Korea.

33 Task Force 77 (TF77), the Seventh Fleet's Carrier Strike Force, was charged with the aerial interdiction of enemy supply lines in North Vietnam and Laos and close air support in South Vietnam. TF 77 operated from Yankee Station, a fixed point in the South China Sea just north of the DMZ, and Dixie Station, a staging area in the South China Sea south-west of Cam Ranh Bay.

34 'Pacification', a term that was originally avoided, became increasingly respectable. Despite elaborate programmes and intricate statistical systems for measuring progress, in the final analysis the US, or for that matter any foreign troops, were limited in what they could do to pacify the countryside or to root out the Viet Cong 'infrastructure' which seemed to infest all of South Vietnam.

35 On the eve of 1968 there were 485,600 US servicemen and 59,300 FWMF personnel in South Vietnam. The South Vietnamese armed forces had grown to 798,000.

36 Westmoreland left Vietnam on schedule. In no sense was he relieved by the President as MacArthur had been. His departure, however, was clouded by the aftermath of the Tet offensive in 1968 and the ambiguous battles of Hué, Khe Sanh and Saigon. Creighton Abrams, his successor, was more popular than Westmoreland. Abrams was burly and bear-like; Westmoreland was stiff and starched. Moreover, after Nixon's inauguration, Abrams' mission was quite different from Westmoreland's. Under the new president, Abrams' mission was to extricate US troops from the war under a programme of withdrawal euphemistically labelled 'Vietnamization'. This he did well. His one significant operational initiative was the Cambodian incursion, temporarily a tactical success, but ultimately counter-productive.

37 'Vietnamization' was essentially the phased turning-over of the conduct of the war to the South Vietnamese and the withdrawal of US forces. All US combat forces were out of South Vietnam by August 1972.

38 *Lam Son 719*, the ill-fated incursion into Laos, had as its objective the supposed major North Vietnamese supply base at Tchepone. Some 20,000 South Vietnamese soldiers and Marines were involved. The operation began on 8 February 1971. Tchepone was reached on 6 March and found abandoned. Losses during the withdrawal were extremely heavy. In all, South Vietnam lost 9,000 men and much materiel. Casualties amongst supporting US units totalled 1,462. Enemy strength was estimated at 36,000.

39 The Easter Offensive was a conventional cross-border invasion. There were three prongs to the attack: one in the north across the DMZ and from Laos, one in the centre coming down through the Central Highlands, and one in the south coming out of Cambodia and threatening Saigon. The only US ground combat units remaining in-country at that time were the 3rd Brigade, 1st Cavalry Division, and 196th Light Infantry Brigade.

40 The massive air support flown by the US Air Force and Marine units in reaction to the Easter Offensive was code-named *Linebacker*. These operations were cut back in October 1972 in response to supposed progress in the peace negotiations in Paris. When these negotiations broke down in December, President Nixon ordered a heightened campaign, designated as *Linebacker II*, against the Hanoi area by US Air Force and Navy aircraft.

41 The ultimate cost for the US in Korea was 157,530 casualties, of whom 33,629 were battle deaths and 20,617 were other deaths. In Vietnam the cost was 210,988 US casualties, of whom 47,239 were battle deaths and 10,446 were other deaths.

Korea to Kampuchea: the Changing Nature of Warfare in East Asia 1950-1986: Part II

PROFESSOR ZHANG JINGYI

Since the end of World War II, there have been no fewer than a hundred wars, large and small, on this planet. But rare are the wars to compare with the four fought in East Asia – the Korean War, the first and second Indochina Wars and the Vietnamese invasion of Kampuchea – in terms of scale, duration, lethality, extent of great power involvement and impact on the global strategic balance. In three of these four wars, not only the two super-powers but also the largest developing country, China, were either directly or heavily involved. Large parts of the two peninsulas were ruined, with heavy casualties on all sides.

It was on these two peninsulas, after paying tremendous costs, that the United States painfully, gradually and coolly realized the limits of its strength. The Soviet Union took advantage of its principal adversary's deep involvement in the Indochina War to increase rapidly its own military capabilities in an expansion that has shocked the world. However, the good days did not last long and by the 1980s the Soviet Union began to feel over-burdened. As for China, ever since its founding it has been dragged into all these wars, without exception. Beijing has been forced to make heavy national sacrifices in an effort to seek a secure and stable environment for peaceful reconstruction. In the face of such difficulty, China succeeded not only in standing firm on its own feet as a newly-born country, but also in embarking on its long-desired 'Four Modernizations' while playing an increasing role in maintaining stability and peace in the Asian-Pacific region and the world. Because of the consequences of these wars more and more people came to realize how wars in East Asia, a region remote from the Western concept of the centre of the world, can change the global balance of power and correlation of forces.

Not surprisingly, experiences and lessons drawn from wars of such scale and with such profound consequences can prove rich. In these wars all sides suffered from miscalculations and mistakes yet, at the same time, achieved some successes. The United States was able to concentrate enough troops for the surprise Inchon landing less than three months after the outbreak of the Korean War, at a time when it had brought millions of servicemen home. The next month saw China reacting with gallantry and efficiency though its own civil war had not yet ended. After decades of discussion and debate, many of the experiences and lessons from the Korean War seem obvious, but just imagine what challenges people faced when, after they had become accustomed to the style of World War II they suddenly found themselves involved in another style of war greatly different in terms of the battlefields, adversaries and international context. It was like suddenly entering a tunnel from the bright sunshine, and having to feel the way in pitch-darkness. No matter what the issue, identifying national interests, making a decision to enter a war, choosing the proper force structure, weapon systems or tactics, and, finally, judging the timing, conditions and manner in which to end the conflict, all presented new problems.

For many Americans, as General Matthew B. Ridgway has said, the Korean War was the first time they 'became acquainted with the concept of limited war'. In China's case, it was the first time its forces had crossed its border and fought on foreign territory, directly engaging the army of the Western super-power. Naturally, uncertainty prevailed on both sides. People all over the world worried about the possibility of a disastrous new world war. They feared particularly the use of the atomic bomb. Yet neither fear was realized.

General MacArthur had been confidently looking forward to a Christmas victory on the banks of the Yalu River, while Mao Ze-dong had prepared for yet another withdrawal into the mountains to fight a guerrilla war. Nevertheless, despite a bloody war fought over three years, the opposing forces ended almost in the same positions from which they had begun. Had there not been ruins, nothing would have remained to remind people that there had been such a 'limited', yet all-out war. Just as the Korean War did not proceed as the antagonists had planned, so other East Asian wars were to prove unpredictable. All the timetables set for wars to achieve a rapid decision, including the French plan to restore the colonial order in Indochina, the American design to 'block the Communist flood' southwards and the Vietnamese attempt to establish an expansionist 'Federal Indochina', proved to be mirages.

New weapons and new tactics appeared one by one in these protracted confrontations between the modern Western concept of war and the ancient Oriental art. The most spectacular examples, of course, were the new air weapons. The earliest engagements between combat jet aircraft occurred in the Korean War. In the 1960s people witnessed the revolutionary impact of helicopters on ground operations and tactics. The 1970s saw precision-guided missiles demonstrate their miraculous effects on modern warfare.

At the same time, traditional weapons and tactics were used innovatively. In Korea, the Chinese forces refined the tunnel warfare used by guerrillas during the anti-Japanese war into a means for powerful positional warfare, so as to enhance the power of the regular army and effectively neutralize US air and ground superiority in firepower. The Americans tried to kill hens with knives meant for butchering oxen, i.e., to accomplish conventional operational and tactical missions using strategic bombers. The war became the more cruel as each side attempted to exploit the adversary's weaknesses and its own advantages.

Last but not least, there was yet another innovative development: the adversaries opened a new 'battlefield', the negotiating table. They adopted another means of operation – negotiation – and threw into action new 'troops', the diplomats. Both in the Korean and Indochina Wars, the two largest 'limited' wars so far, more than half of their duration was spent on both these 'battlefields', as the two sides engaged each other in simultaneous but different forms of warfare. Never before had there been seen so delicate an art of combining 'bloodshed politics' and 'non-bloodshed politics'. They were used secretly and openly in various forms, such as 'talking after fighting', 'fighting while talking' and 'promoting talking through fighting'.

Yet, looking past these dazzling changes, there was also something familiar. The Korean War was fought by large armies on both sides, employing mobile positional warfare. The two Indochina Wars were fought by the Vietnamese against the French and later the Americans with guerrilla warfare against counter-insurgency, air defence against air attack and only in the final stages, set-piece actions between larger formations. The Vietnamese invasion of Kampuchea has shown that Hanoi simply changed its role while the drama remained the same. Although weapons and tactics might have been improved or changed, the dilemmas facing commanders remain almost the same: quality versus quantity, replenishment versus attrition; the short haul versus the long, etc. Additionally, no matter how important naval and air forces might have been in these wars, ground forces remained the decisive factor. The overwhelming numerical superiority of the Chinese and North Korean ground forces successfully confronted the superior firepower of the US army.

Finally, the principle of unconditional surrender applied by the World War II alliance was not reasserted in the three wars in East Asia which have been ended so far. In the current Kampuchean war it seems likely not to be reasserted either. The compromises achieved in these wars reflected the fact that, in resolving international conflicts, the role of military force declined somewhat, while political factors increased in importance. Of course, the domestic aspects of the conflicts differed. In Vietnam, the compromise achieved by Washington and Hanoi led to the ultimate defeat of South Vietnam.

Just a rough review of some facets of these wars is enough to open a well spring of questions. For example, why were the major powers unable to avoid significant involvement in these East Asian wars, yet not get involved to such an extent in wars elsewhere? Why couldn't they fight as freely as they should have, and why were victory and defeat sometimes difficult to define, while gains and losses were difficult to calculate? In an effort to answer these questions the following factors seem worth considering:

(1) The post-World War II international environment is, of course, of vital importance in understanding the causes of these wars. The past four decades, especially the first two, were a period when the world power structure was being reshaped. The pre-World War II colonial powers were either defeated or, greatly weakened, were often unwilling to give up their colonies, while the colonial peoples, including those in East Asia, with their pent-up desire for independence, were determined to crush the colonial system. Thus conflicts were unavoidable. Furthermore, the blueprint for a new world order, designed by the two new super-powers at Yalta in February 1945, could not be turned into reality without a dialogue through force. This was even more true in East Asia than in Europe because the demarcation lines there were not drawn as clearly as in Europe.

Shortly after the peak of the national independence movement had passed, Asian local antagonisms inherited from history became a new source of conflict. In a nutshell, the soil for wars was fertile indeed.

(2) The special geostrategic location of East Asia also played an important and rather delicate role in shaping the special features of wars in the region. From a global strategic viewpoint, East Asia is a front of secondary importance compared with Europe. But analysis should not stop here. East Asia has an importance second only to Europe (which for strategic purposes includes the Middle East) and any advance or setback, any gain or loss in East Asia will have a vital impact upon the super-power global confrontation. Thus neither super-power could afford to stay out of any of the conflicts thus far, and because of the huge war potential of the local adversaries, were forced to throw into these wars unparalleled forces and war materiel. Furthermore, because East Asia is not the most important aspect of super-power confrontation, involvement in conflicts there is less sensitive, less risky and permits more room for manoeuvre. It has thus been easier to make a decision to go to war in this theatre than in Europe.

The other side of the coin was that even though the super-powers were involved in an East Asian war, their major security concerns would always remain focused on Europe. Their flexibility was thus limited in both action and scale. For example, in Korea the United States failed to take the action that was required militarily, which called for bombing the important industrial and logistic base of North-east China. In Vietnam, air action was taken only against Hanoi. For the same reasons and political concerns, the US strategy of 'gradual escalation' was implemented only at the conventional level. Though it was debated no nuclear action was taken.

It is obvious that the special geostrategic position of East Asia has been serving both to promote and to limit wars there, which explains why so many major powers have directly and repeatedly confronted each other on the battlefield yet have not escalated their clashes to a world war. Naturally, such wars make complicated demands, not only political but also of commanders, at the strategic, operational and even tactical levels.

(3) When the origins of a war are explored the decisive role played by the perspective of the highest decision-makers cannot be neglected. In the first two of the past four decades, ideological factors were far more influential than they are today. US leaders alleged they would 'contain Communism' in the 1950s, and the 'Domino' theory served as an important argument for the US entry into the Vietnam War; while the then 'Socialist Camp' decided to take action to safeguard the victory of proletarian revolutions. Such considerations played a considerable part in shaping decisions and summoning people and allies to war. Of course, from an historical point of view there is no reason to blame those who took decisions for their naïvety, but there is ample proof of over-reaction. Even after US troops encountered Chinese People's Volunteers, General MacArthur refused to change his policy.

(4) The natural environment, as shown in the Korean and Vietnam Wars, still stubbornly governs the style and conduct of wars according to its own logic, almost irrespective of advances in science and technology.

The two peninsulas share some common features, of advantage and disadvantage to all combatants. Geographical dimensions are limited: the Korean Peninsula is only 330 km wide at the 38th Parallel, and the width of Vietnam is even less at the 17th Parallel. In both cases the land is narrow while the coastline is long. Terrain and weather are complex. North Korea is mountainous, woody and has many rivers. Winter temperatures are low as −40°C. In Vietnam, on the other hand, there is typical subtropical terrain and weather, with paddy fields everywhere and a long rainy season. The overwhelming air and naval superiority of the US forces gave them flexibility in striking at the enemy's transportation lines and logistic support structure. It also made attacks possible from the rear along the whole coastline, while keeping the US air and sea replenishment system almost untouched. The picture on land, however, was enough to give any commander of a modern force a headache. Freedom of movement and the use of firepower was greatly limited. Although in Vietnam US forces were helped by the development of reconnaissance sensors and the use of helicopters and special forces, they still failed to deal effectively with the Vietnamese guerrilla warfare that spread all over the rural and urban areas.

North Koreans, Vietnamese and Chinese had to be prepared at all times for the opening of another front. Their use of reserves was therefore severely constrained, and logistic and transportation difficulties prevented large-scale mobile operations. But, at the same time, the complicated terrain and weather patterns provided ideal conditions for them to exploit their traditional strengths in attacking the enemy closely at night. Geographical factors affected logistics in different ways. The US advantages in advanced means of transportation and more secure communications had to be set against the problems of fighting a long way from the home base. The weakness of their adversaries was compensated for by fighting at home or 'next door'.

Another very real, yet often neglected, consequence of geography was the psychological strength that derives from defending the homeland or the territory that guards it. To mobilize and fight a distant war presents many more difficulties, even for a just cause.

(5) Finally, and far more significant is the social factor, described by Michael Howard as 'a forgotten dimension of strategy'. This should never be forgotten when analysing wars in East Asia, because most nations in the region have suffered at the hands of colonialists for at least a century, and thus have inherited a strong tradition of striving for national independence. In their long struggle many of them accumulated rich war experience, especially of guerrilla warfare. No matter what domestic differences there were, national coherence remained strong. Once invaded by outsiders, people stuck together and turned on the enemy. The events in Kampuchea are but the most recent example of this. Furthermore, most countries have abundant human resources and the people are capable of enduring extreme hardship. The level of economic and social development is still low and, while inferior in material strength, people can sustain a low standard of living more easily. The potential capability for prolonged wars is amazing. No matter that invaders might look strong or succeed in winning the initial phase of war, it is extremely difficult for them to maintain a long and stable occupation. On the contrary, they will be bogged down and defeated in the long term.

The factors listed above might not have covered all the decisive ones, but certainly include those that made a vital impact on East Asian wars. How the nature of warfare in the region will change will depend upon the extent to which future environments influence these basic factors.

In comparison with four decades ago, the most significant change is that most former colonies have won their independence. Strategically, this means that no major world power will have vast colonies as an uncontested rear and a rich source of manpower and materiel reserves in any future war. This is clearly a silent but powerful stabilizing factor, not as sensational as the nuclear balance but nonetheless a deterrent to war reaching world-wide scale.

Further dramatic changes can be seen in the evolution of the superpowers themselves. After forty years they have accumulated economic strength and built up their military power to an unprecedented level, but neither has succeeded in building a satisfactory world order. On the contrary, they find that the increase of their power lags behind the challenges facing them and, compared with former decades, their capacity to control world affairs and their allies has greatly weakened. In all aspects of their confrontation, whether nuclear or conventional, there is deadlock. In their efforts at a breakthrough or to stabilize their position, they have to rely increasingly on allies whose sense of solidarity or 'collective consciousness' is shaken, and on other medium and smaller countries who are much more difficult to deal with.

In East Asia, as everywhere in the world except for Kampuchea, where people are still fighting to safeguard their territory and sovereignty, and in the Taiwan Strait and the Korean Peninsula where the vital issue of reunification remains unsolved, the struggle for national independence is now over. The major concerns today are economic construction and the conquest of backwardness. Accordingly, domestic turmoil which has its origins in political development falling behind economic growth has become more and more the chief source of instability. Nonetheless, in North-east Asia, one of the most sensitive regions in which the interests of the major powers intersect, peace has been maintained for more than three decades. What is most consoling is that China has managed to muddle through its decade of turmoil with a self-adjusting capability rarely seen. It has decided to modernize, and is therefore able to contribute more powerfully to regional stability. In the absence of serious policy mistakes, strategic trends in East Asia seem likely to be more effective in deterring major war.

The special and delicate geostrategic position of East Asia will remain basically unchanged in the short run, but the role it will play in deciding peace and war and in the global power structure is quite different from its position before the 1970s.

First, the rapprochement between the US and China in the 1970s was a historical strategic change, which played a role in re-establishing and stabilizing the world balance of power and in deterring the escalation of the invasions of Afghanistan and Kampuchea into wider conflicts. Second, the world is getting smaller as a result of the advance of science and technology and the development of economic interdependence. European, East Asian and global strategic interests are more and more interwoven so that the strategic situation in East Asia will be more directly linked to that in Europe and *vice versa*.

Third, after decades of economic development in most East Asian countries, their tremendous achievements and vitality have suddenly been noticed by the world. The economic and political position of East Asia will continue to change at an even more rapid pace. Of course, it will not replace Europe as the world's political and economic centre because the countries in the region differ in their levels and rates of progress, but the possibility of Europe and East Asia being of roughly equal importance in the future cannot be entirely set aside.

Fourth, it should be recalled that while East Asia may be of secondary strategic importance to the super-powers, for China and other East Asian states it is and will always remain their primary concern. To super-powers, it is a front where they can fight when they see the chance of victory and withdraw when they see the risk of a loss, but China enjoys no such flexibility. That is why for decades, and in the face of difficulties of all kinds, China has been involved in, and sometimes even been forced to engage totally as a major party in, wars in East Asia. It is difficult to see this situation changing, given China's strategic location. Since the super-powers seem more reluctant to be involved in direct military confrontation, either because they do not have the necessary strength or are becoming wiser, China's decisive role in East Asian security affairs is certain to grow, irrespective of support or opposition.

The degree to which technological advances can overcome natural and social environments, and thus change the style and conduct of warfare in East Asia, may be debatable. Generally speaking, economic and technological progress in the region has brought great changes in such matters as transportation and communications, which have a direct impact on operational activities and battlefield conditions. Compared with the early post-World War II period, modern forces will be better able to overcome terrain and weather difficulties, so that the intensity and tempo of regional warfare could change.

However, it is unrealistic to suppose that science and technology will make traditional factors invalid. For example, future wars in East Asia would not necessarily be fought only within limited geographical areas and once outside these, it is hardly possible even for a super-power to concentrate its troops and weapons to the same density as in the European or Middle Eastern theatres, if only because of the sheer size of the region. For specific periods, on specific limited fronts, operations may be mounted with a density and tempo similar to the European theatre, but on the whole this will be unlikely. Furthermore, countries in East Asia will not make economic, technological and social progress at the same pace and simultaneously reach the level of development of North American and European countries. So future wars in East Asia, if there are any, are likely still to be wars of a different scale, density and tempo, ranging from primitive to semi-modern ones, though weapons and tactics may be improved. If it is still too early to reach conclusions about the extent to which technological advance has changed the nature of warfare in East Asia, the following characteristics which are unchanged, or basically unchanged, might be listed:

a) Compared with Europe, the theatre has great breadth and depth, allowing more room for manoeuvre;

b) The wide varieties of terrain and weather will complicate requirements for weapons and equipment as well as tactics;

c) The ocean and the long coastlines mean that naval and air operations will have increasing influence, but ground forces will still play the decisive role;

d) Nuclear weapons, strategic or tactical, for deterrence or war-fighting, would not have the same effect as in Europe, except in Japan;

e) The importance of technology and quality will increase, but taken as a whole, factors such as quantity, logistic capability and efficiency, strategic and tactical mobility and, in particular, morale will be more important;

f) Protracted rather than short wars will remain the common pattern, characterized by strategy and tactics based upon extensive use of guerrilla warfare;

g) The support of the local population will remain the most decisive factor. The bitter Vietnamese experience in Kampuchea is but the most recent proof of this law of war, despite Vietnam's own thirty-year experience in a war of national liberation.

The greatest change in subjective factors since the 1950s is the reduced influence of ideology in the minds of decision-makers. And in recent years, national leaders are looking more and more to Sun Tzu's principle of subduing the enemy without fighting, or its modern equivalent, 'force without war'. Rather than moving quickly to the use of military force, the more delicate art of comprehensively applying economic, political, diplomatic and military pressures is being developed. This will certainly influence the nature and conduct of future conflict in East Asia and elsewhere.

Finally, this brief study of different facets of East Asian wars in the past four decades helps not only in assessing potential changes in future wars in the region, but also in better understanding old experiences and lessons, which is no less important. War is a complex social phenomenon influenced by a large number of factors, of which few remain constant or static. No single factor, no matter how decisive, plays its role independently. It is the synergism of all factors that determines the outcome of war. War in general, and in East Asia in particular, demonstrates repeatedly that the combination of material and morale factors makes the greatest contribution to the strength of a nation at war. Yet, no matter how strong a nation may be, it will be defeated if its strength is used in the wrong place, at the wrong time and against the wrong enemy. Fighting under identical conditions, a nominally weak nation may prove the stronger and be victorious when its strengths are properly used. Therefore, it is not a single factor (weapon or man) or a group of factors (material and morale, the environment or political conditions) that is decisive. What is decisive in winning a war is the art or general strategy of using forces. As Sun Tzu said more than 2,000 years ago, 'what is of supreme importance in war is to attack the enemy's strategy'. Any 'strong' force has its weakness while any 'weak' force has its strengths. Only those who can evaluate all the relevant factors and who can design an effective strategy will win. In an examination and analysis of East Asian wars, past and future, these might be useful words to keep in mind.

The Soviet Union, East Asia and the West: the Kremlin's Calculus of Opportunities and Risks

HARRY GELMAN

Some eighteen months have now passed since Mikhail Gorbachev became the leader of the Soviet Union, enough time for him to have left a visible imprint upon Soviet policy in East Asia. In appraising what Gorbachev has done, and what his hopes and intentions are likely to be in the region, four broad questions seem appropriate. First, what lines of policy – military, political, economic – did he inherit? What Soviet vested interests have been created by the momentum of past policies to impinge on Gorbachev's choices? And what have been the effects of past Soviet behaviour on the Soviet position in the region? Second, what objective changes have been occurring in the Asian-Pacific political environment? To what degree have they been linked with developments in the West? To what extent do trends confronting the Soviet Union threaten to complicate or worsen the Soviet overall position, and to what extent do they open new opportunities for Soviet policy? Third, what has been Gorbachev's response to date? What aspects of his behaviour in Asia are a continuation of long-established Soviet policies, and what aspects contain innovations? To what extent is he likely to break new ground in the future? Fourth, what are the probable consequences of the present mix of Soviet policies for Western interests?

Gorbachev's inheritance
When Gorbachev became General Secretary in March 1985, the outstanding feature of Soviet policy in East Asia for many years had been the continuing Soviet military build-up. In progress for two decades, this build-up has cumulatively brought about a fundamental change in force posture, carrying with it an even more radical improvement in the Soviet position in the balance of forces in the East than have the various Soviet force improvements simultaneously carried out in the West. For a variety of reasons to be discussed below, however, a striking discrepancy has always existed between this growing absolute and relative strength of the Soviet military position in East Asia and the continued weakness of Soviet

political influence in the region. This discrepancy has long been quite frustrating to the Soviet leaders, and the thrust of Gorbachev's endeavours in Asia today is to see what can be done – without sacrificing Soviet military advantages – to narrow the gap.

THE MULTIPLE PURPOSES OF THE BUILD-UP
The Soviet build-up has proceeded in stages, with different purposes superimposed as time went on. Underlying all else has been the accumulation of firepower on China's northern frontiers since 1965, a process that saw the number of Soviet divisions stationed around China in the semicircle from the Pamirs to the Pacific rise from about 17–20 in Khrushchev's time to more than 50 in the 1980s. This change was driven in the first place by Soviet perception of Chinese hostility in the mid-1960s, reinforced by the Chinese political challenge to the legitimacy of the Sino-Soviet borders and then dramatized by the border clashes of 1969. The bulk of the Soviet forces facing China today, however, were in place by the early 1970s; since then manpower reinforcement has been slowed to a trickle, although new low-category divisions have been gradually activated over the years to keep the divisional total steadily rising. Modernization of weapons and equipment, though, has never slowed and – particularly since the late 1970s – has proceeded with little lag behind the modernization of Soviet forces in Europe. In one organizational respect, the Far East has, in fact, led the way: because of this region's special requirements for self-sufficiency and co-ordination of very widely dispersed forces against multiple potential adversaries, a high command was activated for the Far East Theatre of Military Operations (TVD) at the end of 1978, several years before this was done elsewhere around the Soviet periphery. Like the ground force divisions, Soviet tactical airpower in Siberia and the Far East has been, and remains today, mainly designated against China. On the other hand, the Soviet naval build-up in the Far East appears to have accelerated since the 1970s even as the land build-up slowed, and is directed primarily against US and Japanese forces in the region, and only secondarily against China. A combination of motives seems to have driven the naval increases. A desire to be able to defend SSBN in the Sea of Okhotsk bastion appears to have been a major factor, particularly after the evolution of SLBM technology increased the importance of all the bastion areas in the late 1970s.[1] A wish to impress and to intimidate Japan has been an increasingly important consideration over the same period, as Soviet-Japanese friction grew over Soviet retention and militarization of the 'Northern Territories', and as Japanese-American military co-operation expanded.

A third factor has probably been a desire to put pressure on available US naval resources and to raise the political costs in the Far East of any US inclination to shift forces elsewhere in time of crisis. In the first instance, to some degree this affects the US ability to move units from the Pacific to the Indian Ocean to help compensate for the predominance of Soviet land-based power in South-west Asia. More fundamentally, it affects the political viability of the US option to swing forces from the Pacific to the Atlantic to assist NATO in time of war.

Finally, the growth of Soviet naval power in the Pacific is also used in a secondary function as part of the deterrent against China, particularly since the emergence of the Soviet base at Cam Ranh Bay and the development of Soviet-Vietnamese naval co-operation.[2]

The last major dimension of the Soviet build-up involves the Soviet regional nuclear delivery systems, most notably today the *Backfire* medium bomber and the SS-20 IRBM. The ninety or so *Backfire* in the Far East have been divided fairly evenly between those allocated to the Soviet Irkutsk Air Army – apparently designated primarily against China and secondarily against Japan – and those allocated to Naval Aviation, primarily for operations against US carriers. Meanwhile, since the late 1970s the three-warhead SS-20 has become the main Soviet instrument of nuclear deterrence and nuclear pressure against China, replacing certain older M/IRBM and supplementing some ICBM used for this purpose in depressed-range configuration. The SS-20 also serves a secondary purpose in relation to Japanese and American facilities in the Far East. The deployment of this missile in Asia appears to have been somewhat accelerated in the mid-1980s – precisely in the period since the atmosphere of Sino-Soviet relations began to improve in Brezhnev's last year.[3] Deployment in eastern Siberia has now reached a total of at least 171 missiles, and has risen over the last few years from one-third to about two-fifths of all Soviet SS-20.[4] Planned deployment in Asia may not yet be completed.[5] Although the arrival of the SS-20 in these numbers has given the Soviet Union a very large margin of effective regional nuclear superiority over all its possible or potential adversaries, it has also become a major political handicap, for reasons explored below.

THE FOUR SOVIET FORWARD DEPLOYMENTS
In addition to inheriting this long process of accumulating military manpower and armaments in the East, Gorbachev has also inherited a series of Soviet forward deployments in Asia over the last two decades. These include, in chronological order, the deployment of five Soviet divisions to Mongolia since the late 1960s to bring pressure against China;[6] the militarization since the late 1970s of the four Northern Territories claimed by Japan south of the Kuriles, to bring pressure on Japan and to help defend the Sea of Okhotsk; the creation of Soviet bases at Cam Ranh Bay and Da Nang since early 1979 in return for Soviet support for the Vietnamese invasion of Kampuchea (Cambodia) and Soviet deterrence of China; and the invasion of Afghanistan since December 1979. The cumulative effect of these four moves forward over the years has been to strengthen

further the overall Soviet military position in Asia but, as in the case of the SS-20 deployments, at great political cost for Soviet relations with a number of Asian states.

In sum, these Soviet military policies and efforts to advance have created protracted challenges for national interests: for China, because of Soviet geopolitical encirclement; for Japan, because of the Northern Territories issue and the threat conveyed by Soviet naval, air and SS-20 deployments; for Pakistan, because of the grave threat that would be implied by consolidation of the Soviet position in Afghanistan; and for some if not all of the ASEAN states, primarily because of the analogous threat that would be created for Thailand by Vietnamese success in consolidating unchallenged domination of Kampuchea by force of arms.

All these causes of Soviet tension with Asian states have been superimposed on older and more general sources of Soviet political weakness in the Far East. In the broad curve of Asia from Pakistan to Japan, India is the only non-Communist state with which the Soviet Union has been able to establish a good long-term working relationship; and, except for the case of Mongolia, relations with all the Communist states have historically been, to say the least, unstable. Great cultural differences and various unhappy memories of the past (in the cases, for example, of Japan, China, South Korea, and even to some extent of North Korea) have been exacerbated by a traditionally maladroit Soviet diplomacy. Moreover, for many years, the relative stability of most of the region has given the Soviet Union few political openings, while the growing weaknesses of the Soviet economy over the last decade has rendered the USSR more and more a marginal economic factor estranged from the dynamism of the region. The remoteness of much of the region from the centres of Soviet military power and from the foci of Soviet anxieties and ambitions has also reinforced a traditional Soviet tendency to give the more distant portions of the Far East a secondary priority.

The trends making for change
Against this background, however, some trends in the Far East have been changing, and now offer somewhat more scope for Soviet policy.

THE ALTERED CHINESE POSTURE
The most important such change by far has been the Soviet ability to exploit, since 1982, China's new willingness to expand Sino-Soviet commercial and cultural intercourse, despite the Soviet refusal to make any concession to China's major geopolitical demands. Over the last five years, China has continued to enunciate these demands under three headings ('the three obstacles'): a reversal of the build-up of forces facing China, and reduction of the forces east of the Urals to the level of Khrushchev's day; cessation of Soviet support for the Vietnamese war effort in Kampuchea; and withdrawal of Soviet forces from Afghanistan.

Throughout this period, China has maintained that satisfaction of these three far-reaching demands – or at least, significant movement to begin to satisfy them – is a prerequisite for an undefined 'normalization' of the relationship. But China's readiness to go on in any case with incremental steps to improve the atmosphere of the relationship has evidently inculcated a certain contempt in Moscow for the seriousness of this Chinese contention about normalization.[7] By the time Gorbachev took power, experience had apparently produced a general assumption in the Soviet elite that time would continue to produce a flow of further minor Chinese unilateral concessions – in the form of additional small moves towards an unacknowledged normalization – without the necessity to make large geopolitical sacrifices to Chinese interests.

Nevertheless, this expectation has by no means rendered the Soviet leaders happy or complacent about their position in the Sino-Soviet-American triangle. Whatever the facts about normalization, and despite the altered diplomatic atmosphere, the Soviet Union has continued to regard China as a major opponent of its interests around the rim of Asia, pursuing relations with the US that are much broader and more intimate than those with the Soviet Union, co-operating closely with the US on some matters of security importance to the USSR and more loosely with Japan on others, and in particular co-ordinating with the US a long-term struggle to frustrate Soviet ambitions in Indochina and Afghanistan. Soviet reluctance to contemplate major geopolitical concessions to China has thus been driven over the years as much by pessimism about Soviet ability to change Chinese behaviour on these fundamental issues as by optimism about Soviet ability to obtain further *gratis* concessions from China on secondary issues.

TRENDS THREATENING THE AMERICAN COUNTERBALANCE
In addition to the modifications which have taken place in the Sino-Soviet relationship, some secular trends in the Far East over the last few years have begun to erode the political underpinning for the American military presence in the region which helps to counterbalance Soviet military pressure. Although these trends have not yet gone very far, and although it is by no means clear that they will ever become a serious impediment to the US regional force posture, they have undoubtedly been sufficiently suggestive to offer enticements to the new activists in Moscow. In the Philippines, a combination of circumstances has raised a long-term challenge to the political viability of the large American naval and air bases at Subic Bay and Clark Field which are the mainstay of US operations in the Southwest Pacific. In recent years, the growth of a Communist rural insurgency has been fostered by economic deterioration in the Philippine hinterland and by the ineptness, brutality and massive corruption of the Marcos regime. The increasing polarization of society against Marcos also brought into question the Philippine relationship with a

US government long seen as supporting him. The removal of Marcos in February 1986 by forces supporting Corazón Aquino, and the encouraging posture adopted by the US towards this change, have for the time being halted the deterioration of the considerable Philippine consensus still supporting the traditionally close relationship with the US. But a large minority on the left is continuing to press for the removal of the bases, and could eventually make headway if President Aquino falters.

In South Korea, where the relationship with the United States has been equally close for four decades, a different set of circumstances has produced visible strains of various kinds in the last few years. The rise of a new generation who do not remember North Korea's temporary overrunning of the South in 1950 has coincided with the rapid growth of the South Korean economy and the consequent expansion of a middle class increasingly impatient with the restraints imposed by the military-dominated government. Growing opposition pressures for faster movement towards democracy have been accompanied by some violent demonstrations and previously unseen expressions of anti-Americanism by some radicalized students antagonized by the American relationship with the government of President Chun. These developments have also coincided with a more general growth of South Korean nationalism and resentment of the effects of US protectionism upon South Korean economic relations with the United States. All this poses little immediate threat to the American military presence in South Korea, which continues to be seen by a consensus as an essential guarantee for South Korean security against the ambitions of the North. But for the first time seeds of doubt have been planted for the future.

Southward in the Pacific, a much more marginal US security relationship has already been more seriously affected. As a result of the New Zealand Labour Government's refusal to accept American nuclear ship visits, the ANZUS Treaty has been disrupted. Simultaneously, some mini-states of the southern Pacific, angered over friction with US tuna fishermen, have moved to sign fishing treaties with the Soviet Union, and in one case, to open diplomatic relations with Moscow. Thus, conditions have emerged for the gradual emergence of a Soviet presence in a part of the region where it had hitherto not existed.

A final, more general Far East trend worthy of Gorbachev's attention has been the economic slow-down observable in parts of the region over the past few years, evoking predictions from some Western observers that, over the longer term, this loss of dynamism could, in some places, radically increase societal strains hitherto precluded by the benefits of rapid growth.[8] Many of the states of the region have been adversely affected by the prolonged slow-down of the US economy, the leading trading partner, and virtually all have been injured to some degree by US protectionist pressures.

Gorbachev's advisers are likely to recommend that the Soviet Union search for ways to exploit any emerging political consequences.

Gorbachev's responses

Given the momentum of existing Soviet policy in the Far East and the new trends just described, how has Gorbachev reacted?

In the first place, while he has now made some noteworthy new gestures towards China, he has not yet demonstrated readiness to make more than token changes in long-established Soviet policy on the issues which have most fundamental importance to Asians and which have contributed most to the general weakness of the Soviet political position in the region. In these decisive aspects of Soviet behaviour, he has shown thus far somewhat less flexibility in Asia than in Europe. Quite recently, he has hinted at last that the Soviet Union might pull some of its forces back from Mongolia as a symbolic gesture to China, and he has offered to begin negotiations with China – reminiscent of the MBFR (Mutual and Balanced Force Reductions) negotiations long in train in Europe – on the possibility of eventual mutual reductions in Asian conventional ground forces.[9] For the present, however, he has provided no good evidence of willingness to halt the continuing broad Soviet force build-up in the Far East which confronts China and Japan. He has remained unprepared to bargain with Japan over any of the Northern Territories or indeed to slow the process of their militarization, to withdraw Soviet support for Vietnam's war in Kampuchea, or to halt the effort to assure permanent absorption of Afghanistan into the Soviet sphere.

In the latter case, he has certainly displayed some impatience with the protracted Soviet military campaign, announced a token withdrawal of a few Soviet regiments and professed a desire for a settlement. But he has made it fairly clear that only a settlement facilitating consolidation of total Soviet political control will be acceptable. He has therefore used the negotiation process primarily as a vehicle to help erode the Pakistani domestic consensus for support of the Afghan insurgents, while increasing sporadic cross-border military harassment and heavy bilateral diplomatic pressure against Pakistan, and escalating the ferocity (and efficiency) of Soviet efforts to crush the Afghan rebels.

All Gorbachev's efforts to improve Soviet relations with others in the Far East are conducted against the background of this 'given' in Soviet policy, the effort to consolidate and legitimize advances staked out in the 1970s. The greater activity he has displayed in new approaches to China, Japan and the ASEAN members is thus intended to probe the willingness of these states to expand dealings with the Soviet Union without significant Soviet concessions on the matters of greatest concern to them, and thereby eventually to move towards incremental acceptance of the *fait accompli*. To this end Gorbachev however, has shown greater awareness than his predecessors of the importance of Soviet flexibility on inessentials.

JAPAN

The shift to this new Soviet demeanour – the so-called 'smiling offensive' – has been most striking in Asia in the case of Japan. There, Soviet diplomacy had long been remarkably hamstrung by the contemptuous attitudes of such officials as Foreign Minister Gromyko – who had invariably refused to visit Japan while Tokyo maintained its claims to the Northern Territories – and the implacable Central Committee functionary Ivan Kovalenko. Gromyko's removal from the Foreign Ministry – desired by Gorbachev to facilitate tactical changes in many spheres – appears to have prepared the way for the Soviet decision to send his successor, Eduard Shevardnadze, to Tokyo in January 1986. As the Japanese soon discovered, this Soviet shift did not reflect any change whatever in the Soviet position that the status of the Northern Territories is a non-subject, but it is symptomatic that Gorbachev did subsequently find it possible to compromise with Japan for the first time on a secondary issue of emotional significance to Japanese, that of visits to Japanese grave sites in the Northern Territories.

In general, therefore, the Gorbachev posture towards Japan has signalled a new Soviet readiness to probe Japanese readiness to expand their relations and perhaps to increase the export of technology and capital to the USSR,[10] in the absence of any Soviet concessions on the issue most important to Japan. There seems little doubt that the Soviet experience with a more permissive China over the last five years has served as a model for this approach. Yet the scope for future Soviet progress with Japan in this way still seems to be constrained by a multitude of very powerful factors: the continuing impact of the Northern Territories issue; the political consequences of Soviet SS-20 deployments and the Soviet naval build-up around Japan; the uncertainties about the future of the Soviet-American relationship; and, not least, the limitations imposed on the growth of Soviet-Japanese trade by the contraction of Soviet hard currency earning capacity and Soviet economic weaknesses more generally.

CHINA

Meanwhile, the Chinese experience with Gorbachev has undergone a rapid evolution, with several ups and downs. Initially, during the first six months of the Gorbachev era, some, if not all, Chinese leaders evidently renewed the hopes – which had risen during the Andropov regime but had fallen in Chernenko's time – that long-term conciliation of the Soviet Union might some day elicit significant Soviet concessions. Encouraged by Gorbachev's reformist aura and his public statements professing good will towards China, Beijing multiplied signals to Moscow in the spring and summer of 1985. For some weeks it suspended polemical attacks on the USSR over Indochina and Afghanistan; it publicly rediscovered that the USSR was a socialist country; on one occasion it referred to Gorbachev as 'comrade' and it applied this term repeatedly to Vice Premier Arkhipov, welcoming him effusively to China. China has now accepted the principle of a long-term trade agreement sought for many years by the Soviet Union. Beijing not only authorized a further large increase in trade,[11] but agreed in principle to accept Soviet assistance in refurbishing 17 Chinese plants and the return of some Soviet experts for this purpose, a politically neuralgic point for China ever since Khrushchev's sudden withdrawal of all the Soviet experts in 1960.

After late 1985, however, the Chinese demeanour became perceptibly cooler. China was evidently quite disappointed at Gorbachev's initial reaction to the two items of bait which China has repeatedly dangled before the Soviet Union in exchange for movement regarding the 'three obstacles': the restoration of party-party relations, and the restoration of top-level contacts. Although both have long been desired by the USSR, Gorbachev at first offered to pocket both without paying for them.

Thus the tacit Chinese offer to restore party relations with the Soviet Union in return for such payment – which China has advertised by announcing willingness to restore such relations with countries in Eastern Europe[12] – evoked an invitation from Gorbachev to China to send representatives to attend the 27th Soviet Party Congress, which was duly refused in the absence of any Soviet concession regarding the three obstacles. Similarly, intense sparring appears to have gone on between the two capitals in late 1985 over the issue of whether and when an exchange of Foreign Minister visits should be scheduled; ultimately, China declined to schedule such visits for the present in view of Soviet obduracy. During the winter Gorbachev proposed a summit meeting without preconditions but it was rejected by China; in response, China is reported to have offered to hold a summit meeting with Gorbachev in return for Soviet concessions on even one of the three obstacles, a notion Gorbachev felt obliged to reject with great firmness.[13]

In general, the Gorbachev leadership, while continuing to decline to make significant concessions regarding the three obstacles, showed great eagerness to portray the continued growth of Sino-Soviet economic and cultural relations as being tantamount to a political rapprochement. The Chinese displayed signs of irritation at these Soviet pretensions, which were voiced particularly by Deputy Foreign Minister Kapitsa in December 1985, and which China apparently interpreted as intended to maximize Soviet leverage in dealings with the United States.[14]

In response, China ceased in 1986 referring to Arkhipov, or any other Soviet leader, as 'comrade'; significantly intensified polemical attacks on the USSR over Indochina and Afghanistan; agreed first to a British and then to an American naval port visit to China; arranged to purchase military avionics from the US; and sent the Chief of Staff of the People's Liberation Army (PLA) on a formal visit to Washington. Equally important, early in 1986 China joined with Japan, France and Britain in successfully urging the US to toughen President Reagan's reply to Gorbachev that year on the INF issue in order to protect Asian interests threatened by the SS-20 build-up.

By the summer of 1986, this firmer Chinese stance appears to have induced Gorbachev at last to make some conciliatory gestures touching on Chinese security interests, although thus far only of a token nature. In his speech in Vladivostok on 28 July, he stated – the first time by a Soviet leader – that the USSR was 'discussing' with Mongolia the question of withdrawing a 'considerable' part of the Soviet troops stationed there. He did not say when such a withdrawal might be carried out, how many troops might be withdrawn, or where they might go. The most likely possibility – a pull-back of one or two of the five Soviet divisions in Mongolia to neighbouring Siberia – would not reduce the total of Soviet forces opposite China and would not satisfy the Chinese demand for complete removal of the military threat posed by Soviet forces in Mongolia. Yet by raising for the first time the possibility of a token Soviet pull-back, Gorbachev clearly intended to suggest to China that conciliation of the Soviet Union might some day bring greater concessions.

In addition, Gorbachev proposed – also for the first time – to begin negotiations with China about 'balanced' reductions in conventional ground force levels in the Far East. In view of the great asymmetries in the nature and disposition of the forces concerned,[15] of the discouraging precedent set by the USSR in the European MBFR negotiations, and of Gorbachev's reluctance to reduce the Soviet nuclear firepower advantage which Chinese troop levels are intended to offset,[16] the prospects for such negotiations did not appear brilliant. Nevertheless, once again Gorbachev evidently sought to encourage Chinese hopes.

Taken together, these two Gorbachev statements will probably serve to strengthen those currents in the Chinese leadership that have believed that long-term conciliation of the Soviet Union may in the end pay security dividends. For the present, however, the military realities facing China have not changed, and the two contrasting aspects of the Sino-Soviet relationship continue to move along widely divergent tracks.

SOUTH-EAST ASIA
Meanwhile, in approaches to the non-Communist states of Southeast Asia and the southern Pacific, where – except for Indochina – the Soviet political presence has long been very weak, Gorbachev has energetically pursued those modest initial goals made appropriate by circumstances in each locality. In dealings with the ASEAN states, his numerous emissaries have dropped the hectoring tone sometimes used on earlier occasions[17] and have vigorously sought, as with China and Japan, to bypass the key political issues in order to enlarge bilateral economic and cultural relations.[18] Further east in the South Pacific, Gorbachev has followed up on the opening already created for the Soviet Union with some local mini-states by the behaviour of American tuna fishermen and the regrettable lassitude of the US gov-

ernment. A fishing treaty with Kiribati (the former Gilberts) has been signed, and diplomatic relations established with the government of Vanuatu (the former New Hebrides). The latter is a new regime which has also pointedly established such ties with Libya. Beyond this, Gorbachev and his propaganda apparatus have made a very elaborate effort to capitalize on the spontaneous spread of anti-nuclear sentiment in the southern Pacific, a subject returned to later.

THE PHILIPPINES

In the special case of the Philippines, the Gorbachev leadership is obviously preparing a long-term effort to improve Soviet assessments as well as Soviet capabilities to influence events in a place where both had long been very weak because of the overwhelming predominance of US influence. The weakness of Soviet assessment was dramatized by the remarkable miscalculation of the likely course of events during the 1986 post-election crisis; the Soviet Union, which had flattered Marcos shamelessly and attacked his US liberal critics for many years, was alone in clinging to him to the very day of his departure, to its subsequent embarrassment. The USSR is handicapped, among other things, by the fact that it has the allegiance of the smaller of the two Communist parties of the country, but not of the larger one which leads the guerrilla struggle in the countryside. Both, however, participate in the international front organizations which are under Soviet control, and all sectors of the radical left share with Gorbachev the goal of eliminating the US military presence from the country.

The focus of Soviet diplomatic and propaganda efforts is therefore to assist the left in the years to come in the protracted political struggle against the US bases,[19] a matter which has now been permanently placed on the Philippine political agenda. From the Soviet perspective, the eventual advent of a radical nationalist government hostile to the bases would be at least as desirable as the victory of a Communist faction independent of Soviet control. American departure from Subic Bay and Clark Field, should it ever occur, would considerably elevate the importance of the Soviet position at Cam Ranh Bay, to the detriment of the interests of many states throughout the Far East.

NORTH KOREA

Of all the recent modifications of Soviet policy in Asia, the one that has the most disturbing potential is the decision, since 1984, to resume the cultivation of the relationship with North Korea. During Chernenko's brief reign the divided Soviet Politburo, although paralyzed and ineffectual in so many other respects, took one action in the Far East which has opened a new policy path for Gorbachev: it invited President Kim Il Sung to visit Moscow, after many years in which he had evidently not been welcome. The coolness manifest in Brezhnev's demeanour towards North Korea throughout the 1970s –

reflected, above all, in the refusal to supply advanced military weapon systems desired by Kim – was now abandoned by Brezhnev's successors.

Gorbachev evidently concurred in this decision; he has followed through with visible consequences since becoming General Secretary. MiG-23 fighters and SA-3 SAM (surface-to-air missiles) sought by North Korea since 1970 have at last been forthcoming.[20] Although important reservations remain on both sides, the tone of mutual references has become several degrees warmer, and high-level contacts have multiplied. The Soviet Union, after years of reticence, has resumed referring to the relationship as a military alliance. Repeated mutual visits by air squadrons have not only been held but publicized, deliberately intimating to the world a degree of integration in air defence, and thus hinting at Soviet readiness to participate in the air defence of North Korea in the event of hostilities, while at the same time avoiding a public Soviet commitment to do so. High-powered Soviet military delegations have visited North Korea, and Soviet naval flotillas have twice ceremoniously visited Wonsan, the second time including the helicopter carrier *Minsk*. The Soviet Union has provided stronger public support for the various North Korean demands regarding the Korean Peninsula, and Soviet propaganda – unlike that of China – has continued to reinforce North Korea's fervid denunciations of an alleged US-Japanese-South Korean aggressive military alliance.[21]

In return, the USSR has obtained North Korean permission to overfly North Korea when staging reconnaissance flights from the Soviet Far East,[22] furnishing the USSR, among other things, with greater opportunity to collect information about Chinese, American and South Korean military dispositions, some of which data may possibly be passed on to North Korea. North Korea, which disliked the Vietnamese invasion of Kampuchea, has muffled its differences with Soviet policy in Indochina. The North has given strong support to Gorbachev's various initiatives in Europe and his global propaganda themes, but only rather terse and qualified support for his broad Asian security proposals. There have been repeated rumours – further stimulated by the Soviet naval visits to Wonsan – that the Soviet Union has sought air or naval base or staging rights of some sort from North Korea, but as yet no reliable confirmation that Kim Il Sung has acquiesced. On the whole, thus far the North Korean *quid pro quo* for the new Soviet favours seems somewhat meagre.

The reasons why the stiff-necked North Koreans have gone even as far as they have to propitiate the USSR are fairly clear. In several senses time is running out for Kim Il Sung. The growth of the South Korean economy is leaving North Korea further and further behind, and the accompanying gradual enhancement of South Korean military capabilities – symbolized particularly by the acquisition of F-16 fighters – threatens increasingly to erode the still-considerable overall North Korean military advantage. The solidification of South Korea's international position has proceeded in parallel, and this process promises to pass a watershed with the 1988 Olympic Games in Seoul. China, which in any case is incapable of furnishing North Korea with the advanced military systems it has lacked, has made clear its intention to go on expanding its trade relations and other contacts with South Korea and to maintain its good relations with the US. Meanwhile, North Korea's effort in Rangoon in October 1983 to blow up the South Korean leadership – a desperate act reflecting North Korea's sense of time pressure – proved a fiasco which further weakened its international standing. The prospect of securing an early US troop withdrawal from South Korea which would leave the South more vulnerable – thought promising in the late 1970s – has now faded.

In short, the prospect of extending his control over the whole of the Korean Peninsula – the central goal of Kim Il Sung's life[23] – has thus also been fading, and at an accelerating pace. North Korea has had ample motive therefore to seek assistance and enhanced international leverage by improving its relations with the Soviet Union.

The multiple Soviet motives for change are also rather obvious. The Soviet political position has long been very weak throughout North-east Asia, and weaker in both halves of the Korean Peninsula than that of China. In a period of new Soviet efforts to compete more vigorously for political influence in every part of the world, a change in Soviet demeanour towards North Korea is not surprising. The opportunity to administer even a marginal setback to China in the competition for regional influence is, of course, also welcomed. The Soviet General Staff will no doubt look forward with anticipation to whatever advantages for the Soviet regional military position, however marginal, the Soviet Union can pry out of Kim Il Sung. Meanwhile, the USSR, much to its chagrin, thus far has been essentially excluded from North Korea's unsuccessful efforts, brokered by China, to secure a tripartite meeting with the US and South Korea. The USSR will now presumably hope at least to be better informed on any developments in that direction. And finally, the Soviet leaders probably also hope that through this opening to North Korea they can gain better insight into the succession process there, assess the chances that Kim Il Sung's eldest son Kim Chong-il will win out in the forthcoming succession struggle, and perhaps stake a claim to some influence with the victor.

However, all these good reasons do not obscure the fact that there has been at least a modest shift in Soviet priorities. Not all the considerations which influenced the Soviet Union to maintain its distance from the North in the 1970s have vanished. In addition to Brezhnev's obvious anger in this period over North Korea's tilting towards China and over what he saw as great ingratitude for Soviet assistance, the Soviet leaders were clearly alarmed at Kim Il Sung's repeatedly demonstrated adventurist proclivities, which they feared could some day drag them into an unexpected and undesired clash with US forces on the Korean Peninsula. Gorbachev certainly continues to have no desire for such a clash, but both Kim Il Sung and the surrounding political circumstances retain a capability to bring the Soviet Union, and all concerned, sudden and unpleasant surprises.

The internal tensions and upheaval now being generated by the struggle to shape the political succession and to revise political institutions in South Korea are being watched with great anticipation by the North Koreans, who may feel in retrospect that they missed an opportunity to take greater advantage of the disturbances that followed the assassination of President Park in 1980. Most North Korean calculations are likely to be focused on the transition year of 1988, which they hope will usher in a period in which their endless political struggle to force a US withdrawal from South Korea can be waged more vigorously and with greater resonance in the South. In this situation, the possibility of misjudgments and rash ventures on the part of North Korea in response to unforeseen developments is likely to be enhanced, particularly against a background of evolving tensions in the North Korean elite over the North Korean succession. Thus, although Gorbachev is likely to continue to urge caution on the North Korean leadership, the pursuit of a closer relationship with this unpredictable regime has inevitably implied acceptance of a marginally greater degree of risk than the Soviet Union was willing to accept in Korea ten years ago.

THE REBIRTH OF 'ASIAN SECURITY'
Along with all his other initiatives, Gorbachev has sought to supplement his bilateral efforts in Asia by attempting to breathe life into the vague 'Asian Security' concept first launched without success by Brezhnev in 1969. To this end, he has expanded on proposals made by Mongolia in 1981 – obviously at Soviet behest – for the conclusion of non-aggression and non-use-of-force treaties in Asia and for the holding of an Asian Security Conference. During a visit by Rajiv Gandhi to Moscow in May 1985, Gorbachev proposed an 'all-Asian forum', explicitly modelled on Helsinki, to deal with Asian security matters. The theme has been persistently pressed by Soviet propaganda and in Soviet bilateral contacts with Asian leaders since that time.

Although a statement by the Soviet government in April 1986 expanded this concept to include the 'Asian-Pacific region' generally – and thus, the US as well – the great bulk of Soviet exhortations to Asians on this subject refer to Asia alone and seem clearly designed to imply a community of interest between the USSR and Asians not shared with the United States – indeed directed against the United States which is depicted vehemently in many of these exhortations as the enemy of peace in Asia. A similar preference for a European Security Conference without the US had been displayed in Soviet early diplomatic and propaganda efforts on that issue in the 1960s, until political realities forced a change in tactics.

As they did in Europe, the Soviet leaders are seeking through this Asian security campaign to make use of anti-nuclear sentiment to weaken Asian willingness to co-operate with the US against Soviet purposes. To this end, Soviet propaganda alludes to such disparate phenomena as Indian desire for a nuclear-free Indian Ocean, New Zealand's quarrel with America over nuclear ship visits, the efforts promoted by Australia, New Zealand and some Pacific island states to foster a nuclear-free zone in the southern Pacific, and North Korea's recent demand that the Korean Peninsula be made such a zone. In its efforts to find support from any quarter for the Asian security notion, the USSR has also been disposed to throw into the Asian security stew North Korea's demands for the departure of US forces from South Korea and Vietnam's proposals for a Kampuchean settlement essentially on Vietnamese terms. (It may be noted that the last item in this 'peace' agenda is, of course, unacceptable to China as well as many other states, and therefore seems ill-advised for the Soviet purpose of reassuring China that the Asian security campaign is now directed solely against US interests, and not against those of China.) Overall, the ultimate purpose of the 'Asian Security' notion seems to be to find a way to identify the US in Asian eyes with the nuclear danger, despite the preponderance of Soviet nuclear forces in Asia, to polarize Asian sentiment against the US as a threat to 'peace', to weaken Asian association with American countervailing military power, and thus to erode over the long term Asian opposition to acceptance of Soviet geopolitical gains.

Many of these themes will sound familiar to those who had close experience with the strenuous, but ultimately unsuccessful, Soviet anti-INF campaign waged in Europe during the first half of the 1980s. It is highly symptomatic of the thinking of the functionaries in the Central Committee apparatus who plan these endeavours that the Soviet Union, despite its setback in Europe, apparently remains convinced that there is important leverage to be gained through an appeal to anti-nuclear sentiment on the other side of the world.

The Soviet Union is undoubtedly particularly encouraged by the spontaneous spread in the Pacific of the notion of nuclear-free zones, now given token endorsement even by ASEAN.[24] This concept has long been encouraged by the Soviet leaders in different parts of Europe, despite poor chances of acceptance, in the expectation that mere agitation of the issue will help over time to erode further NATO's political base of support for a nuclear deterrent – thus giving greater weight to those conventional military asymmetries favouring the Soviet Union – and more generally to serve to promote the growth of political fissures between some Europeans and the US. In the Pacific, the Soviet Union sees the growth of anti-nuclear tendencies, above all, as a phenomenon that can be used to embarrass and to hamper the predominantly naval power of the US confronting the predominantly land-based power of the Soviet Union. To this end, it has sought to encourage the fears of states in East Asia and the Pacific about the prospect of increased super-power naval contention, in effect using its own naval build-up as a means of political attack upon the American naval presence. Along the same line, in July Gorbachev advanced proposals for 'talks on the reduction of naval activity in the Pacific, above all nuclear-armed ships'.[25] In all these endeavours, Gorbachev has sought to create an asymmetry in Asian fears: the Pacific is the subject, Siberia is not. The notion of a nuclear-free zone involving significant areas of Soviet territory is not on the Soviet agenda in Asia as in Europe.

The US Navy's relationship with Japan is obviously the most important object of these Soviet calculations but it is by no means the only such object, nor, from the Soviet perspective, the most promising. In particular, the Gorbachev leadership evidently hopes that the nuclear issue can be used to strengthen the long-term political attack on the American bases in the Philippines. During a visit by Deputy Foreign Minister Kapitsa to the Philippines in the spring of 1986, Kapitsa went so far as to claim publicly that former President Marcos had given a pledge to the Soviet Union to impose a nuclear port ban on American use of Subic Bay, demanding that this alleged precedent should now be respected and implemented.[26] As already noted, Gorbachev himself made a hostile allusion to the Philippine bases in July. Variations on this theme are likely to be pursued in the future by all of Gorbachev's diplomatic and propaganda instrumentalities, including the international front organizations.

Beyond this, Gorbachev is likely to hope for some 'transfer effect' upon Europe eventually, if not immediately. That is, the Soviet leaders are now likely to be waiting to see whether over the next few years existing anti-nuclear tendencies within some of the socialist parties of Northern Europe will be given new impetus by the specific examples posed in the last year by the ruling Labour Parties of New Zealand and Australia: the former, by imposing a ban on nuclear port-calls and pressing the issue to the destruction of a security relationship with the US; and both, by promoting to fruition the South Pacific Nuclear-Free Zone.[27]

The political effects of the INF issue
Yet, despite these particular trends in the Far East which the Soviet leaders find encouraging, in other respects – which are probably more important – the Soviet Union is itself highly vulnerable politically in Asia on the nuclear issue. Most fundamentally, this is because the Soviet Union has assumed a somewhat greater degree of regional dependence on nuclear weapons in Asia than in Europe. The Soviet manpower advantage and the contiguity to huge divisional reserves in European Russia with which the USSR has sought to overawe

Western Europe since World War II obviously do not exist in the Far East, and never can exist. The prolonged build-up against China has assembled conventional forces with a firepower advantage sufficient to threaten and to exert permanent pressure upon China, or if necessary to occupy important areas of Chinese territory. They do not, however, suffice to constitute a war-winning and war-ending capacity against a country of China's size and manpower without the support and use of nuclear weapons, on both the tactical and regional level. At the time of the Sino-Soviet border skirmishes in 1969, it was not the repeatedly-demonstrated Soviet superiority in conventional firepower but the public and private Soviet threats of nuclear attack – what the Chinese publicly termed Soviet 'nuclear blackmail' – that compelled China to cease aggressive border patrolling and bring the series of firefights to an end.[28] Two decades later, although the Sino-Soviet relationship has been significantly improved and become far less tense, the logic of the Soviet military posture *vis-à-vis* China, like the logic of NATO's traditional posture *vis-à-vis* the Soviet Union, continues to imply a strong impulse towards escalation. This is one of the reasons why China since the early 1970s has found Soviet professions regarding no-first-use, and offers of a no-first-use treaty and a non-aggression treaty, not credible and not acceptable.

In sum, while the SS-20 and other Soviet nuclear delivery systems in Europe are intended in the first instance to give free rein to the Soviet manpower and conventional force advantage by paralyzing NATO's inclination to escalate, the comparable systems in Asia are intended primarily to provide a decisive supplement to other Soviet firepower in compensating – and over-compensating – for the large and permanent Chinese manpower advantage. Over the years, the Siberian SS-20 have of course acquired additional missions: to counter the gradual growth of Chinese nuclear capabilities; to threaten and attempt to intimidate Japan in its relationship with the US; and to target some American facilities in the Far East. The continued primacy of the anti-China mission of the SS-20, however, although denied by the Soviet Union today, has been acknowledged by some Soviet writers in the past and by some Chinese spokesmen more recently.[29]

In the 1980s, rapid growth of the SS-20 deployments in Europe – where the Soviet Union is facing a significant land-based counter-deployment – was roughly matched by the pace of SS-20 deployments in Asia, where no counter-deployment comparable to the one in Europe has been in prospect, and where the Soviet nuclear advantage continues to be much greater than the Soviet margin in Europe. These phenomena have inevitably evoked increasing concern from China and Japan, the major Asian states principally threatened by the new deployments. Moreover, by early 1986 evidence was beginning to emerge suggesting that the SS-20 issue had become an issue tending to heighten a sense of shared security interests between West European and Asian elites. This was not always the case. In 1983, at the height of the Soviet campaign against NATO's INF deployment, the question of what compromise the West might consider to settle the INF question had a strong potential to create a visible conflict between European and Asian interests. In the spring of that year, Japanese and Chinese leaders had made vigorous public protests against Gromyko's insistence that the USSR had the right to move to Asia any SS-20 rendered surplus by an INF agreement in Europe. Some months later when Andropov retreated from that position, pledging – with important qualifications – to freeze deployment in Asia if an agreement acceptable to the USSR were reached in Europe, Asian leaders termed this insufficient, insisting that any such agreement must be global and must encompass significant SS-20 reductions in the Far East. It is evident, however, that until NATO's INF deployment actually began, if the Soviet Union had been willing to accept a compromise legitimizing part of that deployment, some European governments under severe pressure from domestic anti-INF movements would have been strongly tempted to recommend acceptance without insisting on reductions in Asia.[30] Japan and China were clearly concerned at this possibility that the Soviet Union might buy from Europe release from the 'global' restriction.

This threat to Asian interests was not brought to fruition because of Soviet obstinacy in refusing to legitimize any NATO INF deployment whatever for the sake of a settlement. After that deployment actually commenced, however, the situation was significantly changed for Asia by the subsequent decline of the mass anti-INF movement in Europe. In early 1986 when Gorbachev made a major retreat which his predecessors had refused to contemplate, at last accepting the principle of zero Soviet and NATO INF deployment in Europe on condition that France and Britain halted their independent nuclear modernization, he found that this concession had come too late to disrupt the NATO consensus. Not only did France and Britain refuse to halt their modernization, but the West European elites more generally – now relieved of much of the anti-nuclear pressure – took alarm at the prospect of the loss of the 'coupling' supplied by the US missiles which had been brought to Europe with so much difficulty. Meanwhile, the Japanese and Chinese governments made clear to America their intense objection to any INF settlement with the USSR which treated Asian SS-20 differently from those in Europe.

In consequence, a unique international coalition arose in February 1986, with Britain, France and some other European states on one side, and Japan and China on the other side, uniting with some forces in the US Administration to toughen significantly the proposed US response to Gorbachev on INF which had already been leaked in the Western press. One highlight of the resulting formal US reply was a vigorous reiteration of insistence that any INF agreements must embody significant reductions in Asia as well as in Europe.

The firmness of the international consensus on this point could eventually be tested again in the wake of the October 1986 Iceland summit between President Reagan and Mr Gorbachev. Although the Soviet Union on that occasion agreed in principle to major INF reductions in Asia (to 100 warheads) as well as in Europe (to zero warheads) as part of a larger package of arms reduction, the sincerity of this offer remained open to question because it was conditioned by demands for limitations on the Strategic Defense Initiative (SDI) which, from the outset seemed unlikely to be met. Should the USSR in future propose a more modest, separate INF agreement not conditioned by this SDI constraint but limited in scope to Europe, some currents of opinion in both Europe and America could once more be tempted to drop the global requirement in order to secure an otherwise attractive settlement in Europe. On balance, however, it seems improbable that this view would prevail in the West; the interdependence of the security issues raised by Soviet SS-20 deployments in Europe and Asia has by now been too strongly established.

Taken as a whole, the sequence of events since 1983 has served, on the one hand, to induce Japan and China to intensify their mutual consultations on the Soviet nuclear issue and other military matters, and, on the other hand, to convince both of their large stake in the future evolution of European negotiating attitudes. Sino-Japanese conversations regarding Soviet missile deployments and Soviet INF negotiating strategy have been supplemented over the last few years by periodic exchanges of visits between ranking Chinese and Japanese military leaders. Meanwhile, Japan's identification with the preservation of Western security was formally acknowledged for the first time at the May 1983 Williamsburg Summit, and although any Japanese relationship with NATO remains very tenuous, Japanese diplomatic and other bilateral contacts with Western Europe on security matters have multiplied as the INF issue has evolved.

On the other hand, SDI has created some countervailing concerns in the Far East, as in Europe, that US policy could ultimately increase local vulnerability to the Soviet threat. This does not seem to be the case in Japan, where for historical and geographical reasons, Western European worries about the possible decoupling effects of SDI upon the US nuclear deterrent are apparently not widely shared. But it is the case in China, a secondary nuclear power whose leaders share with many in Britain and France a concern that SDI could stimulate Soviet creation of an anti-missile defence that would destroy the credibility of an independent nuclear deterrent.

On the whole, however, Soviet deployment trends in Europe and the Far East and Soviet negotiating strategies have tended to outweigh sufficiently the effects of SDI to encourage a tendency towards convergence of European, US and Asian regional security interests. Although the Soviet nightmare of a European-American-Japanese-

Chinese security phalanx still remains remote from reality, Soviet regional nuclear policy has tended to make it somewhat less so.

Conclusions
Taken as a whole, the panorama of trends examined suggests that Gorbachev's exploration of new approaches in the Far East is still tentative, opportunistic and rapidly evolving. In the near term, the results are likely to be somewhat limited. Thus far, Soviet ability to play on anti-nuclear fears in Asia indeed appears to be substantial; but as in Europe, it may not be sufficient for Soviet purposes. Gorbachev appears to have made little progress to date in his efforts to advance the Asian security notion; no Asian states have been willing to respond to his overtures, except heavily dependent Vietnam and its Kampuchean and Laotian satellites; of course Mongolia; and to a lesser and more ambiguous extent, North Korea. In particular, the three largest and most influential Asian states – China, Japan and India – all continue to show little enthusiasm, despite their widely varying relationships with the USSR and the US. Overall, the specific grievances many Asians have with different aspects of Soviet behaviour seem likely to remain a powerful deterrent against signing on to so blatant a campaign against the US.

On the bilateral plane, Gorbachev's drive to improve and expand Soviet dealings with individual states of the Far East is making some progress, but appears to suffer from two major handicaps. As already suggested, one is created by the grave weaknesses of the Soviet economy, the backwardness of Soviet civilian technology and the inadequacy of Soviet hard currency earning capacity, particularly in a period of sharply depressed world oil prices. Cumulatively, these realities limit what the Soviet Union has to offer East Asia and constrain Soviet ability to participate in the economic development of the region. It seems clear that under the spur of Gorbachev's aspirations to modernize Soviet industry, many Soviet leaders would like to be able to enlarge greatly Soviet imports of advanced technology from the Far East – particularly but not only from Japan. The Soviet Union would also evidently welcome large new Japanese investments in Siberia, and doubtless planned to use an anticipated Gorbachev visit to Japan in 1987 to encourage Japanese joint ventures in the USSR. But while there may well be some Japanese response, its scope is likely to be disappointing to Soviet planners. Although some Soviet trade expansion with Japan and other parts of the Far East is quite possible, the USSR seems condemned to remain for most Asians a secondary and residual trading partner, useful mainly as an alternative barter market to soak up some production rendered surplus by protectionist trends in the capitalist industrialized world. Only a catastrophic acceleration of those trends – and a severe outbreak of trade warfare – would be likely to alter this picture materially.

Superimposed on these economic constraints on the Soviet Union's ability to improve its relations with East Asia are the self-generated political handicaps already reviewed. The implementation of the Gorbachev strategy most clearly voiced by his propaganda chief Aleksandr Yakovlev, to outflank the US by enhancing Soviet relations with America's allies and friends, has so far suffered from one peculiar difficulty in Asia: Soviet unwillingness to make important political concessions to this end to anyone.

The first hint of a crack in this facade has now appeared, with Gorbachev's offer of a partial troop withdrawal from Mongolia and of force negotiations with China. Yet the very limited nature of these changes – in the first case, primarily symbolic, and in the second, still completely ambiguous – offers little evidence as to the likelihood of more serious Soviet concessions to Asia. All other aspects of Soviet behaviour in the region are not encouraging in this regard and suggest an intention to seek new asymmetrical military changes advantageous to the Soviet position in the overall Far East balance of forces while tenaciously retaining earlier advances.[31]

More profound concessions, and a readiness to contemplate genuine geopolitical compromise with the interests of China, Japan, the United States, ASEAN and Pakistan, would appear to require far-reaching changes in long-established assumptions of the Soviet elite consensus, and indeed radical changes in the balance of power within the elite, on a scale which is not yet visible on the Soviet political horizon. A certain loosening-up and displacement within the long-frozen Soviet foreign policy bureaucracy is now in progress and has already brought marginal benefits to Soviet tactics in Asia. More such changes are possible as time goes on, and would probably bring further benefits, on the margin. The eventual retirement of Mr Kovalenko, for example, would certainly be interpreted as a good sign in Japan, and the departure of his Central Committee colleague Oleg Rakhmanin would presumably be similarly regarded in China. Yet personnel shifts of this sort do not seem likely to suffice to bring Soviet geopolitical concessions to Asia of the kind required, without profound modifications in the leadership thinking which has driven Soviet military policy in Asia over the last two decades. It does not yet appear likely that Gorbachev will bring about a transformation of these dimensions in the next decade. And to the degree that minor improvements in Soviet political standing in East Asia do emerge in the next few years without any such major substantive Soviet concessions, this is likely further to entrench the reluctance of the Soviet elite to contemplate significant sacrifice of existing military advantages.

Finally, given this probable continuity in the underlying postulates of Soviet behaviour, the most severe challenge to the security interests of the states interacting with the USSR in East Asia will centre on their ability to deal with those independent processes of change which it is seeking to exploit. In the next decade, this will mean, above all, assisting change in the Philippines and the Korean Peninsula without allowing the Soviet Union a new geopolitical windfall or permitting a new military explosion.

Notes

[1] That is, the development of SLBM by the late 1970s with sufficient range to reach the US from Soviet home waters elevated the strategic importance of protected adjacent areas – such as the Sea of Okhotsk – in which SSBN could be stationed.

[2] A sizeable Soviet-Vietnamese joint naval and amphibious exercise is reported to have taken place for the first time in April 1984 around Haiphong, an area not distant from China. See Georges Tan Eng Bok, *The USSR in East Asia* (Paris: The Atlantic Institute for International Affairs, March 1986), p. 53. In March 1985, a Chinese article asserted that because of the Soviet position at Cam Ranh Bay, Soviet naval units 'by moving northward ... can blockade China by sea and launch a joint converging attack on the country'. (*Shijie Zhishi* (Beijing), No. 6, 16 March 1985).

[3] See the discussion in: Harry Gelman, 'Soviet Far East Buildup: Motives and Prospects', pp. 40–55, in Richard H. Solomon and Masataka Kosaka, (eds) *The Soviet Far East Buildup: Nuclear Dilemmas and Asian Security*. (Dover, MA: Auburn House, 1986)

[4] As of early 1986, the USSR was reported to have some 270 SS-20 launchers in European Russia, out of a global total of 441. (*Baltimore Sun*, 25 February 1986)

[5] In May 1983, the USSR was alleged to have commenced building enough SS-20 bases in Siberia to accommodate well over 200 of these missiles when completed, given the customary number of missiles per base. (*Los Angeles Times*, 8 May 1983)

[6] Since the 1971 India-Pakistan War, Soviet forces on China's northern borders have served the secondary function of inhibiting Chinese military response to military initiatives by Soviet clients to China's south – most notably today, of course, Vietnam. This geopolitical function is one of the reasons the USSR has failed until now to make even a token withdrawal of forces from Mongolia, where they perpetually threaten the North China plain. This motive was unofficially acknowledged by an unidentified Soviet spokesman on one occasion ('Follow up Interview with a Soviet Colonel', (*Detente* (Leeds), no. 2, February 1985).

[7] To quote one external observer: '*Moscow-Pékin: que reste-t-il à 'normaliser'?*' (Headline in *Le Monde*, 22 October 1985)

[8] Richard Holbrooke, 'East Asia: The Next Challenge', *Foreign Affairs* vol. 64, no. 4, Spring 1986.

[9] *Tass*, 28 July 1986.

[10] In a 28 July 1986 speech in Vladivostok, Gorbachev raised the possibility of joint ventures with Japan in Siberia.

[11] A Soviet article has implied that China also agreed to extend the balancing of Sino-Soviet barter trading accounts over a five-year period, instead of continuing to insist that the barter account be completely balanced every year, a politically-motivated Chinese stipulation since the 1960s. (*Sotsialisticheskaya Industriya*, 13 June 1986)

[12] In the summer of 1986, a Chinese Foreign Ministry spokesman went out of his way to make this point unusually explicit, asserting that there were 'no difficulties' in the way of restoring party ties with the East European countries. (*International Herald Tribune*, 3 July 1986)

[13] *Wen Wei Po* (Hong Kong), 22 January 1986, 8 March 1986.

[14] In early June 1986, Hu Yaobang is reported to have told a Polish visitor that 'the Soviet Union says one thing and does another', adding: 'The Soviet Union talks a lot about improving and normalizing relations with China but at the same time continues activities such

as flying spy missions against China. Since the beginning of this year we have counted about thirty of them'. (AFP, Hong Kong, 22 June 1986.)

[15] In general, the picture is one of much larger Chinese forces relying mainly upon their superior numbers – and China's space – to help offset a great Soviet advantage in conventional and nuclear firepower. Because of geographical imperatives (the proximity to the frontier of the Trans-Siberian railway and Soviet cities), the bulk of the Soviet forces are also much closer to the Sino-Soviet border than the bulk of the Chinese forces. China has just completed a large unilateral cut in the size of its army, while Soviet firepower facing China has continued to grow.

[16] Soviet spokesmen have maintained that Soviet nuclear missiles in Asia are needed to counter US nuclear forces in the western Pacific, and particularly US aircraft carriers. In view of the obvious impracticality of attempting to use SS-20 against carriers, this argument is hardly credible. It is clearly being put forward as part of the Soviet political attack on the US naval presence in the Pacific.

[17] On a visit through South-east Asia in the same month Gorbachev came to power, Kapitsa was reported to have issued numerous hardly-veiled threats against Thailand, insisting that Bangkok must come to terms with an irreversible situation in Kampuchea, and allegedly going so far as to intimate that unless ASEAN acquiesced in Vietnam's terms for a settlement, Vietnam was likely to respond by support for subversive guerrilla movements in the region. This line was probably later considered counter-productive by the USSR and by August 1985 the Soviet tone towards Thailand had softened considerably. (*The Nation* (Bangkok), 7 August 1985)

[18] For example, by purchasing Thai exports rendered surplus by US protectionism, and by pressing for an expansion of the flow of Thai students to the USSR.

[19] In his Vladivostok speech, Gorbachev called for the removal of the US military presence from the Philippines.

[20] These belated deliveries no longer have the military implications they would have had 15 years ago, since the weapons involved no longer represent new Soviet technology. The USSR has recently delivered fresher technology to others, most notably India. This circumstance is one of several indications of some continued Soviet wariness regarding North Korea. Nevertheless, the shift in Soviet policy to permit the delivery of the MiG-23 and SA-3 is important to both Moscow and Pyongyang.

[21] The USSR has a built-in propaganda advantage here. It has poor relations with Japan and is confronted by US-Japanese military collaboration against the Soviet build-up, and therefore has no inhibitions about portraying that collaboration as also menacing the Korean Peninsula. China has good relations with Japan, has no objections to US-Japanese military ties directed against the USSR and therefore cannot conveniently support Pyongyang in linking those ties to South Korea.

[22] *Jiji Press*, (Tokyo), 19 September 1985; *Washington Times*, 15 October 1985.

[23] In the opinion of this observer, North Korea's various dealings with South Korea over the last two years regarding bilateral contacts do not yet suggest any attenuation of this central North Korean purpose.

[24] The USSR has probably interpreted as another sign of the political potency of the anti-nuclear issue the remarkable posturing which China, a nuclear power, felt it expedient to adopt on the issue of nuclear naval port visits. In the wake of New Zealand's dispute with the US on this matter, China considered it useful to profess to agree with New Zealand regarding an anti-nuclear principle which it obviously does not apply to its own nuclear warships in Chinese ports. The USSR will also doubtless recall that during the Soviet anti-INF campaign in Europe, China for similar reasons adopted a propaganda posture of benign neutrality towards the West European anti-INF movement. More recently, by accepting British and US naval visits, China appears to have begun to edge away from its professions of agreement with New Zealand.

[25] Tass, 28 July 1986. Gorbachev also proposed talks on unspecified 'confidence-building measures' (CBM) in Asia. One of the unsuccessful Soviet

aims in the recent CBM conference in Stockholm was to secure restrictions on NATO naval activities, and it is likely that the USSR had in mind, in addition to the advantages this would provide in Europe, the usefulness of the precedent this would establish for similar discussions in the Pacific.

[26] *Business Day* (Quezon City), 30 April 1986. The USSR evidently calculates that efforts in this regard will be assisted by ASEAN's recent gestures regarding a local nuclear-free zone. Although ASEAN's endorsement of the concept was *pro forma* and half-hearted, it has increased the delicacy of the issue in Manila.

[27] It is true that the South Pacific Nuclear-Free Zone as eventually agreed upon was designed so as not to inhibit the passage of nuclear-armed ships, thus avoiding immediate practical consequences for US naval operations in the Pacific. Nevertheless, the long-term political consequences are not likely to be insignificant.

[28] See Harry Gelman, *The Soviet Far East Buildup and Soviet Risk-Taking Against China*, R-2943-AF (Santa Monica CA: The Rand Corporation, August 1982).

[29] At the end of 1983, one senior adviser to the Chinese government stated: 'The Russians say that the SS-20 missiles are not targeted on China but on Japan and the United States. But in truth, I believe they sited the SS-20 missiles in Asia to employ military means of threat for the purpose of exerting political pressure on China'. (Huan Xiang interview in *Der Spiegel*, 26 December 1983). During the renewed Soviet negotiations with the US on the INF issue in the autumn of 1986, the USSR is reported to have privately justified its resistance to US demands for proportionate SS-20 cuts in Asia by alluding to its need for these weapons to offset Chinese capabilities. (*Baltimore Sun*, 2 October 1986.)

[30] Indeed, the Nitze-Kvitsinsky 'Walk in the Woods' formula discussed in July 1982 would have been such an arrangement, freezing SS-20 missiles in Asia at ninety, the Soviet deployment level estimated by the West at that time.

[31] Should it materialize, Soviet consent to some reductions in SS-20 deployments in Asia as a by-product of an INF settlement in Europe would indeed reduce the nuclear pressure on China and Japan to a proportionate degree. Even after reductions, however, the Soviet theatre nuclear advantage would almost certainly remain much greater in Asia than in Europe. Thus, the Soviet package proposal at the Reykjavik Summit in October 1986 would have permitted no INF warheads in Europe but 100 in Asia, while leaving shorter-range systems in both theatres as yet unlimited.

Soviet Influence in East Asia and the Pacific in the Coming Decade: Part I

PROFESSOR ROBERT A. SCALAPINO

In the years ahead, momentous decisions confront the Soviet Union with respect to its Asian-Pacific policies. Already, Soviet specialists on Asia, in and out of official positions, have been requested to re-examine Moscow's Asian policies, exploring possible alternatives, especially in situations where matters have not gone well. Mikhail Gorbachev's Vladivostok speech on 28 July 1986 is an indication of the first fruit of those efforts. How far innovations will go, how fully proposals will be translated into concrete agreements, remains to be seen. A major power always finds it difficult to execute bold new policies. Traditions accrue, weighing heavily not merely upon actions, but on the attitudes underwriting them. Bureaucracies in particular are uncomfortable with change. They do not want to tear down or even significantly alter the edifices they have so laboriously built and defended. And above all, the USSR is a bureaucratic polity. Thus, before effectuating genuine changes of policies, a leader must change officials, especially at the all-important middle levels where the 'experts' zealously defend their handiwork. Gorbachev recognizes this fact, as is illustrated by the personnel changes taken and in the offing. But it remains to be seen whether such changes will be sufficient to sustain fresh attitudes and policies.

The Soviet Union also has a formidable military establishment, one that has commandeered huge technical-scientific resources in recent decades, used them to good effect and, in the process, acquired extensive authority. While the Soviet military has constituted a pressure group *on* the party rather than the dominant force *within* the party as in China earlier, no CPSU General Secretary can slight military views. The degree to which this will be a restraint on new approaches in Asia remains to be seen, but it will not be negligible.

Another formidable limitation lies in the Soviet Union's geopolitical circumstances, a situation largely beyond the capacity of leaders to alter. Despite the extraordinary change that modern science has wrought in matters of time and space, some conditions cannot be changed. The USSR remains a vast land empire, its eastern reaches extending deeply into Asia; it is thus destined to co-exist with another empire, that of China, with a negligible buffer-state system to separate these two giants. The eastern portions of the Soviet Union, moreover, have long been its weakest, least populated, most alien parts. From these central facts stems a psychological mood characterized by a continuous Russian defensiveness with respect to East Asia and the mutual apprehensions of both Soviet and Chinese leaders.

These are the constraints on policy innovation. But the motivations for change are powerful. They begin with the ardent desire to have greater energy and resources to tackle the serious and accumulating domestic problems.[1] A high-cost, high-risk foreign policy can only be harmful to this goal. Soviet leaders also recognize that after Europe, the Asian-Pacific area is the most critical, both with respect to key bilateral relations and in terms of the global balance with the United States. Moreover, as suggested, Asia represents for Soviet leaders a continuum of peoples and land with their own territory, hence, a region inseparable from issues of empire. Here, domestic and foreign policies have a symbiotic relationship. Is it the perception of Soviet Kazakhs, Uzbeks, Buriats and Mongols that they are being protected against incorporation into a Chinese empire while participating in modernization, Soviet-style? Do they feel that they are truly Soviet citizens, with racial and cultural barriers fading away? Or is it their perception that they are forcefully held hostage to Russian imperial interests, serving as buffers but with limited opportunities for self-fulfilment? And what is the Chinese perception, conscious and subconscious?

On the other hand, if Asia is inextricably related to Soviet domestic concerns, it is equally vital to the Soviet quest for recognition as a global power, at least co-equal to the US. In North-east Asia, the nations destined to be the major powers of the twenty-first century meet. Here, resources, human as well as natural, promise an unequalled economic dynamism. In Asia, moreover, political competition among the democratic, Leninist and authoritarian-pluralist systems is most active, now and for the foreseeable future.

If the importance of the Asian-Pacific region to the USSR is self-evident, it is also clear to the Kremlin that, on balance, the Soviet Union's Asian policies stand in need of alteration. There have been recent gains: an expanded presence, notably military; the acquisition of a new ally, Vietnam, and (disputed) control over an additional buffer region, Afghanistan; the shift from open animosity towards normalized relations with China; a similar trend towards North Korea; and, most importantly, the maintenance of special influence in India through various regime changes. The low point for Soviet Asian policies came in the mid-1970s, when very little was going well despite the US-South Vietnamese defeat in Indochina.

But when all of the gains have been tabulated, they fall appreciably on the debit side of the ledger. The basic Soviet problems, moreover, cut across bilateral relationships, affecting Soviet influence throughout the region. First, the economic position of the USSR in Asia is extraordinarily weak. Such meaningful economic intercourse as takes place is principally that in which Soviet outflow greatly exceeds intake. Military, developmental or 'life-support' assistance is provided to aligned states with limited return. Here, as in East Europe, the USSR is paying a heavy price to retain influence. Perhaps the strategic returns make the costs worthwhile. But the crucial fact is that the Soviet Union lies almost wholly outside the Asian economic mainstream, able to benefit only in the most limited fashion from the dynamic Asian-Pacific developments of recent decades.

In the political realm, the Soviet position has eroded badly. There was a time when, for many Asian elites, the image of the USSR was that of a revolutionary government in the forefront of the struggle against Western imperialism and, at the same time, a state offering a programme of social justice and rapid economic growth – the New Democracy, it was called. The Asian Communist movements were solidly affiliated with their ideological 'motherland' and even non-Communist nationalist movements throughout the region frequently accepted a united front strategy, or looked upon Moscow as a useful counterpoint to their principal antagonists. That era has ended. The Leninist legacy remains potent in parts of Asia, including China – testimony to its utility when backward societies seek a one-generation, forced march towards modernization. But the image of the Soviet Union among articulate Asians today is no longer that of a vanguard nation. Rather, it is seen as another nation-state – economically underdeveloped, politically conservative, culturally foreign, militarily powerful and strongly nationalist. Contemporary Asian revolutionaries seek their own path. Some fly the banners of religious fundamentalism. Others claim their roots in aspects of their indigenous cultures. Self-proclaimed Marxist-Leninists are also to be found, but even among them, few see their spiritual home in Moscow. When they turn to the USSR for aid, it is out of self-interest, not a sense of political identity or emotional camaraderie. Lying in the same ideological bed, they dream different dreams. As nationalism triumphed over Marxism in Russia, so has it triumphed in Asia. If there is a challenge to Asian nationalism, it comes not from the cosmopolitan appeal classically associated with Marxism, but from religious, regional and racial-ethnic cleavages.

The economic and political insufficiencies plaguing the USSR in the Asian-Pacific region naturally affect the Soviet strategic position. Both super-powers pay a heavy price to maintain their strategic position in the area, but in comparison with the US, the alliance-alignment structure of the USSR in Asia is minimal and more fragile. In North-east Asia, the only true Soviet ally is Outer Mongolia, more a burden than an asset in strategic terms. Improved relations with North Korea, while giving the USSR certain strategic opportunities, do not as yet constitute a firm alliance. In South-east Asia, the forging of the alliance with Vietnam has provided the Soviet Union with progressively more meaningful strategic returns –

but at a sizable cost economically and, more important, politically in terms of other relations in the area, and notably with China. Moreover, even now, Vietnam, in the classical fashion of a small state hedged in by major nations, is seeking greater manoeuvrability. That will not come easily, but as the USSR itself realizes, Vietnam's present degree of hostility towards China is untenable in the long run and, from Moscow's standpoint, probably undesirable. But how will the accommodation with others, and particularly with China, be made? Can it be done without cost to Soviet interests?

Even the special relationship with India, cultivated through sophisticated Soviet policies and nurtured by Indian leaders' perceptions of their needs, will require new inputs in the future. As Indian economic growth advances, that nation's requirements are correspondingly changing. Already, India is entering the age of high technology, with a need for global markets. Can the Soviet Union meet these and related needs?

This brief survey should indicate why Soviet leaders tend to frame the issue in catch-up terms and harbour a generally defensive psychology even as they often pursue policies of an expansionist nature. Siberia, still a relatively remote and backward, if potentially rich, part of the Soviet Union, lies exposed to the emerging Chinese giant. The yellow peril is alive and well in the consciousness of the average Russian, supplementing the attitudes of his leaders. Further, there is the close-in power of the United States, contained in the Seventh Fleet and the network of bases in the region. Coupled with the US forces in the Indian Ocean and in Europe, American power has achieved a global nature which the Soviet Union still finds difficult to duplicate. Hence, the concentration has at least until recently been upon quantity – of conventional forces in Europe and strategic forces for both theatre and global purposes. And the US does not stand alone. For all of the problems that attend its alliances and alignments, the US has strategic ties of significance with Japan and South Korea, a low-level strategic relationship with China, and strategic connections of varying types with the ASEAN states as well as with Australia and the newly independent states of Micronesia. Notwithstanding the advent of the nuclear age, and the presumed decisiveness of intercontinental warfare in case of a Soviet-American conflict, the Soviet leaders appear to worry about such traditional concepts as encirclement and a two-front war.

If this analysis is accurate, either as a depiction of the facts or as a Soviet view of the facts, the stage has been set for an exploration of how Soviet policies might be altered or augmented to improve the position of the USSR in the Asian-Pacific region. Such a mission would have to include an assessment of the feasibility of such changes as might be desirable in the abstract. And, as suggested, the evidence indicates that Gorbachev and his new team have been actively engaged in that process. They are asking, in the words of Lenin, what is to be done?

Soviet economic policies and Asia

The supremely important arena for change lies in the economic field. This is also likely to be the most difficult task, since it relates quite as much to Soviet domestic as to foreign policies. Indeed, a crucial variable affecting its Asian policies in their entirety is the direction – and the results – of efforts to improve the Soviet economy. Put simply, the key issue is whether attempts to make the system work better will succeed, and whether if they fall short, Soviet leaders will undertake structural changes at least as bold as those being ventured in China.

Upon the answers to these questions rests the potential for greater Soviet involvement in the mainstream of Pacific-Basin economic interaction. Thus far, General Secretary Gorbachev has relied essentially upon the time-honoured methods of Khrushchev and others to work within the system, albeit with a flourish and style which demonstrates his formidable talents as a politician. Large-scale purges of managers and party cadres have been conducted in a drive to root out corruption and incompetence, at the same time testing new talent. Exhortations to display more initiative at the regional and local levels pour forth, as do appeals for a new work ethic. On the international front, moreover, there are growing indications that Soviet leaders want to turn outward to a greater degree: requests to join GATT (General Agreement on Tariffs and Trade), at least as an observer; an expressed desire to participate in various Asian-Pacific economic organizations; heightened receptivity to joint ventures with enterprises in capitalist States; and the interest in placing trade high on the agenda in bilateral talks.

To date, however, there are few indications that Soviet leaders are contemplating the type of structural reforms that would point in the direction of 'market socialism'. Capital investment continues to flow strongly into heavy industry and energy projects, with state expenditures in agriculture continuing to be substantial, but little evidence of an enhanced commitment to consumer industries or a relaxation of restraint on market forces. If the past is any measure, Gorbachev and his new team will have to go much further in reform efforts to truly revitalize the Soviet economy. It follows that if the old system is left essentially intact, the capacity of the Soviet Union to interact in a significantly new manner with the East Asian economies will be hampered. Some advances, to be sure, are not only possible but likely. Trade with China will continue to grow. Acquisition of technology from Japan will expand via joint ventures and other means. But under conditions of relatively very small structural change in the Soviet economy, the USSR is likely to remain largely outside the Asian economic mainstream.

If one assumes, however, that at some stage, Gorbachev or his successors move towards more basic reforms, the potential of the Soviet Union to play a substantial economic role in the Asian-Pacific region would be considerably enhanced. Soviet resources are bountiful. Managerial talent and a skilled labour force could be harnessed to much greater productivity under more rational policies. And the potential domestic market is vast. If serious structural reforms were contemplated, the Soviet Union would need credits in greater amounts and more diverse forms, including concessional loans as well as funds from international lending agencies. Interest in technology transfer from countries like Japan would be greatly increased. Strict reliance upon compensatory or barter trade would give way to more flexible arrangements as the USSR sought to take advantage of the productive facilities of the steadily enlarging community of NIC (Newly-Industrializing Countries).

While Siberian development would not receive high priority in the initial phases of economic reform, given competitive needs and costs, a greater emphasis upon economic decentralization and regional autonomy would allow the Soviet Far East much broader latitude in associating itself with the economies of its neighbours. In some degree, Siberia would become a part of the soft regionalism now emerging in North-east Asia with Japan as its vortex. This, in turn, would legitimize the Soviet desire to participate as a full member in the multilateral undertakings that exist or will emerge in the Pacific region.[2]

At this point, it is impossible to estimate the chances for significant economic reform in the Soviet Union in the near or intermediate future. Such a development, if it comes, will be driven by a combination of internal and external pressures: from within, the demands of younger urban generations desirous of a new life-style, many of them from the privileged classes; from without, growing competition from more dynamic societies, including some in the socialist orbit, buffeting national pride and raising gnawing questions pertaining to Soviet leadership and security. The next century will not be kind to laggard economies.

Thus, one cannot rule out a process of accelerating change that will propel the USSR beyond a Stalinist economic order in the course of the next several decades. If this trend develops and can be sustained, it will provide powerful impetus for meaningful strategic arms limitations and other forms of tension reduction without making the Soviet Union any less competitive in its drive for recognition as a global power. And while such a course would encompass some degree of decentralization and a heightened role for market forces, it would not mean a departure from socialism, namely, a shift to an economic order governed largely by the market. Rather, it envisages some form of market socialism. As in the case of China, therefore, the continuing challenge would be how to integrate the centralized, controlled economy – still likely to be dominant – with the decentralized, guided economy and the market economy. With this challenge, moreover, will go a second – namely, how to retain or reorder a value system and the legitimacy of political institutions derived from an earlier economic order.

Quite possibly, no tidy answers to the Soviet Union's economic problems, or at least answers acceptable to Soviet leaders, will be found. Compromises involving certain structural changes with a continuation of many elements of the old system may ensue, with experimentation a continuing feature and numerous contradictions a part of the scene. Whatever the future, the central thesis here holds: the compatibility of the Soviet economy with that of the mixed economies of the Asian-Pacific region is irrevocably connected with trends within the USSR. But there is another side to this coin: the ability of the market economies to resolve key problems in their mutual economic relations will also affect the relative strength or weakness of the Soviet Union as an international economic actor. In the context of a protectionist, warring community of market-oriented states, the Soviet position might well be enhanced, even if its economic inputs were less than decisive.

The political elements of a Soviet Asian policy
When the political factors that will underwrite future Soviet policies in Asia are assessed, the picture is clearer. To put the matter simply, the political appeal of the USSR to Asia will be that of a nation – and a people – sharing common goals and objectives, namely, peace and development. The USSR will not project itself as the agent of revolution. The age of political revolution is over for most Asian states. In the period ahead, there will be few, if any, systemic changes in Asian polities.[3] To make a revolutionary appeal, therefore, is to be out of phase with the times. There is considerable evidence to indicate that the Soviet Union understands this fact.

Thus, the Soviet emphasis will be upon state-to-state, not comrade-to-comrade relations. It will reiterate the theme that revolutions cannot be exported and, generally speaking, it will adhere to that theme. To be sure, it will take advantage of especially tempting targets of opportunity. But even where conditions are reasonably promising (such as in the Philippines), it will be cautious, not wishing to risk existing diplomatic relations by rendering support to a movement whose chances of success are at best dubious.

This is in harmony with political trends within the Soviet Union. If one wishes to chart Soviet political behaviour at home and abroad, it is best to set the works of Marx and even Lenin aside, and read modern treatises on nationalism and balance of power politics. In some limited settings, Soviet leaders will stress their role as the vanguard of socialism and leader of the socialist world – but towards the internal community at large, the emphasis will be upon the USSR as a responsible citizen of an independent globe, prepared to do its part to avoid the holocaust of war, to abide by international law, and to right injustices between rich and poor ('imperialists' and others). In the latter regard, however, rhetoric will continue to be much more powerful than action. There is no indication that the Soviet Union is prepared, now or in the foreseeable future, to launch a broadly-gauged economic assistance programme directed towards the so-called Third World.

Soviet security policies in Asia
To what extent will future Soviet security policies in the Asian-Pacific region mesh with or contradict political declarations? Herein lies a serious problem for Moscow. Soviet spokesmen will continue to insist that their military build-up in the region is a defensive response to a threat initiated by the United States. In actuality, the build-up began as a response to a perceived threat from China. In any case, it has been sufficiently rapid and sufficiently large to pose problems for many Asian states, especially since it has been coupled with assistance to Asian nations with a proven expansionist record – namely, North Korea and Vietnam.

A significant scaling down of Soviet strategic deployments in Asia can take place only in the context of a comprehensive strategic arms limitation agreement with the US, global in its coverage. Given the domestic exigencies confronting both nations and the external pressures upon them, some agreement is very likely after a process of intensive, painstaking negotiations. Even with such an agreement, the USSR will continue to maintain between one-third and one-quarter of its existing military forces in the Asian-Pacific region, and far from withdrawing from any of the strategic positions or bases now held, it will seek to make its coverage more complete.[4] Tactical adjustments will be made, especially when they offer political advantage. Adjustments of border troop-dispositions and modest territorial concessions have already been proferred, and more may follow. In Asia, however, Soviet leaders are very cognizant of the fact that in the long term, it is likely to be the *Asian* rather than the *American* quotient of the security problem that requires the greater attention. Indeed, the importance of Asia to the USSR in security terms is certain to grow as the next century approaches, and this fact already concerns Soviet policy-makers.

Sino-Soviet relations
It remains now to examine the future of the key bilateral and regional relationships to which the Soviet Union is a party, using the preceding general analysis as the context.[5] A second crucial variable in addition to that of the Soviet domestic course must be weighed at this point: the varying perceptions of national interest held by the Asian political leaders when they contemplate relations with the USSR. Given the different circumstances in which these leaders find themselves, responses to Soviet overtures will not be uniform.

Let us commence with Sino-Soviet relations since they are perceived to be of central importance both by Moscow and by others.[6] Gorbachev's Vladivostok speech unveils the approach the USSR will use in seeking to improve relations with Beijing. The proposals outlined in that speech had obviously been subject to intensive review and discussion at the highest party levels, and they covered a range of fields: troop reductions in Mongolia and, after negotiations, along the broader reaches of the Sino-Soviet border; minor boundary concessions in connection with the Amur River islands; troop withdrawals in Afghanistan, albeit with the timing and extent conditional upon reduced assistance to the Mujaheddin; on the economic front, the renewal of joint water management projects in the Amur River basin, and co-operation in the development of a railway linking Xinjiang with the Soviet republic of Kazakhstan; and, in the scientific-cultural realm, Soviet training of Chinese astronauts for a joint space mission.

These proposals signal the new, forthcoming tone Soviet leaders intend to inject into their Asian policies, and especially the policies aimed at China. They also indicate that Moscow now appears willing to move away from its long-standing technique of concentrating upon proposals of a broad, relatively meaningless nature such as 'Asian collective security' and 'treaties of friendship and non-aggression', while eschewing the settlement of specific grievances and problems. The new approach is virtually certain to pay some dividends. At the same time, euphoria by the Chinese or other Asians is unlikely and would be very premature. A great deal of hard bargaining lies ahead with respect to the specifics. Indeed, Moscow may be disappointed by the fact that after earlier signals that the Chinese would be forthcoming if progress were made on any one of the three obstacles, Deng and others now indicate that their principal interest is with a favourable resolution of the Indochina issue, and Soviet policies must speak to this before genuine progress in Sino-Soviet normalization can take place. Beijing, of course, realizes that even if the military concessions in these proposals are made, they do not basically alter the current Soviet strategic position in the Asian-Pacific region, nor with respect to China specifically. Soviet power, nuclear and conventional, would still encircle China in massive degree. Nor would Sino-Soviet economic relations be greatly advanced, since the factors that will govern future trends here are much more fundamental. Thus, while not minimizing the political significance of Gorbachev's move (heightened by its timing in connection with certain current developments in China), the truly critical determinants of Sino-Soviet relations remain to be affected.

Looking ahead to the next decade, the most likely prospect is that of a Sino-Soviet relationship which is normal but cautious. Both societies have every reason to avoid high levels of tension as they tackle the extraordinarily complex tasks of internal reform and development. Thus, war or the type of incidents created out of ideological disputation, boundary controversies, or a refusal to communicate, are unlikely to occur. Some Soviet observers believe that the domestic trends in China, economic and political, will lend themselves to much closer Sino-Soviet ties. With the Chinese-style New Economic Policy having failed to run its course, they argue, Beijing will find stability in a revitalized relationship with Moscow. Perhaps. But it would seem more logical to assert that closer ties, especially in the economic realm, would emerge from a similar pattern of reforms in the two countries.

One cannot rule out the possibility that as a reaction to the failure of current changes, a new leadership would take China back along the route of self-reliance and centralization, evoking Mao's name in the process. Whether that would actually lead to closer ties with the Soviet Union is a debatable question. In any case, the more likely prospect is that of a China which continues to turn outward, seeking assistance from the industrial world. In such a setting, Sino-Soviet economic intercourse will increase, and if Soviet reforms are effective, it can increase more rapidly. Even under optimal conditions, however, China's primary economic ties are apt to be with the market economies – the economies best equipped to be of assistance in its quest for foreign exchange and the other requirements of rapid development.

Since both the USSR and China act very much in the fashion of other nation-states, the key issues of the future are twofold: economic development and security. If the Soviet Union can only be of secondary importance to China's development (and vice versa), security relations hinge upon positive assistance. As has been seen, the USSR has now proffered certain tactical concessions on security matters, concessions entirely feasible without jeopardy to basic Soviet security. Such actions, while largely symbolic, can aid in the creation of a more relaxed atmosphere. The Soviet Union can also encourage a compromise on the Indochina issue, promoting a coalition government in Kampuchea 'friendly' to both Beijing and Hanoi, with its neutrality guaranteed by external forces. A limited rapprochement between China and Vietnam could then follow, ending one of the primary obstacles to Sino-Soviet 'normalization' without requiring Moscow to alter its ties to Vietnam or its military arrangements in the area.

At some point in the not too distant future, this development, or one similar to it, may occur. It is also clear that Gorbachev wants to reduce the Soviet military presence in Afghanistan, hoping that the indigenous structure built can carry an ever greater share of the burdens. The result of these efforts will be to present a new image of the Soviet Union as a nation less threatening to its Asian neighbours, constrained in its military actions, and anxious for peaceful, political compromises on outstanding issues. But as noted, the Soviet Union will still encircle China with a military force far more formidable than any it has had to confront in its 5,000-year history. In addition, the USSR will maintain a priority of influence in a number of the small peripheral states around China that constitute such a buffer system as exists, among them, Mongolia, Vietnam and Afghanistan.

Even with respect to North Korea, which China regards as well within its sphere of influence, Moscow has signalled that it intends to make its presence felt.

There is no chance, therefore, that the Chinese concerns about the Soviet threat will be removed, although this threat will be perceived as one of pressure rather than invasion, as is the case now. Nor is there any chance that the Soviet Union will cease to be concerned about the China of the next century. As has been indicated, reasonably or unreasonably, Soviet leaders – and the Soviet populace – have a deep fear of a massive, resurgent China which seeks to reclaim its historic position as the dominant power of Asia. From time to time, Soviet spokesmen have even suggested the need for a coalition of Asian forces, such as an Indian-Vietnamese-Indonesian alignment, to counter the threat. Whatever the future may be, it is the fate of two empires to have to live, cheek by jowl, with no significant buffer system separating them. Both are highly nationalistic and determined to be recognized as major powers. These are not the conditions that promote a trusting, tension-free relationship, however much the interests of both countries are served by the avoidance of conflict.

Soviet-Japanese relations
From a Soviet perspective, the problems presented by Japan are different. First and foremost, Japan is seen as an instrument of American security policy – the means, as one Soviet military figure put it, whereby US strategic forces 'can get close enough to our territory to spit on it'. Past Soviet efforts to cultivate pacifist or neutralist forces in Japan, sporadic and without spirit, have come to nought. The predominant psychology behind Soviet policy towards Japan has been 'treat them tough'. From time to time, concessions have been floated such as Khrushchev's proposal of returning two of the four northern islands to Japan in exchange for a peace treaty, and various economic overtures, but the norm in Soviet-Japanese relations has been aloofness and hostility. Even in unofficial exchanges, except for certain visits pertaining to business, meetings have been cool and marked by minimal agreement.

One hesitates to make such generalizations, but the fact is that those Russians and Japanese who count, with rare exceptions, do not like each other. Racial stereotypes are advanced as explanations for political behaviour and policies. It must not be forgotten that the Russians and Japanese have fought two fully-fledged wars against each other this century and have been involved in a number of hostile 'incidents'. After World War II, moreover, there can be no doubt that the USSR was determined to have its revenge for past humiliations and with an eye to its own historic interests in Northeast Asia, insistent that Japan never be allowed to rise again. In sum, the subjective conditions encompassing Soviet-Japanese relations, and possibly the objective conditions as well provide fewer incentives for Soviet concessions to Japan for the sake of improved relations than in the case of China.

Nevertheless, is a change in the Soviet stance in the offing? Could Shevardnadze's moderate words betoken an effort to create a new image of the USSR in Japan as elsewhere?[7] The appropriate answer to this question would seem to be 'yes, but'. A small group of Soviet specialists (not all of them) have long argued privately that Soviet policies towards Japan have been too rigid. In the years ahead, a cautious policy based on the cultivation of specific Japanese constituencies without making major concessions, especially of a security nature, will be pursued. A decade hence, economic relations between Japan and the USSR, especially the Soviet Far East, will be considerably expanded. Japanese high technology will be tapped and, as suggested earlier, under conditions of significant Soviet reform, business and financial relations could go much further. The USSR will be hard pressed to provide products for the Japanese market – an inhibiting factor. But ventures like the Sakhalin natural gas project currently under way will proliferate, and tourism will become a major Soviet industry, with the Japanese a natural clientele.

On the security front, much hinges on the nature of US-Soviet arms agreements. A far-reaching accord that eventually covered the Asian-Pacific region would permit or require some reduction of Soviet SS-20 in the Asian sector and other adjustments. As noted earlier, however, it is exceedingly unlikely that the Soviet Union will downgrade the strategic priorities accorded this theatre, and particularly in North-east Asia where its central facilities are located. It will surely continue to contest the efforts of US-Japanese forces to bottle up its fleet in the Sea of Okhotsk and surrounding waters. A key question is whether the Soviet Union is prepared to make a dramatic gesture such as returning the two smaller northern islands to Japan in exchange for an agreement that they would be permanently demilitarized. Such an act, costing little strategically, could create political fissures within Japan, and is probably being considered, despite an ingrained Soviet distaste for abandoning territory anywhere.

For the time being, advances in Soviet-Japanese political relations are likely to rest with summitry, a possible trip by Gorbachev to Japan. Prime Minister Nakasone has made it clear that this would be welcomed. In addition to being of personal advantage to the Prime Minister, it would signal further progress in Japan's entry into the world as more than an economic power. And for the USSR, it would mark a clear departure from the policies of the past, typified by Gromyko's disdain for Asia in general and Japan in particular.

However, Soviet leaders, while quite prepared to take advantage of problems in the US-Japan relationship, fully expect that alliance to survive in the decade ahead. Their principal goal will be to build economic ties which are of benefit to the USSR and which provide a growing constituency within Japan for a non-antagonistic, accommodating policy towards the Soviet Union. There is a reasonable chance that some progress will be made in this direction in the years ahead, but much depends upon the Soviet economy and upon the international climate, especially Soviet-US relations.

The Soviet Union and Korea
Meanwhile, Soviet leaders have signalled quite clearly that they do not intend to be excluded from the Korean Peninsula, or any settlement of issues that may evolve there. Moscow neither likes nor trusts Kim Il Sung, and, in general, it has long taken a dim view of developments in North Korea, regarding it as 'a *strange* country'. Nonetheless, Moscow recognizes that a succession looms ahead at some point and that within North Korea policy changes have been under discussion. It has not been happy with proposals, including those for tripartite negotiations, that would exclude it, especially since it views its role in providing Pyongyang with military and economic assistance as critical to North Korea. As Sino-Soviet relations have got better, it has been possible for North Korea to improve its relations with Moscow in exchange for augmented assistance without unduly exercising Beijing.

The USSR, however, must walk a narrow line. It has gained certain military privileges from North Korea recently, including the right of overflights and port visits. China cannot be happy about these developments, even though the official line is an insistence that nothing is amiss. The USSR does not want to jeopardize improvements in Sino-Soviet relations over Korea. Nor does it want another Korean War. Hence, its policy must be a cautious one. Looking ahead, the most logical development would be for it to move gradually towards a *de facto* two-Koreas policy, as China has done. The two Koreas are most unlikely to be reunified peacefully in this century. It is not even clear that the Soviet Union would relish a unified Korea under whatever political banner. It suspects that, in the long run, Korea will either fall into the Chinese sphere of influence, as it did historically, or be more closely identified with Japan and the West. A Soviet Korean policy which retained Moscow's influence with the North through aid, while at the same time having access to the South Korean economy, as it does to the economy of West Germany, may well be the direction in which the USSR moves, albeit more haltingly than China, due to the close ties already existing between South Korea and the US and Japan. As has been seen, however, the similar ties possessed by West Germany have not deterred Soviet economic overtures.

The Soviet Union in southern Asia
The Soviet Union now has a physical presence in South-east Asia, and that will not be abandoned. At the same time, neither this region nor the South Pacific will be an area of primary significance to the USSR. Soviet interests – and concerns – regarding North-east Asia and South Asia will continue to be much greater. Vietnam is tightly

bound to Moscow, economically, politically and strategically – more tightly than any other Asian state except the Mongolian People's Republic. At some point in the next decade, as has been suggested, those bonds will be somewhat loosened as a new generation of Vietnamese seek greater flexibility and independence. If the shift is managed properly, this development will not be wholly disadvantageous to the Soviet Union, since it will help to ease relations with China and with some of the ASEAN states. The aid-base arrangement with Hanoi, however, is likely to remain – a monument to the Soviet determination to be a global power.

It is conceivable that in a situation like that in the Philippines, the USSR may be tempted to enlarge its contacts with elements of the 'disloyal opposition'. This is not certain, however, first because the New People's Army (NPA) and its Communist Party have not so far been oriented in the Soviet direction and, second, because Soviet leaders are well aware of the potential repercussions throughout the region should they be discovered as benefactors of any guerrilla movement. Nor are they confident that the NPA can win at this time. Ironically, Soviet contacts in the past have been with elements of the urban labour movement and the old Communist Party of the Philippines, both of which rendered allegiance to Marcos, as did the USSR itself. The Soviet Union will step up its cultural relations programme throughout South-east Asia, taking an increased number of students to the USSR and in other respects cultivating people-to-people relations, but it will exhibit care in going outside legal channels.

South Asia, as noted, is of much greater importance to Moscow, now and for the foreseeable future. Here, one must start with Afghanistan. Soviet strategy will surely be to seek a gradually reduced military presence, as has already been signalled, hoping that the issue of the invasion can be defused internationally. There is virtually no chance, however, that the USSR will accept defeat in Afghanistan. Whether a type of 'neutralization' is devised that preserves some independence for Afghanistan while guaranteeing official friendship towards the Soviet Union, or the country is governed by individuals installed and kept in power by Moscow, the USSR will not permit a restoration of full independence. Consequently, it is certain to have problems here for a very considerable period of time – problems which complicate relations with Pakistan, Iran and other Middle Eastern states.

Meanwhile, having expended much energy and major resources upon India, the Soviet Union now enjoys the fruits of its labours and ardently hopes that these can be preserved. Up to now, diverse Indian leaders have seen it in India's interest to maintain close ties with the USSR, despite official adherence to non-alignment. Future uncertainties stem from two factors – one economic, the other political. Can the Soviet economy serve India adequately in the years ahead? It can be predicted with reasonable confidence that India will be much more fully integrated into the global market economy in the course of the coming decades, ever more in need of high technology, foreign investment and markets. As has been suggested, only if the Soviet economy itself keeps pace with these developments will Soviet-Indian economic relations maintain the past mutual benefits. On the political front, there exists a question as to whether at some point, India might undergo upheavals leading to systemic change. The odds seem against this. In its own, somewhat chaotic fashion, India has preserved parliamentarism for nearly four decades, with one brief lapse. Moreover, the decentralization of power which has recently taken place can actually help in the preservation of the democratic system, since it allows greater flexibility. Yet the level of communal and religious strife, the profound weakness of the Congress Party, and the uncertainties surrounding future leadership raise doubts. Could India be forced at some point into a choice between heightened authoritarianism and separatist states, or possibly some combination of these? Even if this were to occur, its potential repercussions upon Soviet-Indian relations cannot be predicted, since the precise course of Indian domestic affairs cannot be plotted under these conditions. One can only say that it is most unlikely that the Indian Communists in any of their several forms would dominate the scene, but the Soviet Union has never been dependent upon Indian Communists for influence. The probable course of India, in any case, is evolution not revolution, and the chief Soviet worry should be whether that evolution will bind India ever more firmly to the market economies, both economically and politically.

Summary

A few conclusions are warranted:

First, the domestic policy decisions made by Soviet leaders in the period immediately ahead will have a deep influence upon the scope and nature of Moscow's Asian-Pacific policies, as well as upon the image of the Soviet Union in Asia. To a unique degree, domestic and foreign policies will be intertwined in the coming years, with economic considerations more compelling than at any time since World War II.

Second, while neither culture nor ideology can be ignored in evaluating Soviet foreign policy, the element overwhelmingly dominant is the elite's calculation of Soviet national interest. The USSR is acting and will continue to act as a major power, responding like a traditional nation-state to perceived threats to its two supreme concerns: security and national development.

Third, in similar fashion, perceptions of national interest by Asian leaders will play the crucial role in their varying responses to current and future Soviet overtures.

Fourth, the Soviet Union has the opportunity in the decade ahead to improve its economic and political position in Asia from the present relatively low point and, under new leadership, may well do so.

The USSR under Gorbachev is likely to be a far more formidable competitor than the USSR under his predecessors. It is still uncertain, however, whether the Gorbachev Administration can respond effectively to the key concerns of Asian leaders.

Fifth, the security issue is a case in point. No single power will dominate the Asian-Pacific region in the years ahead. To many Asian states, however, the Soviet Union represents a security threat, primarily because its forces are close-by, massive and still increasing. Acknowledging that the outcome of US–USSR negotiations will be one crucial variable, one can still assert that the vital test will be whether the USSR is prepared to go beyond tokenism and help to create the conditions under which far more minimal security provisions – its own included – would be warranted.

Finally, in the last years of this century, the USSR will probably make its greatest gains in Asia simply by advancing its relations with key Asian-Pacific nations from hostility to normalcy, in the process adding the economic, cultural and political inputs necessary to that end. It is unlikely to be able to build an enlarged network of alliances, or even to establish new alignments. Yet, if a decade hence, the region is essentially at peace with itself and others, and the Soviet Union has established *normal* relations with the states of that area – and most particularly with China, Japan and the United States – it will have made major strides over its position today.

Notes

[1] See John Lukacs, 'The Soviet State at 65', *Foreign Affairs*, Fall 1986, pp. 21–36.

[2] Recent studies of Siberia in its relation to Soviet policies and the Asian-Pacific region are John J. Stephan and V.P. Chichkanov (eds), *Soviet-American Horizons on the Pacific* (Honolulu: University of Hawaii Press, 1986), and Allen S. Whiting, *Siberian Development and East Asia* (Stanford, CA: Stanford University Press, 1981).

[3] Essays dealing with Asia's political future from various perspectives are to be found in Robert A. Scalapino, Seizaburo Sato and Jusuf Wanandi (eds), *Asian Political Institutionalization* (Berkeley, CA: Institute of East Asian Studies, 1986).

[4] For recent studies on the Soviet strategic position in Asia, see Richard H. Solomon and Masataka Kosaka (eds), *The Soviet Far East Military Buildup: Nuclear Dilemmas and Asian Security* (Dover, MA: Auburn House Publishing Company, 1986).

[5] An earlier survey of Soviet relations with the key East Asian countries, with essays also on the military and economic dimensions of Soviet Asian policies, is Gerald Segal (ed.), *The Soviet Union in East Asia: Predicaments of Power* (London: Heinemann, 1983).

[6] For additional data, see the Paper by Jonathan Pollack on pp. 56–75.

[7] For further discussion of Soviet policies towards Japan, see the Paper by Harry Gelman on p. 10.

Soviet Influence in East Asia and the Pacific in the Coming Decade: Part II

PAUL DIBB*

'Russia is a border state; it is the European frontier with Asia.'
S.M. SOLOVYOV, (nineteenth century Russian historian)

Although Europe remains the region of key concern, the Soviet Union has vital security interests in East Asia and the Pacific.[1] Over half of Soviet territory is in Siberia and the Soviet Far East. US forces capable of nuclear strikes on Soviet territory are based or home-ported in the region in Japan, South Korea, the Philippines, Guam and other Pacific islands. China – the only Asian power with nuclear weapons – is a latent security problem for the USSR. And Japan – which has the third largest economy in the world – remains the most important US ally outside NATO and identifies the Soviet Union as its most likely military threat.

East Asia and the Pacific present many more uncertainties for Soviet policy than does Europe, for the maintenance of peace in the region is subject to fewer agreements and understandings. Difficult and intractable territorial issues persist, and there are no multilateral security arrangements involving the USSR in East Asia. Soviet military power in East Asia must be capable of undertaking a greater variety of tasks than in Europe because it has to be directed against China, US forces, Japan and South Korea, as well as in support of its distant ally Vietnam. Moreover, the USSR does not have the protective territorial glacis in the region that it has in Eastern Europe. As seen from Moscow, Soviet Pacific territories are a distant possession flanked by hostile or potentially hostile states.

It will be a primary Soviet objective over the coming decade to correct this state of affairs and to improve its influence and standing in the region. This Paper examines the means available to the Soviet Union for improving relations with key states in the East Asia and Pacific region. It begins by analysing the domestic aspects of Soviet security policies in the region, a subject often overlooked in Western commentary.

Domestic dimensions of Soviet security policy
Its Siberian territories provide the USSR with a forward strategic position in the region, in close proximity to the major Asian powers of China and Japan and just across the Bering Sea from the United

States. From this secure base, the Soviet Union has developed the most powerful military forces in the region. Siberia offers the USSR great strategic depth for the dispersed location of its population, military industries and some of its intercontinental ballistic missile (ICBM) silos. It also contains one of the two major Soviet bases for fleet ballistic missile submarines.

From the security of its Pacific bastion, the Soviet Union can threaten Japan, most of America, the sea-lanes between those two countries, as well as US bases in Guam, Hawaii, the Philippines and Australia. From across the long border it shares with China (and from Mongolia), the USSR is able to pose a military threat to the security of China's western provinces and Manchuria. It also shares a common border with North Korea and could readily provide it with combat assistance.

Historically, the Far East Theatre has been of secondary importance, as Soviet planners have placed greater emphasis on supporting Soviet forces opposite NATO. In the last decade, however, the USSR has devoted considerably more attention to increasing the sustainability of its forces in the Far East because of the long lines of communication and the need to support large theatre forces opposite China and Japan.[2]

The Far East Strategic Theatre (GTVD) encompasses the USSR's largest continental theatre of military operations. After the Western Strategic Theatre, it has a high priority in Soviet force structure planning and the allocation of defence resources. About one-quarter of the Soviet army, air and navy forces are deployed in the theatre, as well as over one-third of its submarine- and land-based strategic nuclear forces and almost two-fifths of its regional nuclear forces. The High Command for the Far East Theatre (TVD) now has the control of all army, navy and air force units in the area, and possibly theatre nuclear forces, to prosecute 'combined-arms' operations. This theatre command covers Siberia, the Soviet Far East, Mongolia, China, the Koreas, Japan and Alaska.[3]

There are also economic factors which increase the importance of the area in Soviet policies. As resources in its European territories become exhausted or uneconomic to exploit, the Soviet Union will become increasingly dependent on Siberian energy and minerals which will be essential for the development of the national power. In future years, Siberia will account for almost the entire increase in Soviet production of energy and fuels, many non-ferrous metals and energy-intensive chemical products.[4] During the remainder of this century, the centre of gravity of the Soviet economy will gradually shift eastwards and Siberia will become increasingly important in Soviet national planning perspectives and security concerns.

These economic trends will reinforce Soviet concern to maintain a strong military presence in Siberia. Although there are undeniable rival pressures for investment and human resources between the European and Asian parts of the state, there can be no doubt that Siberian energy and raw material supplies are seen as indispensable to the future economic and military power of the USSR. Moreover, the dominant Russian element in the Party apparatus is likely to view the development of Siberia, which has been settled predominantly by Russians, as a higher priority than the development of the racially different territories of Soviet Central Asia.

External aspects of Soviet security policies
External developments, especially the emergence of a growing intelligence and defence relationship between the US, Japan and China, have added to Soviet concerns about the long-term security of its distant eastern flank. As the then Chief of the General Staff of the Soviet Armed Forces, Marshal N. Ogarkov, put it in *Kommunist* in July 1981:

> The broadening of military-political links of the USA with China and with a Japan which is going in the direction of militarization creates a long term military threat to our eastern frontiers.

The Soviet political leadership must have observed that, since Ogarkov made this statement some five years ago, substantial military co-operation between China and the US has not developed, but there are other adverse security trends which cast shadows over the Soviet eastern territories. The rapid development of the Chinese economy, with the assistance of the US, Japan and Western Europe, will inevitably strengthen China's military potential in the long run. The Soviet Union must reckon with the emergence of a powerful China one day, and the spectre of the potential of over a billion Chinese, who are racially and culturally so different, haunts the Russian mind.

Japan, too, despite its modest military capabilities at present, clearly has a considerable military potential and the Soviet press talks incessantly about Japanese 'militaristic ambitions'. Such propaganda is designed to undermine Japan's alliance with the US and a more realistic Soviet concern must be that the Japanese economy will outstrip the Soviet economy within the decade. The USSR will then slip from being the world's second largest economy to the third.

A further problem for the Soviet leadership is that, unlike China and Japan, the Soviet Union is not an Asian country. It is not accepted in this sense as a regional power, but is seen as a rather arrogant European power, relatively recently arrived in the area. Other European colonial powers have lost their Asian possessions, but the USSR continues to occupy territory taken from China and Japan.

The security of Siberia
If the USSR is concerned about its peacetime influence in the region, it also has some worries about the vulnerability of Siberia in a global war. The Soviet leadership probably feels that its nuclear and conventional forces in the region are a sufficient deterrent against a major attack. The USSR has provided the Far East Strategic Theatre in recent years with substantial, modern forces which are capable of

providing adequate capability in war against the US and its allies in the Pacific and of neutralizing China. In the event of a war in Europe, however, the USSR would be forced to engage in rapid offensive operations to bring about a quick termination of US attacks on the eastern front and to avoid becoming enmeshed in a prolonged conventional ground war in China.[5]

There are several compelling reasons for such a strategy. First, if a war in Europe occurred, the Soviet Union would regard the campaign there as the decisive one, and a prolonged war in East Asia would detract from its ability to achieve a quick victory in Europe. Second, prolonged large-scale military operations in East Asia would be beyond the logistic capacity of the USSR to support, given that it had at the same time to support a major campaign in Europe.

According to the US Department of Defense, Soviet ground and naval forces in the Far East Theatre can sustain *defensive* conventional wartime operations for more than 100 days.[6] The prepositioning of large quantities of war materiel in the Far East reduces the dependence on logistic assets from the USSR's western industrial centres for resupply during the initial period of a war, but the Trans-Siberian Railway would be a critical supply line to the Far East in a war exceeding 100 days. The Pacific Fleet is especially dependent on this railway for the supply of war materiel. Its remoteness would make reinforcement of the fleet exceedingly difficult during wartime.[7]

The US has stated that, in the event of war with the USSR, it reserves the right to strike the Soviet Union where it is weakest. US nuclear strikes on the railway and storage capacities for ammunition, fuel and other war materials, as well as on the limited defence manufacturing infrastructure of Siberia, would 'break the back' of the country, effectively detaching Siberia from European Russia. Such a fundamental weakening of Soviet military resources in Siberia could increase the prospect of a Chinese assault against the USSR.[8]

Soviet objectives and means of exerting influence

The Soviet Union's main peacetime objective is to shift 'the correlation of forces' (*sootnoshenie sil*) in East Asia and the Pacific in its favour.[9] It would like to see the US excluded from military bases and alliances in the region, Japan detached from its alignment with America, China as a friendly power which acknowledges Soviet preeminence in the world Communist movement, Vietnam and North Korea as compliant allies, the extension of Soviet influence to the ASEAN states and the small island countries of the South Pacific, and the break-up of the ANZUS Alliance.

In many ways, however, the USSR is 'the odd man out' in East Asia, having little influence except in Indochina, North Korea and Mongolia. Although militarily the most powerful country in the region, it has not yet been able to translate its growing military strength into comparable political influence. In no other region of the world is there such a major discrepancy between Soviet military power and political influence.

Compared with thirty years ago, the Soviet *military presence* in the region is much more impressive, but Soviet *political influence* is much less. China and Indonesia are no longer friendly powers, the Soviet brand of Communism is no longer seen as the wave of the future, and Soviet relations with Japan are cool and estranged. To the south, the Soviet Union now has a major presence in Indochina, but, it has little influence among the ASEAN countries or in the South Pacific. The one major Soviet gain in recent years has been Vietnam, which now provides the USSR with its most important forward naval base (at Cam Ranh Bay and Da Nang) outside the Warsaw Pact.

In terms of its global political and ideological policies, East Asia must be assessed as a spectacular failure for the USSR. Its diplomacy in the region has been marked by a toughness and rigidity which has served Soviet interests poorly and has earned the hostility and enmity of most of its Asian neighbours. To a large extent this is a direct result of its growing military build-up. There is a basic contradiction in a Soviet policy which pursues an incessant expansion of military power in the region whilst allegedly seeking improved political relations.

The Soviet invasion of Afghanistan, its alliance with Vietnam and the increasing display of Soviet military power in the region have alienated an enormously complex and diverse part of the world. To change this fundamental shift in the Asian balance of power will be no easy task for the Soviet leadership. Its heavy-handed approach to Asians, its obsessive concern with military security and its espionage and subversive activities, have caused it to miss major opportunities to improve relations with China, Japan and the ASEAN countries over the last decade.

While the US has friendly relations with Japan, China, South Korea, Taiwan, the members of ASEAN and most of the countries of the South Pacific, the only Soviet major ally in the region is Vietnam. Its other friends, Mongolia, Kampuchea and Laos, count for little as regional powers, and in North Korea the Soviet Union has to compete with China for influence.

The Soviet Union now faces a more assertive United States which is pursuing a vigorous containment policy and a military build-up of its own. There is also an increasingly strong military relationship between the US, Japan and South Korea, a *de facto* alignment of China with the West against the USSR, substantial Japanese rearmament, an ASEAN which is suspicious of and alert to Soviet ambitions in South-east Asia, and an ANZUS that – so far at least – has been successful in denying the USSR a major presence in the South Pacific. Taken together, these developments represent a potentially critical challenge to Soviet power and prestige in the region.

The Soviet Union's economic presence in East Asia is even less substantial than its political presence. The USSR can provide neither a major market for East Asian products nor technology and investment on the scale required. It has a substantial economic presence only in Indochina, Mongolia and North Korea – countries which have a dismal economic performance. The cost of Soviet military and economic aid to Vietnam in particular is quite heavy, amounting to over $US 12 billion since 1978. The financial strain of supporting Vietnam is reflected in a statement by G.A. Aliyev, a member of the Politburo, in Hanoi in 1983 when he said:

> Let me say frankly that in helping Vietnam develop its economy, the Soviet people have to share with you even things they are also needing.[10]

There are indications that the Soviet leaders expect Vietnam to make better use of the aid it receives. During the visit by former General Secretary Le Duan to Moscow in June 1985, a joint declaration stated that Vietnam would strive to fulfil its commitments to the USSR and to make their economic relations 'more balanced and more mutually advantageous'.

Trade with East Asia amounts to only about 7% of total Soviet trade. Almost half of it is with Japan, and most of the rest is with Soviet allies – Mongolia, Vietnam and North Korea. Soviet trade with China is worth only one-tenth of China's trade with Japan. The Soviet Union is a significant purchaser of Malaysian rubber and palm oil, Australian wool and New Zealand meat. Singapore provides bunkering, victualling and repair facilities for Soviet merchant ships. But it is difficult to see how the USSR could exert more than a limited influence on the overall economic welfare of the East Asian countries.

The USSR has the largest fishing fleet in the world, and the declaration by many countries, especially in the North Pacific, of 200-mile fishing zones has encouraged an increase in its more distant fishing operations in South-east Asia and the South Pacific. There must be concern that fishing agreements – including the possibility of access to port facilities – with the poor island states of the South Pacific will give the USSR opportunities for political influence. (Harry Gelman deals with this in his Paper on pp. 3–26.)

Other than this, there are few prospects for any major breakthroughs in Soviet economic influence in East Asia and the Pacific. For almost 20 years now, the USSR has made considerable efforts to attract Japanese and US investment in Siberia, but both countries are wary of the potential strategic and political implications of improving Siberia's infrastructure and general economic strength.

In stark contrast to its relatively poor political and economic influence in the region, the Soviet Union has an impressive military position. It has concentrated in the area 53 divisions, having available some 14,000 tanks and 10,000 artillery pieces, some 2,000 combat aircraft and helicopters, as well as 88 attack and cruise-missile submarines and 85 principal surface combatants.[11] Ground force strength has increased almost threefold in the last 20 years. Fighter aircraft have increased sixfold, from less than 200 in 1965 to about 1,300 now, and the helicopter force also grew rapidly over the same period from about 60 to 500. Major surface ship numbers have increased from 50 in 1965, and some of the Soviet Union's most modern naval units have joined the Pacific Fleet in recent years, including two *Kiev*-class aircraft carriers and a *Kirov*-class battle cruiser. Yet, according to the Chairman of the Department of Strategy at the US Naval War College, the size of Soviet naval forces in the Pacific and Indian Oceans does not yet compensate for the superior quality of US naval forces, nor is it likely to do so in the immediate future.[12]

The overwhelming weight of the Soviet military presence in the region is in the North Pacific, where it sees the main threat to the homeland. Soviet forces have been used sparingly in combat in regional conflicts in Korea, on the Sino-Soviet border, and in Vietnam. But large-scale military exercises and the regular display of military power in the region are often used by the USSR to influence the perceptions of regional states about the relative military balance between the USSR and the United States. The Soviet Union constantly seeks to impress China and Japan in particular with the realities and preponderance of Soviet military power.[13]

Out-of-area military deployments average 25–30 ships and submarines operating in the Pacific outside home waters. In addition to ballistic-missile submarine patrols, there are normally intelligence collectors off the west coast of the US, Hawaii and Guam, and a patrol ship in the Korea Strait. In the South China Sea the Soviet Naval Squadron generally includes about two or three attack and cruise-missile submarines and six to eight surface combatants. Since late 1984 a Soviet air unit consisting of 16 naval Tu-16 *Badger* bombers, eight Tu-95 *Bear* long-range reconnaissance and ASW aircraft, and a squadron of 14 MiG-23 *Flogger* fighters, has been deployed in Vietnam.

Soviet use of ports and airfields in Vietnam assists Soviet Indian Ocean deployments and improves surveillance capabilities in the South China Sea. In peacetime, the use of Vietnamese facilities is a valuable military asset, giving a power-projection capability in South-east Asia and providing much greater flexibility for extended naval operations in the South China Sea, the straits of South-east Asia, and the Indian Ocean.

From Vietnam, the Soviet Union can undertake regular intelligence collection and ASW missions against US naval units operating in or passing through the South China Sea, deploy units near the US naval base at Subic Bay in the Philippines, and operate against Chinese naval forces and installations off the southern coast of China and on Hainan Island.

The Soviet military presence in Vietnam has introduced a new element into regional security perceptions and a concern that the USSR has placed itself in a position from which it can more readily threaten the sea-lanes which pass through the strategic waterways of South-east Asia. From its bases in Vietnam, the USSR could respond rapidly to a crisis in the region. In the event of crisis in the Northwest Indian Ocean, in which the Suez Canal may be denied, Cam Ranh Bay could be used to generate naval reinforcements.

The Soviet Union does not, however, enjoy naval or air dominance in the region.[14] The costs for the USSR in attempting to threaten sea-lanes in the region are high, even if it were prepared to accept the risks which would be involved in such an unprecedented military action. As a major maritime power with global naval and commercial interests, it would be impossible for the USSR to adopt a position of denial in respect of any one set of straits used extensively for international navigation, without incalculable repercussions affecting other such straits through which it might wish to deploy.[15] The most likely circumstances for Soviet interdiction of South-east Asian waterways would be global war rather than regional conflict.

Prospects for relations with key states and regions
As a global power and as an East Asian regional power, the Soviet Union will undoubtedly seek more influence in regional affairs.[16] More attention will be given to the region in the coming decade than has been traditionally the case in the post-war period. Under a succession of Soviet leaders – Stalin, Khrushchev and Brezhnev – this part of the world was treated with a mixture of great Russian disdain and a lack of sensitivity towards Asian culture and historical values. Soviet diplomatic intemperance, the unrelenting build-up of its military power and the refusal to negotiate over outstanding territorial issues have served to alienate Asian powers.

The new leadership under Gorbachev will want to change this adverse situation. For the last 28 years, Soviet foreign policy under the guiding hand of Gromyko has been almost single-mindedly preoccupied with relations with the US and Western Europe. Gorbachev has signalled that more attention will be paid to other parts of the world, and already there have been attempts (most notably in his Vladivostok speech of July 1986) to improve relations with China and Japan, proposals for Asian collective security have been resurrected, and moves to establish a greater Soviet presence in the South-west Pacific have been initiated.

Addressing the 27th Party Congress on 25 February 1986, Gorbachev described the Asian and Pacific region as one of growing importance. The increased attention now being focused on East Asia has been demonstrated by a series of visits to the area by Gorbachev himself, by Foreign Minister Shevardnadze and other high-ranking leaders.[17]

Gorbachev's Vladivostok speech was an attempt to present Soviet policies towards Asia and the Pacific in a new light. He emphasized the importance the USSR places on economic and strategic developments in the Asian-Pacific region. The speech contained a scattering of vague 'initiatives', offering relatively little of substance, but wrapped in a package of reasonableness and conciliation. There were no substantial concessions with regard to the Soviet military build-up or the major territorial and strategic issues affecting relations with Japan and China. Until these issues are settled and political relations are improved, it is difficult to see that the Asian-Pacific region will be the source of capital, technology and markets Moscow wants.

China and Japan are at the top of the Soviet Union's priorities and new diplomatic and economic initiatives can be expected. In his Vladivostok speech Gorbachev claimed that 'a noticeable improvement' had occurred in Soviet relations with China. During 1985, more than 60 Soviet delegations went to China and parliamentary groups exchanged visits for the first time since 1960. The sixth round of Sino-Soviet talks aimed at normalizing relations ended in Moscow on 14 April 1986. The persistence of basic divergences, however, is reflected in Vice-Premier Li Peng's statement that the basis for any further improvement in relations is the taking of 'concrete steps and eliminating obstacles'.[18] The Soviet leadership's eagerness to advance relations with China seems unlikely to reach the point of overcoming these serious strategic obstacles in the foreseeable future. It remains to be seen how China will react to the first tentative suggestions of Soviet troop withdrawals from Afghanistan and Mongolia. So far, China's reaction has been to dismiss these Soviet initiatives as lacking substance. The priority issue for China is the removal of Vietnamese troops from Kampuchea.

The Soviet motive for improving relations with Japan at present is largely economic and technical, particularly with the aim of securing Japanese technological expertise and investment funds for the development of Siberia. But, as with China, there are fundamental obstacles in the way of improved relations. The most important of these is the territorial issue of the Soviet occupation of the four islands, which Japan regards as its Northern Territories. Shevardnadze's visit to Tokyo in January 1986 was the first by a Soviet Foreign Minister for ten years. It marked a major step forward in that the two Foreign Ministers 'held talks on the conclusion of a peace treaty, including the problems which might constitute the content of such a treaty' (meaning the territorial issue). They agreed to continue these discussions at further consultations of Foreign Ministers to be held at least once a year. It is doubtful, however, whether the Soviet Union will change its position in any substantial way on the territorial issue. In Vladivostok Gorbachev demanded co-operation with Japan 'free from problems of the past', which seems to indicate that the Northern Territories are not negotiable.

Indochina will continue to be a Soviet priority. The alliance with Vietnam in November 1978 was the USSR's most dramatic gain in the region since its alliance with China in the 1950s. Vietnam is also one of only three non-European members of the Soviet dominated CMEA (Council for Mutual Economic Assistance) – Cuba and Mongolia are the other members. The Soviet Union will go to considerable lengths and pay heavy financial costs to ensure that Vietnam remains within its orbit. Vietnam receives all its arms and most of its aid and essential imports from the USSR. The Soviet Union is also closely allied with Kampuchea and Laos and supplies about $US 170 million a year of military and economic assistance to these two countries. All three countries are thus being bound more closely into the Soviet Bloc.

There are inevitable strains in the Soviet relationship with Vietnam but, as long as the latter sees China as a threat, it will need Soviet support. For the USSR, the desire to improve its relations with China will require careful handling, for Vietnam must fear that any significant improvement in Sino-Soviet relations could occur only at its expense. For the foreseeable future, however, the confluence of Soviet and Vietnamese basic strategic interests seems durable.

North Korea has moved somewhat closer to the Soviet Union in recent years, having long maintained a balance between the USSR and China or, at times, withdrawn into isolation from both countries. President Kim Il Sung made his first visit to Moscow for 23 years in May 1984, and since then there have been numerous high-level exchanges. Foreign Minister Shevardnadze's visit to Pyongyang in January 1986 confirmed the Soviet leadership's interest in improving co-operation with North Korea. Major new agreements on economic and technical co-operation for the period 1986–90 have been signed, and the USSR is also supplying more sophisticated military aid, including MiG-23 aircraft. In return, it appears that the USSR has received permission to make military over-flights of North Korea by Tu-16 reconnaissance aircraft, Tu-95 *Bear* G strike aircraft, and Tu-95 *Bear* D naval intelligence collectors.

It seems improbable, however, that North Korea will totally align itself with the USSR. The North Korean leaders will continue to see some value in maintaining a degree of balance in their relations with China, even if they tend to favour the Soviet Union for military reasons.

Elsewhere in the region, among the ASEAN countries and in the South Pacific, the USSR has been unable to achieve any major penetration since the failure of its close relations with Indonesia over 20 years ago. Soviet military support of Vietnam, continued backing for Vietnam's occupation of Kampuchea, and military presence in Cam Ranh Bay are important factors in the continuing coolness of the ASEAN countries to the Soviet Union. This may change somewhat now that the USSR is moving to a more 'smiling' policy, involving greater diplomatic and economic flexibility in the region.

As an opportunistic power with global ambitions, the Soviet Union will probe for areas it can penetrate at relatively low cost. The slowing down of the ASEAN economies and the narrow economic base of the island states of the South Pacific offer the prospect for greater Soviet trade involvement, economic aid and the negotiation of fishing agreements. The ASEAN and South Pacific countries will remain basically anti-Communist and wary of Soviet penetration, but economic realities may force them to turn to the USSR in some instances. The fragility of the economies of the islands of the South Pacific makes them particularly vulnerable to Soviet offers of fisheries agreements, port visits for cruise ships, and requests for resident missions to service these activities.

The Soviet Union can be expected to exploit anti-Chinese sentiments in Malaysia and Indonesia, political instability in the Philippines and Thailand's border conflict with Vietnam to improve its own position in these countries. It has strong latent interests in Indonesia, which it sees as the most powerful country in ASEAN and as the bulwark of anti-Chinese sentiments in the region. It has recently made offers of aid worth $US 180 million, which Indonesia declined. The Soviet Union will be alert to any opportunities that may arise in the post-Suharto era to foment trouble in Indonesia.

The prospect of the Soviet Union dislodging its major adversary, the US, from its position of prominent influence in South-east Asia and the South Pacific is not at all promising. Nevertheless, it will seek to encourage any developments which could see the US lose its military bases in the Philippines and the ANZUS Treaty relationship between New Zealand and the United States further undermined. Soviet calls for confidence-building measures that involve the security of sea-lanes in the Pacific and the exclusion of certain oceans from anti-submarine activities are not likely to receive a positive response from the US.

Proposals for an Asian collective security agreement in East Asia, which the USSR has put forward in one guise or another since 1969, have received no support except from the Soviet Asian Communist allies. The latest proposal, in April 1986, for an 'all-Asia forum' – which calls for a meeting of Pacific Basin countries on security, 'including economic security' – is unlikely to be successful.

Conclusion

The Asian-Pacific region is assuming a greater salience in the new Soviet leadership's view of the world. In the past, Soviet foreign policy, in focusing on the US and Europe, had neglected a region which was fast becoming more important in economic, political and strategic terms. Gorbachev's new approach to the region has been characterized by an energetic campaign to improve Soviet relations with virtually all countries in the region.

In bilateral relations, the ideological struggle is being played down and economic, cultural and state-to-state links are being emphasized. There will be a more sophisticated differentiation between countries in the region. And the Soviet Union will seek to exploit regional rivalries, as well as to put forward initiatives concerning arms reduction, nuclear-free zones and confidence-building measures.

But while Gorbachev's style is exemplified by a more conciliatory and pragmatic approach to the region, he also shares his predecessors' confrontational view of relations with the outside world. The Soviet military build-up in the region can be expected to continue. And there is no sign that the USSR is about to make major policy changes or significant concessions on any of the principal regional issues, particularly those relating to Japan and China and the Soviet military presence in Vietnam.

Overall, the Soviet Union faces a formidable array of diplomatic, ideological, economic and strategic obstacles in the region.[19] These will work against any fundamental change in the adversarial relationship that it has with major regional powers. It will, however, probe for weaknesses, and the region will need to be alert to potentially unstable situations which the USSR could take advantage of at a low cost, especially in South-east Asia and the South Pacific.

---

* The author is now Director, Joint Intelligence Organization, Department of Defence, Canberra; he was formerly Ministerial Consultant to the Australian Minister for Defence. The views expressed in this Paper are not a statement of Australian Government policy.

Notes

[1] East Asia and the Pacific is here taken to include North-east Asia, Indochina, South-east Asia, the South Pacific, and the intervening ocean areas.
[2] *Soviet Military Power*, US Department of Defense, Washington, DC, fifth edition, March 1986, p. 100.
[3] *Ibid*, p. 13. All strategic nuclear forces are under central control from Moscow.
[4] For a more detailed analysis, see *Strategic Survey 1981–1982* (London: IISS, 1982), pp. 104–8.
[5] *Soviet Military Power, (op cit.*, in note 2) p. 62.
[6] *Ibid*, p. 100.
[7] *Ibid*, p. 63.
[8] Soviet exercises suggest that it does plan against the contingency of a Chinese attack during a NATO-Warsaw Pact war.
[9] *Soviet Military Power, (op cit.*, in note 2) p. 138.
[10] *Pravda*, 1 November 1983, p. 4.
[11] *The Military Balance 1985–1986*, (London: IISS, 1985), p. 29. Over one-third of the principal surface combatants are corvettes. Of the submarine force, 62 boats are attack submarines, more than half of which are 20 years old or more.
[12] Alvin H. Bernstein, 'The Soviets in Cam Ranh Bay', *Quadrant*, Sydney, July-August 1986, p. 49 (reprinted from *The National Interest*, Washington, DC, Spring 1986). US naval forces in the Pacific have almost twice as many large surface combatants (aircraft carriers, battleships and cruisers) as the Soviet naval forces.
[13] There are about 500 Soviet naval movements and 345 aircraft movements a year around Japan. (*Defense of Japan 1985*, Defense Agency, Tokyo, 1985, p. 33).
[14] In wartime, Soviet forces based in Vietnam could be rapidly destroyed by US forces. For example, a US carrier battle group could, with a high probability of success, detect and destroy Soviet naval and air forces operating from Vietnamese bases; B-52 bombers from Guam could destroy Soviet base facilities.
[15] Michael Leifer, 'The Security of Sea Lanes in South-East Asia', *Survival*, January/February 1983, p. 21.
[16] This section has drawn on the *Background Briefs* on the USSR prepared regularly by the Foreign and Commonwealth Office, London.
[17] Shevardnadze visited Japan, North Korea and Mongolia in January 1986. Arkhipov, a Soviet First Deputy Prime

Minister, led the first meeting of the Joint Commission for Economic, Scientific and Technical Cooperation to China in March 1986. Soviet Deputy Prime Minister Ryabov, who visited Indonesia in October 1985, was the most senior Soviet figure to go there in 20 years; in November 1985 he went to Malaysia. A Soviet Deputy Foreign Minister, M. Kapitsa, visited Thailand in April 1986; he then went on to the Philippines to meet the new President Mrs Corazón Aquino.

[18] These (three) obstacles are Soviet military deployments along China's northern borders, Soviet occupation of Afghanistan, and Vietnam's Soviet-supported occupation of Kampuchea.

[19] According to Admiral William Crowe, Chairman of the US Joint Chiefs of Staff, 'every year that peace continues in the Pacific our friends and allies are winning there – and the Soviets are losing' (*US News and World Report*, 4 August 1986, p. 12).

China's Relations with East Asia and the Pacific Region: Part I

DR JONATHAN POLLACK*

China and East Asia in the coming decade
China's emergence as a stabilizing influence in East Asia constitutes the most important development in regional politics and economics of the past decade. Having spent much of the preceding ten years mired in xenophobic isolation and convulsive, almost incomprehensible domestic conflict, the Chinese leadership has devoted the later 1970s and early 1980s to undoing the damage of the past. Economic goals have assumed primacy in Chinese policy-making, with ideological preoccupations largely subordinated for the first time since the mid-1950s. Beijing is seeking to define a hybrid path for socialist development that limits the powers of the country's long-dominant political and economic institutions, permitting a devolution of decision-making authority unthinkable in the past. At the same time, the Chinese are assertively soliciting capital and technology from the capitalist countries, hoping thereby to harness the scientific and technological transformation underway in the industrialized world to the needs of their own modernization programme. The principal objectives for the next decade are to establish the conditions for sustained technological and economic dynamism in the twenty-first century and to achieve an orderly transfer of power from Deng Xiaoping to his designated successors.

Deng's assurances to innumerable foreign visitors that reformist leadership and policies will continue after his passage from the scene bespeak the triumph of hope over experience. In nearly four decades of Communist rule, China has experienced repeated upheaval and political instability. Deng is also aware that the history of arranged successions in Communist systems is abysmal, a fact reinforced by China's culture and history. Rather than an orderly political succession after Deng's death, it seems far more likely that various presumptive successors will manoeuvre for influence and power, with another individual leader ultimately achieving political predominance. This successor could well be someone who would meet with Deng's approval, but to anticipate a smooth transition would be to expect far too much.

These observations do not mean that China will yet again experience a cycle of convulsive, debilitating internal conflict reminiscent of the Cultural Revolution. The cumulative effects of China's movement away from the Maoist era – Mao has now been dead for ten years, more than a quarter of the political life of the People's Republic – are too pronounced and pervasive to permit a turning back of the clock. There has been a cathartic, 'distancing' effect to the dismantling of Mao's legacy that seems far more thorough and wide-ranging than de-Stalinization in the Soviet Union. Even as the Chinese elite debates its country's future directions, the broad contours of national policy and the range of choice confronting the leadership seem increasingly well defined.

The primacy of economics
In Deng's view, China's present policies will continue because they work. During the first half of the 1980s, agricultural and industrial production grew at an annual rate of 11%. Similarly, the Chinese doubled the level of exports and imports from the start of the decade. To guard against excessive optimism and inflated expectations, however, the near-term economic goals appear relatively prudent.[1] China seems quite likely to achieve its development targets for the year 2000 – that is, a gross national product (GNP) of $US 1 trillion, or $800 *per capita*. This would represent an average annual growth rate between 1980 and 2000 of more than 7%, an impressive accomplishment by any criteria.

If China sustains its projected growth rates to the year 2000, then the gap in its aggregate economic capabilities relative to other major powers, although still very large, will be substantially smaller. For example, should China's GNP reach $1 trillion by the year 2000, and should the Soviet economy grow at between 2 to 2.5% annually over the next 15 years, then the gap between the two economies will narrow from approximately 3.5:1 at present to approximately 2.4:1 in 2000.[2] In addition, regardless of continuing *per capita* disparities, an economy of such absolute magnitude will represent a potent international force, with substantial resources available for various national purposes, including the acquisition of military power. Deng's message to his successors is simple: a return to autarky and defiant nationalism would guarantee a future of backwardness, vulnerability and international irrelevance.

Deng therefore sees a direct link between Chinese development goals and the character of China's relations with the outside world. The country's economic accomplishments since the late 1970s have been matched by a steady stream of foreign-policy break-throughs, including near-universal diplomatic recognition, membership and active participation in a far fuller range of international organizations, the development of far closer and more comprehensive relations with the US and Japan, and a Sino-British agreement on the reversion of Hong Kong to Chinese sovereignty in 1997. The outlines of a normal Sino-Soviet relationship have also emerged; only with Vietnam do China's relations still seem largely confrontational. Although territorial disputes of varying intensity persist with several neighbouring states, and Beijing has yet to achieve a political reconciliation with Taipei, China's position in both regional and global politics is barely recognizable when compared with that of a decade ago.

The tasks for the coming decade are to consolidate these gains, to avoid being drawn into a major international conflict and to integrate China more fully within the evolving framework of East Asian politics and economics. The Chinese recognize East Asia as the most dynamic economic region of the world, and they intend to become a major actor in that process. This ambition, however, is fraught with uncertainty. It depends on the adaptability of China's political and economic institutions, a comprehensive upgrading of China's manpower and technical base, and the capacity of Chinese industrial enterprises to enter into meaningful, sustained collaboration with foreign firms. Perhaps most important, it will depend on regional stability, if not tranquillity. Should East Asia become skewed towards conflict, instability and polarization, it would limit Beijing's political and economic options and quite possibly shift China away from its present emphasis on an improved standard of living and industrial and scientific rejuvenation. Thus, the prospects for realizing China's development objectives ultimately depend on a relatively quiescent security environment.[3]

After a period of debate over China's foreign-policy directions during the early 1980s, Deng and other leaders put forward the concept of 'an independent foreign policy'. Its regional implications are threefold: first, China should avoid entanglement in the Soviet-US strategic competition in East Asia; second, at the same time, Beijing should pursue separately better relations with Moscow and Washington, without sacrificing China's vital security interests to either; and third, wherever feasible China should broaden its commercial and technological relations with other regional states, including those with whom full governmental relations are not yet possible. To review the status and prospects for China's foreign-policy course, I shall review separately: China's relations with the super-powers; its ties with the regional Communist states; and links with East Asia's rapid developers.

China and the super-powers
China's foreign-policy agenda has long been dominated by its relations with the United States and the Soviet Union. However, because of Beijing's more differentiated foreign-policy strategy, the balance among the security, economic and political aspects of these relationships has shifted in recent years. In practical if not doctrinal terms, Japan has also been elevated to comparable status in long-term Chinese thinking. Chinese strategic pronouncements repeatedly assert that the international system is undergoing a transformation from a bipolar to a multipolar world. Among these emergent 'poles', however, Western Europe has only nominal political and economic coherence, and the Third World is a highly disparate amalgam of states, with only a fictive claim to unity of purpose and direction. Thus, the prospective list of candidate super-powers reduces to two (China and Japan), with

India, Indonesia and other putative major powers conspicuously absent from Chinese formulations.

Among the super-powers, only the USSR poses a direct challenge to the security of China. Despite continuing overtures to the Chinese since the early 1980s, the essence of Soviet policy in Asia remains intact, altered only by a more skilful diplomatic effort: the undiminished deployment of Soviet nuclear and conventional military power east of the Urals, much of it oriented directly against China; a continuing effort to subjugate Afghanistan and underwrite Vietnam's occupation of Kampuchea; a burgeoning naval and air force presence in Cam Ranh Bay; and an attempt to establish a political beach-head in East Asia, not only in Japan and the ASEAN states but extending to North Korea as well.

Despite China's repeated insistence on the removal of the 'three obstacles', the Chinese entertain few illusions that the Soviet Union will substantially reduce its military strength deployed in Asia. China has tacitly assented to what Brezhnev had long proposed – that is, a decoupling of the Sino-Soviet bilateral relationship from the larger political and military competition, at the same time that China has disassociated itself from closer security collaboration with the West, in particular actions that imply a co-ordinated strategy for countering Soviet power. In his Vladivostok speech of 28 July 1986, Mikhail Gorbachev asserted that 'there has been a noticeable improvement in our relations', asserting further that 'the acceleration of socio-economic development' reflected 'similar' priorities in both states.[4] For the first time, a Soviet leader has indicated a willingness to reduce some of the forces posing an immediate threat to the security of China. The Chinese (including Deng) have responded with a mixture of encouragement and scepticism, reserving judgment on whether Gorbachev's overtures portend a significant change in Soviet policy towards China.[5] But the Soviet Union's latest moves seem certain to breathe new life into the stalled process of Sino-Soviet normalization. Unlike the 1970s, when the antagonisms between the USSR and China seemed stark and unbridgeable, both states find it politically useful to talk and to smile.

Why have the Chinese undertaken actions which five years ago they refused to countenance? Are they likely to take additional steps? Four principal factors explain this reassessment. First, the Chinese seem persuaded that Soviet geopolitical expansion has passed its zenith, with the USSR increasingly constrained by a renascent strategic and technological competition with the US and diminished opportunities for interventions in the Third World. Unlike the 1970s, when Deng and other Chinese leaders castigated Washington for its supposed illusions and irresolution *vis-à-vis* the Soviet Union, the Chinese believe that US assertiveness will continue to inhibit the USSR. Second, Gorbachev seems determined (in word and perhaps ultimately in deed) to revive the long-stagnant Soviet economy, suggesting that the Soviet leadership will be preoccupied in the next decade with an internal economic agenda rather than external expansion. Third,

Gorbachev's rapid consolidation of power and the likelihood of his long tenure in office provides China with substantial incentives for more amicable relations, including the possibility that the new leadership will slowly begin to dismantle the long-entrenched Suslov-Brezhnev policy of implacable hostility and military threat. Fourth, the Chinese believe that the expansion and institutionalization of Sino-American relations and Sino-Japanese relations provides some latitude and leverage in dealings with Moscow but without endangering relations with Washington and Tokyo.

China's internal transformation affords additional insight into its altered Soviet policy. First, the modernization agenda gives China a substantial incentive to keep tensions with Moscow at a manageable level. Second, a much more active Sino-Soviet economic and technological relationship may be appealing to some leaders in China, given that much of its heavy industrial base was furnished by the Soviet Union in the 1950s. Equally important, some segments in the leadership see a natural complementarity between the two economies and the character of their economic institutions.

By forgoing the anti-Soviet rationale which guided Chinese dealings with the West in the late 1970s and early 1980s, while permitting a certain level of Sino-Soviet interchange, Deng has diversified China's political and strategic options. A more credible and active Sino-Soviet relationship does not negate the importance of close relations with the US. However, the earlier posture of unyielding negativism and hostility towards the Soviet Union brought China very little, and held its policy hostage to ties with Washington. A modest but growing Sino-Soviet relationship may also help Deng deflect domestic criticisms of his predominant orientation towards the West. Beijing's strategic objective remains unchanged: a steady growth in China's national power, abetted by US and Japanese technology, which begins to narrow the economic and military gap between the Soviet Union and China. But this can be done quietly, so as not to provoke or alarm leaders in the USSR.

An incremental accommodation with Moscow assumes US tolerance and a measure of Soviet responsiveness. China's repeated pledge 'never [to] attach itself to any superpower, or enter into alliance or strategic relations with either of them' unconditionally limits its security collaboration with the United States, irrespective of Soviet conduct.[6] But this pledge does not permit a free ride for Soviet defence planners. A neutral but more powerful China still requires the Soviet Union to allocate substantial forces against China in peacetime and wartime; this allocation of Soviet military power therefore has clear if indirect strategic benefits for the US. Moreover, China's declaration of strategic independence does not extend to non-binding forms of defence collaboration with the West, including upgrading the technologies employed by China's armed forces. The balance sheet in the Sino-Soviet relationship may give Gorbachev some modest encouragement, but the longer-term implications of the growth of Chinese power tempers overly optimistic expectations.

The Soviet Union also believes it has a major opportunity to enhance economic interchange and technical collaboration with China, a point emphasized by Gorbachev in his Vladivostok speech. A five-year trade agreement coinciding with the planning cycles of both states was signed in 1985, with annual two-way trade scheduled to reach $US 3.5 billion by the end of the decade. Under the terms of the agreement, the USSR will provide heavy machinery, aircraft, motor vehicles, power equipment, railway rolling stock, chemicals, and metals in exchange for Chinese foodstuffs, textiles and various consumer items.[7] More important, it is barter trade, entailing no outlays of foreign exchange. An agreement on Soviet technical assistance, whereby the USSR will modernize 17 enterprises in metallurgy, coal, machine building and chemicals as well as participate in new construction in the power industry, means that Soviet technicians will reside in China for the first time in a quarter century.[8]

To date, however, the logic of Soviet technical assistance has been more compelling than the evidence of increased activity. Moreover, the Soviet Union's own economic constraints suggest that Soviet assistance and trade can only be a supplementary means of upgrading China's industrial, transportation, communication and energy sectors. Although Sino-Soviet trade has increased from a mere trickle in 1980 to approximately $1.8 bn in 1985, it still ranks well below China's trade with its leading economic partners.

China looks instead to increased trade and advanced technology from the West as a far more crucial component of its modernization programme. The US and Japan are especially important in Chinese thinking, since these two economies are expected to furnish the technology that will enable China to leap-frog into a 'new technological revolution' characterizing world development in the latter twentieth century. In addition, the United States has assumed a disproportionate role in the training of Chinese students, more than 15,000 of whom are enrolled in American universities.

Chinese hopes for much closer economic and technological relations with both states were clearly reflected in an essay on relations among the US, Japan and ASEAN written in 1984 by a leading Chinese international relations specialist.[9] Transposing the logic of Soviet-American strategic relations onto US-Japanese economic relations, the author described Washington and Tokyo as the two 'economic superpowers' (*jingji chaoji daguo*) that compete as well as co-operate for investment and markets: 'The competition between the United States and Japan in ASEAN is an extension of the competition between them elsewhere as well as an important link in the overall competition between them'. Under circumstances of heightened US-Japanese economic contention, he concluded, the competition between the two states would grow more intense. The relevance of this assessment seems self-evident: China hopes to be the object of equivalent solicitation, shrewdly playing off the world's two leading capitalist powers against one another.

To attract Japanese and US investment, however, China must do more than declare the door open; it must demonstrate that it works. Many companies regard China as a promising market for the sale of goods and services, but the investment climate remains far more uncertain. The grievance list of foreign firms remains a long one: the extreme difficulty of repatriating profits in hard currency; inadequate safeguarding of intellectual property rights; the penchant of some Chinese enterprises for renegotiating signed contracts when the terms are no longer deemed useful;[10] prodigious infrastructural problems, in particular severe shortages in skilled manpower; and the sheer costs, complexities and frustrations of doing business in China. The Chinese are not oblivious to these issues, and in selected respects have taken steps to reassure potential investors. But China's repeated urgings for foreign firms to adopt a long-term perspective may increasingly fall on deaf ears; such pleas are a tacit admission not to expect too much and certainly not very soon. Until these conditions change appreciably, comparative advantage for foreign companies in local assembly or manufacture remains highly problematic.

These observations diminish expectations of a vast Western technological role in China's industrial development. Senior Chinese officials also acknowledge these circumstances. As Vice Premier Li Peng has observed, foreign trade and investment are 'very important' but not 'decisive'; China 'ultimately . . . relies mainly on its own resources' for national development.[11] Cautioned by the experience of many third-world states, China seems intent on avoiding a major debt problem. Unless Western firms are prepared to provide a major infusion of funds, equipment and personnel, the Chinese will not be able to upgrade comprehensively the technological level of their industrial system for many years to come. US investment in China has surpassed $1 bn, well in excess of any other state, but these funds are concentrated in offshore oil development (thus far a major disappointment), tourism and several large-scale projects, including resource development. With the exception of a few sectors (e.g., integrated circuits, consumer electronics and microcomputers), Japanese and US technological involvement in the industrial system as a whole (as distinct from the sale of products and services) remains relatively constrained, and helps to explain China's active wooing of trade and investment with East Asia's rapid developers and the intermediate capitalist powers.

The asymmetries in China's relations with the two leading industrial powers (especially with Japan) are amply reflected in yawning trade deficits. Until 1983, China was able to maintain a rough balance in its foreign trade with Japan. In 1984, however, loosened restraints on expenditure of hard currency and pent-up internal demand for foreign industrial and consumer items resulted in a trade imbalance favouring

Japan by more than $2 bn; in 1985 the gap grew to more than $5 bn.[12] According to Chinese Minister of Foreign Economic Relations and Trade Zheng Tuobin, 'China is not able to bear any further increase in this burden'; in Zheng's view, both states need to achieve a more equitable balance in trade relations.[13] To narrow this gap, China reimposed far more stringent controls on the expenditure of foreign exchange. But calls on Japan to increase its purchases of Chinese products (notably coal, crude oil, foodstuffs, handicrafts and textiles) seem highly unlikely to rectify China's continuing trade imbalance with its most important economic partner. Despite repeated Chinese urgings, Japan has also remained exceedingly cautious in undertaking major investments in China.

Trade tensions have generated political consequences. In the autumn of 1985, demonstrators on several of China's leading university campuses protested against 'the second Japanese occupation'. Personal interventions by senior Chinese leaders helped dampen the protests, but trade and related problems had tapped powerful sentiments. Recurring disputes over the depiction of Japanese aggression in the 1930s and 1940s in Japanese educational text-books cast an additional cloud over the bilateral ties, with the Chinese warning against a revival of Japanese militarism. Although it is doubtful that the Chinese regard the text-book issue as serious evidence of such a trend, these differences have harmed the relationship.

The Chinese also remain equivocal about Japan's long-term security role in the region. Although conceding Tokyo's legitimate right of self-defence, Beijing has yet to express its views on the appropriate scope of such activity, including Japan's commitment to assume responsibility for sea-lane defence to a distance of about 1,000 nautical miles. This equivocation extends to Chinese views of the US-Japanese security relationship, for which China periodically expresses 'understanding' but never outright approval. Beijing recognizes the need for a response to the growth of Soviet military power in the Pacific, and it has cautiously explored opportunities for upgrading its informal security ties with Tokyo. But China remains troubled by the potential implications of a major increase in Japanese military capabilities and in the scale of US-Japanese security collaboration. Some in Beijing voice quiet concern about the longer-term effects of an enlarged concept of Japanese national security, in particular if it entails a more autonomous regional role and a formal division of labour between Washington and Tokyo.

China's continued ambivalence is most pronounced in its dealings with the US. Despite Beijing's clear intent to avoid dependence on any external power, relations with the US loom very large on the Chinese policy agenda, including China's long-term security calculations. The clarion calls of the late 1970s and early 1980s for an anti-Soviet united front are a distant memory, supplanted by a less obtrusive but far more meaningful acceleration of technology transfer to China.[14] Although the process remains protracted and the Chinese still express complaints about restrictions on sales of particular technologies, the export control machinery is now vastly more permissive, resulting in dramatic increases in the flow of US high technology to China.[15] Simplifications of CoCom procedures have further expedited transfers from various US allies.[16] In addition, an institutional framework for US defence technology transfer has been established, with recent or pending transactions for various military items. The largest of these prospective sales, a $550 million transaction for 55 avionics packages for China's J-8 fighter, will for the first time provide the Chinese air force with a limited all-weather capability.[17]

Without continuing close relations with the US, China's access to advanced technologies needed for industrial and military modernization would become far more problematic. At the same time, the United States has substantial reasons of its own for building a credible, long-term relationship with China. But the Chinese do not view positive Sino-American relations as a blanket endorsement of US policy, even less as a limit on Beijing's freedom of action in its foreign and defence policy. Neither state wishes to put at risk the accomplishments of the past five years, but differing objectives and expectations could limit future opportunities, to the consequent disadvantage of both countries.

Chinese unease about US policy reduces to one principal concern – that a resurgently 'hegemonic' US will exercise its power to the ultimate, if unintended, detriment of China's political and security interests. There is an undeniable irony in this situation, given China's repeated admonitions in the 1970s about American weakness and vacillation. Having castigated the US for its inability or unwillingness to resist Soviet geopolitical advances, Beijing now finds the shoe on the other foot. Chinese strategic analysts depict the mid-1980s as a period of American advance and Soviet retrenchment if not retreat, with the United States pressing its technological, economic and military advantage, thereby seeking to recoup from the strategic setbacks of the 1960s and 1970s.[18]

To the Chinese, the risks of a heightened Soviet-American military rivalry are clear: accelerated expenditures on strategic offensive and defensive forces that degrade the credibility of China's limited nuclear deterrent; US interventions in the Third World that complicate Beijing's accommodation with the United States and present the Soviet Union with new political opportunities; and an escalation of Soviet-American tensions in the West Pacific that threatens to polarize the region and provide the USSR with political openings at China's expense. Finally, some Chinese worry that a more unilateralist US policy might further complicate resolution of the Taiwan question, which China continues to describe as the principal limiting factor in the Sino-US relationship.

In certain instances, China's disagreements with US policy have eroded political support in the US for closer Sino-American relations. What Senator Moynihan has aptly termed China's 'two United States' policy rankles American officials. For example, China implores the US to be far more forthcoming on the transfer of advanced technology, yet at the same time feels free to criticize harshly US regional security and arms-control policy. It backs New Zealand in its dispute with the US, while welcoming the US Secretary of Defense. It endorses growing anti-nuclear sentiment in the Pacific, when the principal consequence could be an erosion of support for the forward deployment of US military power, leaving Soviet nuclear and conventional power unchallenged within the region. In each case, it is less the fact that China disagrees with US policy, and more that China voices its dissent publicly. It remains exceedingly unlikely that such differences will create a major rupture in relations, but these disputes do suggest some of the limits of Sino-American accommodation.

China may feel that protecting its relationships with other political constituencies leaves little choice but to dissent publicly from US policy. At the same time, what some observers view as Chinese ingratitude may reflect the multiplicity of voices now heard in Beijing, with attitudes towards US power and policy increasingly reflecting different bureaucratic interests. Such complexity is likely to characterize Sino-US dealings even more over the next decade. The challenge will be to find common ground on which to withstand the periodic political differences to which the relationship seems likely to be subjected.

The regional Communist powers
Of the three major Asian Communist states, only China has been able to rid itself of the political dogma that long inhibited effective political and economic relations with the non-Communist world. North Korea and Vietnam both remain mired in the past, neither of them demonstrating the political wherewithal or creativity to break loose from their international isolation and ideological fixations. Beyond these similarities, however, the two cases diverge. North Korea represents a first in the Communist world – a system which is both Marxist-Leninist and monarchical. Kim Il Sung's principal preoccupation in his final years in power is to avoid Mao's political fate. By passing power to his son, he hopes to preserve the essence of the political system he created. But Kim's fixation on maintaining North Korea's ethos of self-reliance seems increasingly anachronistic and costly to the regime's long-term health. There are enough stirrings to suggest that the present system will persist only so long as the father lives. Until the elder Kim's passage from the scene, the Chinese intend to nurture quietly those tendencies that they hope will ultimately lead the North in directions akin to China's policy reassessment of the past decade.

Vietnam seems different, as does China's political prescription. Although Hanoi now encourages a range of economic reforms (especially in agriculture), there is no credible evidence that economic flexibility is matched in the slightest by a readiness to compromise on Kampuchea's future. The aged revolutionaries who have shaped Vietnam's politics believe victory is within their grasp. In Hanoi's reckoning, it can only persevere, hoping that war-weariness among the

ASEAN states will ultimately take its toll, and lead to acceptance of Vietnam's domination of all of Indochina. Under such circumstances, China believes that the smallest of political gestures towards Vietnam from whatever quarter will only sustain Hanoi's conviction that time is on its side.

Thus, China views the opportunities and risks in North-east and South-east Asia very differently. In relation to North Korea, it urges flexibility and openness on the part of Japan and the US, and insists that such steps will be reciprocated. By implication, the Chinese suggest that a more forthcoming Western policy towards the North will increase their influence on Pyongyang. In relation to Vietnam, however, China is determined to maintain maximum political pressure, interspersed with intermittent low-level military action. In addition, China has repeatedly turned aside all of Vietnam's calls for the normalization of relations, both public and private. In another context, China has called for the initiation of 'trade and economic exchanges' with all countries that 'have difficulties' in entering into diplomatic relations with China at present.[19] But China deems it inappropriate to make comparable overtures to Vietnam. According to a spokesman from the Ministry of Foreign Affairs, 'China and Vietnam have no trade relations now, nor is the condition available for the resumption of trade'.[20]

The test of wills between Beijing and Hanoi seems likely to persist; it seems equally doubtful that the Soviet Union would put the kind of pressure on Vietnam that would compel Hanoi to alter course. Thus, only a significant change in the battlefield situation, an alteration in ASEAN strategy, or major shifts on the part of the successor leadership generation in Vietnam seem likely to change the Sino-Vietnamese relationship. China judges the costs of continued aid to the Kampuchea resistance as bearable; similarly, periodic military pressure can be maintained along the border without entailing major risks to Chinese security. To be sure, China may be somewhat chastened by Vietnam's pugnacious refusal to alter course; it may be equally chagrined by the USSR's ability to turn its bases in Vietnam into a major strategic asset. In the absence of a Vietnamese withdrawal from Kampuchea, China has concluded, no concessions will be forthcoming, raising yet again the question of when, if ever, peace will come to Indochina.

The stakes in North-east Asia, however, are incalculably bigger. A renewed conflict in Korea would have profound repercussions for China, whose national security calculations remain inextricably linked to the future of the Peninsula. Unlike the past, the Chinese no longer sit with their hands folded.[21] In a period of only three years, they have significantly reoriented their posture towards both North and South Korea, opening *de facto* relations with Seoul, while also setting explicit limits on the scope of political, economic and defence obligations to Pyongyang. As a result of these changes, China enjoys a unique position among the major powers: it alone can deal credibly with both North and South, while also enjoying close links with the United

States and Japan which all three states have used to limit the possibilities of renewed conflict.

China does not pretend to control the obstreperous leaders of the North, but no longer deems inaction a viable policy. Although clearly concerned about any prospective 'tilt' towards Moscow on the part of Pyongyang, it is prepared to take political risks with North Korea and even to accept some negative consequences. Even as Moscow has made political inroads with Pyongyang for the first time in more than two decades, Beijing does not believe that Kim Il Sung will allow himself to become a strategic pawn in the US-Soviet rivalry. Thus, the Chinese have offered declaratory political support for the improvement of Soviet-North Korean relations – deeming it equivalent to China's independent foreign policy – but have also leaked to foreign correspondents in Beijing their concerns about Soviet overflight rights in North Korea which are directed against China.[22] Through such acknowledgments, Beijing has implicitly warned the North that consenting to Soviet activities inimical to Chinese interests will pose political risks.

Beijing does not seek a confrontation with the North, since a predominant Soviet role in Pyongyang would engender a very serious political and security challenge to China. Rather, China seems likely to persevere in its efforts to nudge the North in political and economic directions akin to those it has already adopted. To a certain extent, therefore, Beijing has assumed the role of an intermediary, counselling patience and moderation to Pyongyang, while encouraging Washington and Tokyo to undertake gestures towards the North. With occasional lapses, the Chinese continue to assert that the prospects for a reduction of tensions on the Peninsula have rarely been better. Their optimism assumes that the North can ultimately be weaned from its steady diet of invective hurled at the US, Japan and South Korea, and, conceding the growing chasm in its economic capabilities relative to the South, will ultimately turn away from its version of war Communism.

Chinese actions entail obvious risks. Not only does Beijing reject North Korea's claims of an emergent 'US-South Korean-Japanese military axis' which plots nuclear war against the North; its entire reform programme must be seen by Kim Il Sung as a serious challenge to his decades of Stalinist rule. Although the North Koreans have cautiously assented to the economic and political changes underway in China, they have made it very clear that their own road to modernization will not emulate that of Beijing.[23] Unlike the Soviet Union, however, China shrewdly opted to endorse the arranged succession of Kim Chong-il, however noxious it may have regarded such an action. Thus, the Chinese believe that over time they will wield more influence over North Korea than will the Soviet Union.

In the near term, Beijing will seek to limit the damage deriving from the warming of Soviet-North Korean ties. Although China cannot compete with the Soviet Union in proffering new military equipment to the North, it does not believe that the USSR is prepared to provide significant military assistance, lest the North feel it has sufficient encouragement to initiate hostilities. Neither Moscow nor Beijing desires a resumption of conflict; indeed, a simultaneous Soviet and Chinese role on the Peninsula may impose more constraints on North Korean behaviour than when only one of the two enjoyed a credible relationship in Pyongyang.

Over the longer run, China remains convinced that North Korea must take the painful step of reaching a genuine accommodation with the non-Communist world, including with South Korea. At the same time, China hopes that such actions will contribute to an ultimate rapprochement between the major Western powers and Pyongyang, but not to the detriment of the South. The logic of China's concept of 'one country, two systems', as it pertains to Korea, presumes autonomous political activity in both North and South, with national reunification a much more long-term goal. But the imponderables of the impending succession to Kim Il Sung also weigh heavily in Chinese thinking. Indeed, the USSR may believe that its military assistance provides them with significant leverage with Pyongyang's future leaders where Beijing has little or none. Both major Communist powers therefore await Kim's death, for only then will the prospects for political change in the North emerge with any clarity.

China and the rapid developers
Some of the most dramatic changes in Chinese foreign policy concern Beijing's growing interest in expanded trade and technological ties with the newly-industrializing countries (NIC) of the Pacific rim. Despite Beijing's major diplomatic break-throughs in recent years, a number of East Asian states as yet do not have full official relations with China, including South Korea, Singapore and Indonesia. Economic ties have therefore proved a valuable intermediate step, whereby China is able to explore the modalities of a *de facto* relationship when diplomatic recognition is not yet practicable.

The results of these steps are demonstrable. Starting from near zero at the start of the 1980s, Chinese trade with South Korea now outstrips that with the North by a wide margin, and is likely to grow even greater in the future. Singapore has made a fundamental decision to foster much fuller economic, technical and advisory relations with China, and already ranks among China's ten leading trading partners. Taiwan represents a very special case. Despite Taipei's insistence that it will not permit any form of official contact with Beijing, two-way trade (mainly through Hong Kong) has ballooned in recent years, with some 1985 estimates ranging as high as $US 1 bn. It seems clear that China's desire for trade and other forms of contact has political as well as economic consequences. Moreover, the political implications cut in both directions. On the one hand, China wants to demonstrate its credibility and reliability as a trading and investment partner; at the same time, such linkages prove very useful to countries such as South

Korea in solidifying relations with China. For example, Beijing does not call attention to Singapore's extremely active ties with both Taiwan and China; Lee Kuan Yew is the only world leader who has been a welcome guest in both Beijing and Taipei within the past year, without provoking a response from either.

Indeed, the potential for considerably enhanced collaboration may look increasingly attractive to Beijing and its regional trading partners. There are both economic and political factors in this thinking. China was initially drawn to the experiences of Hong Kong, Taiwan, South Korea and other rapid developers for their possible relevance to its own development options. The notion of export-processing zones which combine Western technology with cheap domestic labour as the engine of economic growth remains very appealing to Beijing, even as the Chinese are undertaking a major reappraisal of the concept. To assess some of the problems with the special economic zones, the Chinese have secured the services of Goh Keng Swee and other retired Singaporean officials; advice from an East Asian NIC seems far more useful than the views of a major industrial power.

How far might China proceed in nurturing ties with the East Asian rapid developers? In the aggregate, the East Asian NIC represent a very potent economic force. Although the technological base of these economies does not approach that of the advanced industrial states, they have made extraordinary strides in a very brief period of time. Indeed, as the Chinese increasingly learn that they must walk before they can run, decisions to acquire intermediate technologies may prove more feasible and more useful. Perhaps most important, increased ties with the NIC may mean reduced dependence on Japan and the US, conveying that for numerous products and services China has alternatives. Over time, China might become more discriminating and focused in its trade and technology ties with the world's economic giants. Similar reasoning pervades China's efforts to broaden its technical and commercial links with the Western European states and with Australia.

These increased dealings may also represent a mutual safety net for China and its smaller neighbours, should protectionist sentiment begin to limit the export opportunities for various NIC in the US. To be sure, goods from the smaller island economies sometimes compete with those of China (e.g., textiles). But the more diversified and developed industrial base in a number of these countries could well provide much needed technology and services for the Chinese development effort.

Moreover, important political trade-offs are at work in a number of these cases. Policy-makers in Seoul, for example, have been quietly gratified by the growth of their 'non-political' relations with China, including athletic competitions, scientific exchanges and various instances of crisis management. As a result, the two states are no longer strangers to one another; the Chinese in particular have a much more developed and differentiated view of the South Korean system. Although diplomatic relations are not yet feasible, the benefits to

South Korea in the present situation are palpable. Should Beijing permit it, therefore, Seoul may gradually opt for a much broader involvement in the Chinese development programme, even in the face of uncertain economic gains.

The Chinese have their own calculations in this regard. Not only have their increasingly visible dealings with the South been a powerful message to Pyongyang; they lend sustenance to China's express desire for expanded relations with virtually all states, irrespective of ideology or social system.[24] China's goals for economic and technological advancement have profound political consequences as well, for effective long-term collaboration within East Asia would be impossible without Beijing acknowledging and acceding to existing regional realities.[25]

The true test for the adaptability of Chinese policies concerns the very special cases of Hong Kong and Taiwan, in particular the latter. Indeed, if economic motivations can be said to underlie Beijing's present-day calculations, its incentives for a 'live and let live' approach towards Taiwan are extraordinary. Taiwan's booming economy is now accumulating foreign exchange reserves at roughly $1 bn a month; its pool of scientific and technical talent is enviable; and its industrial base is growing in complexity and sophistication. Yet how tolerant and patient are leaders in Beijing likely to be? How much diversity and autonomy will Beijing countenance in relations with its long-standing adversary? Are more coercive voices likely to prove ascendant over the longer run? The answers to such issues will speak volumes not only about China's dealings with the outside world, but the transformation of China's own political system.

Some alternative scenarios
Two central, interrelated facts define present Chinese policy-making. First, there is no major conflict within the leadership over the general goal of accelerating China's modernization. Individual leaders differ on specific policy objectives and the directions of the reform effort, and many long-entrenched beneficiaries of the old system continue to resist the changes Deng has introduced. But these disputes are more those of degree than kind, focusing on the distribution of political, economic and institutional power rather than the basic commitment to national development. However, the far more open process of policy debate prevailing in Beijing suggests to some observers that the centre cannot hold. Beyond a certain point, therefore, a more tolerant atmosphere could produce confusion if not chaos, as different parts of the system veer in different directions. In essence, the leadership has yet to address the full implications of the reforms: how much internal political realignment will be permitted? What degree of inequality will be allowed to develop as a consequence of the reforms? How much variation – by sector, by region and by social stratum – can a system predicated on central control tolerate? Answers to these questions will take more time.

The second, indisputable fact is equally important: China is no longer at war with the international system. The country's incentives and opportunities for increased international participation are self-evident, and Deng and other leaders have made the most of them. Although China continues to put forward an alternative view of global development and to urge a major reallocation of the world's economic and technological resources, these calls no longer entail special pleading. The Chinese are not angry, dissatisfied outsiders; they are an active, constructive force on the global scene. The most important implications are within East Asia. The Chinese understand only too well their incentives to offer a constructive and tolerant approach to the outside world, since Hong Kong and Taiwan are their nearest neighbours. Many deem it inevitable that China will emerge as a more powerful and assertive state. It is therefore a question of how China chooses to exercise this power. Since this issue cannot be answered in the near term, most of China's neighbours, as well as the great powers, have opted for an intermediate solution: by giving China an increased stake in existing norms and institutions, the implications of China's engagement in the international system are more likely to be positive than negative. Here as well, the true tests are yet to come, as China seeks to define workable economic, political and security arrangements with the outside world.

Even as optimism prevails in most areas of Chinese policy-making, the uncertainties remain substantial. Five potential categories of unsettling change – much of it beyond China's effective control – could exert a major influence on future Chinese policy. In raising these possibilities, I will not assess their likelihood, but will only briefly consider their possible implications.

The first possibility is a major heightening of US-Soviet tensions in East Asia, not excluding military conflict within the region directly affecting the interests of the super-powers as well as China. In an ideal world, China might wish that neither the USSR nor the US regarded East Asia as particularly important to their long-term interests. The reality is quite different, and Chinese observers call attention to the growing political, economic and strategic significance that the US and the Soviet Union attach to the region.[26] In such an eventuality, China may find it exceedingly difficult to maintain a purely sideline role. Should the US-Soviet regional rivalry grow more heated, Beijing's capacity for political, economic and strategic manoeuvre would become much more difficult. Polarization would ill serve China's interests, and it seems no surprise that China appears discomfited by the warning signs of increased Soviet-American military competition.

The most serious worries about the outbreak of a major conflict will continue to focus on Korea. Notwithstanding endless Chinese assurances about North Korea's peaceful intentions, the continuing build-up of Pyongyang's armed forces near the 38th Parallel evokes growing concern in Seoul, Tokyo and Washington. These anxieties are underscored by the political uncertainties likely to attend the leadership succession process in both North and South as well as the Summer Olympics of 1988, towards which North Korea's attitudes remain very murky. China understands only too well that a renewed Korean conflict would be a nightmare for its interests. The question remains what, if anything, can be done to prevent Pyongyang from undertaking major risks, thereby keeping this scenario in the realm of bad dreams.

A second Chinese worry concerns other potential sources of instability in East Asia. Compared to many areas of the Third World, East Asia has represented an oasis of tranquillity and prosperity in recent years. Yet events on the horizon could unsettle this optimistic picture: political succession in a number of authoritarian political systems with no institutionalized means for the orderly transfer of power (including Taiwan); domestic instability within various societies (e.g., a more active insurgency in the Philippines); or mounting protectionist sentiments in the West leading to a major decline in regional economic growth are all real possibilities. Chinese expectations of increased economic opportunities presume political stability within the region; a prudent planner would remain cautious.

A third scenario concerns the possibility of a major Soviet political break-through in East Asia in conjunction with mounting problems for the US position within the region. Gorbachev's more supple, differentiated approach to the politics, economics and security of the region has already been manifest in a number of cases. The new Soviet leadership may believe that a political backlash against super-power military deployments could redound to its benefit, especially should it result in declining support for the US naval and air presence in the West Pacific. Under such circumstances, the political equation in East Asia could undergo a major shift and force China into major adjustments of its regional strategy.

A fourth potential problem concerns China's future relations with Hong Kong and Taiwan. China's incentives for an orderly transfer of power in Hong Kong are compelling, but there are no precedents or prior experience for Beijing in seeking to manage this process. Indeed, even if the political dimensions of the transition take place fairly smoothly – an outcome many do not expect – the longer-term effects on the character of Hong Kong and the attitudes of its population may not be nearly as amenable to Beijing's control. At the same time, China knows that Taiwan is watching. Major miss-steps in the process could derail Beijing's hopes of engaging Taipei in a gradual accommodation. Thus, a poorly managed outcome on Hong Kong would make the possibility of a peaceful reconciliation with Taiwan incalculably more difficult.

The fifth unsettling set of issues concerns the modernization strategy going seriously awry. It is not clear what would constitute failure of the economic reforms or of the political reforms that Deng declares their handmaiden,[27] but a number of pitfalls and possible misdirections come to mind: a potential resurgence of disruptive nationalism in the context of mounting trade and investment tensions, especially with Japan; a breakdown of political cohesion in relation to simultaneous calls for greater latitude and the reassertion of central control; increased discontent among those segments of the political system that seem less supportive of the reforms, notably the armed forces and the public security apparatus; and a successor leadership more determined to protect China's socialist essence, thereby limiting China's co-operation with the West and expanding areas of Sino-Soviet collaboration. These are only possibilities, not certainties, but each could prove disruptive to China's broader accommodation with the states of the region.

But China's opportunities for international engagement and economic advancement seem far too great for any abrupt departure from present policy. Surprises should never be precluded, but the era of abrupt swings in the Chinese political pendulum may be at an end. The Chinese do not have a road map or a blueprint for their future, but they do have a compass which has guided them very well. It is Deng, the principal architect of China's political transformation, who clearly recognizes the interconnected character of China's internal and external policies: 'China's history over the past few centuries has showed that a closed door policy tends only to backwardness... China has started its new march . . . to improve productivity and raise the people's living standards while adhering to the principles of socialism. The only way to improve productivity is to restructure China's economy'.[28] This reasoning continues to guide Chinese policy in the region and seems likely in time to reshape the political, economic and strategic landscape of East Asia as a whole.

The opinions in this Paper are the author's own, and do not reflect the views of The Rand Corporation or its governmental sponsors.

Notes

[1] See Premier Zhao Ziyang's report on the Seventh Five Year Plan (1986–1990), in *Beijing Review*, 21 April 1986, Supplement, pp. I–XX.

[2] These are only rough approximations, but leaders in Moscow and Beijing both appreciate their implications. My thanks to Charles Wolf, Jr. for calling these comparisons to my attention.

[3] According to Deng, 'our political line focuses on the four modernizations (agriculture, industry, national defense and science and technology) persisting in developing the productive forces. Nothing short of a world war would make us release our grip on this essential point'. 'Build Socialism with Chinese Characteristics', (30 June 1984), in Deng Xiaoping, *Build Socialism with Chinese Characteristics* (Beijing: Foreign Languages Press, 1985), p. 38.

[4] Moscow Television Service, 28 July 1986, in *FBIS-Soviet Union*, 29 July 1986, p. R-14.

[5] See Deng Xiaoping's 2 September remarks to CBS Correspondent Mike Wallace, in *Beijing Review*, 22 September 1986, pp. 4–5.

[6] The above declarations are drawn from Zhao Ziyang's report on the Seventh

Five Year Plan (op. cit., in note 1), p. XVII.
[7] See the article by M. Bureyev in Sotsialisticheskaya Industria, 13 June 1986, in FBIS-Soviet Union, 23 June 1986, p. B2.
[8] Ibid, p. B3.
[9] Pei Monong, 'On the Triangular Relations of the United States, Japan, and ASEAN', Guoji Wenti Yanjiu, No. 4, October 1984, pp. 10–18.
[10] One authority on US-China trade has observed that 'in China, the negotiations begin once the contract is signed'.
[11] Xinhua, 15 July 1986, in FBIS-China, 16 July 1986, p. B2.
[12] 'Trade Gap Challenge', China Business Review, July 1986, p. 1.
[13] See Zheng's interview in Xinhua, 11 November 1985, in FBIS-China, 12 November 1985, pp. D1–2.
[14] Deng has described technology transfer as 'the most important issue' in US-China relations. 'An Interview with Deng Xiaoping', Encyclopedia Britannica Book of the Year – 1986 p. 495.
[15] See Denis Fred Simon, 'The Evolving Role of Technology Transfer in China's Modernization', in Joint Economic Committee, US Congress, China's Economy Looks Toward the Year 2000, Vol. 2 (Washington DC: US Government Printing Office, 1986), pp. 254–86.
[16] The Co-ordinating Committee on Multilateral Export Controls (CoCom) is an organization composed of most NATO members and Japan which tries to control the transfer of sensitive technologies to Eastern Bloc countries.
[17] See the remarks of Edward Ross, Office of International Security Affairs, US Department of Defense, in Martin Lasafer, (ed.), The Two Chinese – A Contemporary View, (Washington: The Heritage Foundation, 28 January 1986), pp. 83–90.
[18] For a forceful statement of Chinese thinking, see Sa Benwang, 'The Reagan Administration's New Strategy of "Flexible" Response', Shijie Zhishi, No. 13, 1 July 1986, in FBIS-China, 25 July 1986, pp. B1-5.
[19] The above offer was made by Premier Zhao Ziyang on a visit to South America. Xinhua, 2 November 1985, in FBIS-China, 20 November 1985, p. A1.
[20] Xinhua, 20 November 1985, in FBIS-China, 20 November 1985, p. A1.
[21] I have discussed these issues more fully in 'US-Korea Relations: The China Factor', Journal of Northeast Asian Studies, Fall 1985, pp. 12–28.
[22] Agence France Presse, 22 June 1986, in FBIS-China, 23 June 1986, p. C1.
[23] In an interview with a visiting Japanese correspondent in July 1986, Party Secretary Ho Dam stated 'we will not copy China's system of opening to the outside world', Yomiuri Shimbun, 5 July 1986, p. 4.
[24] As stated by Premier Zhao Ziyang, 'China strives to establish, resume, or expand normal relations with all countries of the World . . . and engage in friendly co-operation with them. China does not determine its closeness with or estrangement from other countries on the basis of their social systems or ideologies', (op. cit., in note 1) p. XVIII.
[25] See, for example, Wei Yanshen and Gu Yuanyang, 'The Abrupt Rise of the Economy in the Asia-Pacific Region', Liaowang, No. 24, 11 June 1984, in FBIS-China, 6 July 1984, pp. A1–4; and Pei Monong, 'China's Stake and Role in the Economy of the Asia-Pacific Region', Guoji Wenti Yanjiu, No. 1, January 1986, pp. 1–9
[26] See, for example, Xie Wenqing, 'Soviet and US Military Strategies in the Asia-Pacific Region', Guoji Wenti Yanjiu, No. 4, October 1985, in FBIS-China, 13 December 1985, pp. A5–9.
[27] According to a recent speech by Deng, 'The party must not interfere too much . . . Whether all our reforms can eventually succeed or not will, after all, be determined by the reform of the political structure. Reform of the political structure and reform of the economic structure should be interdependent and co-ordinated with each other. Our economic structural reform will fail if we do not reform our political structure', Deng's remarks were reported in Jiefang Ribao, 1 August 1986, p. 1, in FBIS-China, 6 August 1986, p. K1.
[28] Xinhua, 28 August 1985, in FBIS-China, 28 August 1985, p. D1.

China's Relations with East Asia and the Pacific Region: Part II

YAO WENBIN

The situation in the Asian-Pacific region is an important component of the global strategic situation. World peace is indivisible, as the security interests of the peoples of all countries are closely linked. Asian-Pacific questions should, therefore, not be treated independently but, instead, be studied in the global strategic context so as to draw proper conclusions. In this Paper the situation in the Asian-Pacific region and China's policy towards the region will be examined first, after which China's relations with the United States, the Soviet Union and other Asian-Pacific nations will be discussed.

The Asian-Pacific situation
Over the past several years, there has been much discussion of the Asian-Pacific region. Some have predicted that the world economic and strategic centre would move from Europe and the Atlantic to the Asian-Pacific region, and a few went as far as saying that the twenty-first century would be 'the Century of Asia and the Pacific'. I have reservations about this prediction. I am of the opinion that the economic and strategic position of the Asian-Pacific region in the world will be strengthened steadily for some time to come, but this will promote the development of the global strategic pattern in the direction of multipolarization and will not necessarily lead to the replacement of one centre by another.

There are a large number of countries in the region and the situation there is complicated. Not only are there different types of countries but, furthermore, the interests of the two global powers – the United States and the Soviet Union – are involved. Economic development in the Asian-Pacific region is encouraging, but the gravity of the military situation is causing anxiety. In South-east Asia, the Kampuchean War has gone on for eight years. In the Korean Peninsula, there has been military confrontation between the North and the South for thirty-three years. What is particularly noteworthy is that the US and the USSR have competed with each other in strengthening their military power and force deployments, leading gradually to a regional military confrontation between them. It is against this background that the situation in the Asian-Pacific region has aroused ever-growing concern among the peoples of the Asian countries and indeed the whole world.

China's policy towards the region
China is a developing country in the Asian-Pacific region. Being wholeheartedly engaged in carrying out the 'Four Modernizations', it needs an environment of lasting and stable peace. The political, economic and military situation in the region is of particular importance to China. It can be said that China's policy towards the Asian-Pacific region is one of the most important components of its independent foreign policy of peace, the main points of which are as follows:

1) To adhere to the position of peace and make joint efforts together with the Asian-Pacific countries and other countries in the world to turn the Asian-Pacific region into a region of peace, friendliness and co-operation;
2) To be independent and not to enter into alliance or establish strategic relations with any big power or line up with one against another;
3) To oppose any hegemonist threat, intervention and aggression in the region and solemnly declare that China will never seek hegemony;
4) To establish and develop friendly relations with all Asian-Pacific countries on the basis of the Five Principles of Peaceful Co-existence;
5) To lend support to the developing countries in the region in the development of their national economies and in the enhancement of regional economic co-operation;
6) To pursue the policy of opening to the outside world, to establish and develop bilateral economic co-operation with Asian-Pacific countries and take an active part in some activities of existing organizations for multilateral economic co-operation.

It is clear from these points that China's pursuance of an independent foreign policy of peace in the Asian-Pacific region is helpful to the maintenance of a balance of power both in the region and in the world, conducive to the safeguarding of regional peace and stability and in accord with the fundamental interests of China and other Asian-Pacific countries.

Sino-American and Sino-Soviet relations
The development of Sino-American and Sino-Soviet relations and changes in them are important factors influencing the situation in the Asian-Pacific region and even the global strategic situation. Judging from the present position, no fundamental changes will take place in the existing pattern of Sino-American-Soviet triangular relations in the near future, but some progress may be made in both Sino-American and Sino-Soviet relations.

In recent years, the development of Sino-American relations has, on the whole, been steady. Advances have been made in co-operation in some areas by the two countries. The Taiwan issue, however, is still an obstacle in the way of the development of Sino-American relations. With the aim of a peaceful settlement of the Taiwan issue, China has put forward the concept of 'one country, two systems' and a series of policies such as 'three exchanges'. So far, the United States has made no definite, active response. With the Taiwan issue remaining, a certain instability in the development of Sino-American relations is hard to avoid. Furthermore, there is some divergence between China and the US in their approach to some specific questions in international affairs and bilateral relations. Nevertheless, in accordance with the general trend, so long as both sides strictly abide by the three communiqués signed by them, major twists and turns can be avoided in their relations, which will then develop steadily for a long time.

Sino-Soviet relations have improved in the past few years. Economic, cultural and personnel exchanges have been increased to some extent and the atmosphere between them tends to relaxation. But no substantive progress has been made in Sino-Soviet political consultations and so political relations lag behind economic ones. The root cause of this is that the Soviet Union has used the pretext of 'not harming a third party' to evade discussion of the 'three major obstacles' in the hope that these obstacles will gradually 'become obscure' and even 'disappear naturally' through procrastination. In his speech in Vladivostok on 28 July 1986, the Soviet leader Gorbachev advanced proposals for withdrawing six regiments from Afghanistan and some troops from Mongolia. Such a symbolic withdrawal of troops would have little impact on Soviet military strength and deployment in the Asian-Pacific region. Whether Gorbachev's speech signifies a Soviet willingness to change its rigid attitude towards the question of the three major obstacles remains to be seen. China hopes that Sino-Soviet relations will be normalized on the basis of the Five Principles of Peaceful Co-existence at an early date. However, the prospect of this does not depend on Chinese wishes alone. Given the Soviet failure to take practical action to remove the three major obstacles and the continuous maintenance of a military threat to China in the north, south and west, the improvement of Sino-Soviet relations can only be slow and limited. From a long-term point of view, even when Sino-Soviet relations are normalized they would be no more than common relations between two countries and cannot possibly be restored to those of the Sino-Soviet alliance of the 1950s.

China's relations with North-east Asian countries
North-east Asia is a sensitive part of the Asian-Pacific region where there is a grave military situation. However, due to the fact that the various forces restrain each other, relative stability is still expected for some time. To promote stability and peace is China's fundamental policy towards North-east Asia and the countries concerned.

Japan is the only developed capitalist country in North-east Asia. Relations between China and Japan have grown rapidly since their normalization 14 years ago. The trade between the two countries is the largest in China's foreign trade. Japan provides most loans on favourable terms to China. In addition to the signing of a Joint Communiqué and the Sino-Japanese Treaty of Peace and Friendship, China and Japan have confirmed the four principles of 'peace and friendship, equality and mutual benefit, mutual trust, long-term stability' for guiding the development of their bilateral relations. Despite the existence of such questions as the trade imbalance and technological co-operation lagging behind the trade flow, the development of good neighbourly relations between China and Japan is, generally speaking, the main trend. China hopes that the development of Sino-Japanese relations will be steady and enduring. China is willing to do its best to make the next century one of Sino-Japanese friendship and make the friendship between the two peoples last from generation to generation.

The Korean Peninsula is still the scene of military confrontation between the North and the South and represents the most unstable factor in North-east Asia. But taking into full account the situation in the Peninsula itself and in the peripheral countries, including the US and the Soviet Union, it is expected that the state of confrontation instead of intense conflict which has been shaped in the last 30 years and more will continue and that a new Korean War is unlikely.

In recent years, North and South have started a dialogue, resulting in the easing of tension to some extent. This is to be welcomed. China supports the dialogue between North and South and hopes that the momentum of detente in the Peninsula will be maintained and developed. China also supports the holding of tripartite talks by the North, South and the US, aimed at discussing questions concerning a relaxation of tension in the Peninsula. China withdrew the Chinese People's Volunteers from Korea completely as far back as twenty-eight years ago and has long since ceased to be a party directly concerned in the Korean question, accordingly disagreeing with the holding of quadripartite talks to include China. However, as a close neighbour of Korea, China is ready to help facilitate the tripartite talks if need be.

China's relations with South-east Asian countries
The most prominent issue in South-east Asia is the practice of regional hegemony by Vietnam, with the support of the Soviet Union, through armed aggression against and military occupation of Kampuchea. An early end of this abnormal state of affairs is the basic requirement for stability in South-east Asia and also an important aspect of safeguarding peace in the Asian-Pacific region.

The Kampuchean War has been going on for eight years with no sign of an end. Vietnam's claim of the so-called complete withdrawal of all its troops from Kampuchea by 1990 is nothing but a swindle, the essence of which is that Vietnam is attempting to annihilate Kampuchean resistance forces within five years. This is wishful thinking: the history of the War has eloquently proved that the attempt is doomed to failure. The question now is not whether the Kampuchean resistance forces can continue to keep up the struggle, but whether Vietnam, which is wantonly engaging in military aggression and is beset by difficulties both at home and abroad, can sustain the war for long.

The question of Kampuchea may eventually be settled politically, but the key to a political settlement lies in forcing Vietnam to withdraw its aggressor troops from Kampuchea. Only when these are all pulled out will the Kampuchean people be able to decide their own destiny without any outside intervention and build an independent, peaceful, neutral and non-aligned Kampuchea. To this end, China steadfastly supports the Kampuchean people in their struggle to resist Vietnam and endorses the solemn and just stand of the Democratic Kampuchean Coalition Government on the settlement of the Kampuchean question. In the meantime, China hopes that international society will exert greater political pressure on Vietnam. Only when Vietnam is compelled to shrink from the difficulties can the conditions for a political settlement of the Kampuchean question be created.

China and Vietnam had very friendly relations in the past. The current state of Sino-Vietnamese relations stems entirely from Vietnam's policy of aggression against Kampuchea and opposition to China. The key to the normalization of Sino-Vietnamese relations is that Vietnam must put an end to its invasion and occupation of Kampuchea and withdraw all its troops from there. China has declared time and again that if Vietnam withdraws its troops, talks can be held between China and Vietnam so as to improve relations.

China's relations with the ASEAN countries are on the whole good. In recent years there have been many exchanges of visits between Chinese leaders and the leaders of Thailand, the Philippines, Malaysia and Singapore. Trade, economic and technological co-operation as well as cultural exchanges between China and these four countries have developed. China and Thailand have taken a common position opposing Vietnam's occupation of Kampuchea, and co-operation in supporting the Kampuchean resistance forces is good. In the struggle to safeguard sovereignty and territorial integrity waged by the people of Thailand, China has stood firmly by their side. China has supported the proposal of setting up a peaceful, free and neutral region of South-east Asia made jointly by Singapore and other ASEAN nations. China hopes to establish and develop relations of friendly co-operation with ASEAN countries – no matter whether diplomatic relations have or have not been established – on the basis of the Five Principles of Peaceful Co-existence without regard to differences in ideology and social systems, so as to facilitate the maintenance of peace and stability in South-east Asia.

China's relations with South Pacific countries
The South Pacific is a relatively stable area in the Asian-Pacific region. China and other Asian-Pacific countries have attached importance to the efforts made by the South Pacific countries to develop their national economies and safeguard peace in their area. The Chinese government has clearly indicated its support for the common aspiration of the South Pacific countries to establish a nuclear-free zone.

Over the past several years, China and Australia have further developed their friendly relations. The exchanges of visits between the leaders and peoples of the two countries have been increased and economic co-operation expanded. The Chinese and Australian peoples share the desire for safeguarding peace in the Asian-Pacific region and in the world and for developing and building their own countries. The prospects for friendly co-operation between the two countries are good. China hopes that both, in the spirit of mutual benefit and mutual aid, will further tap their potential to promote the development of economic and technological co-operation between them on a large scale.

New Zealand is also a friendly neighbour of China in the South Pacific. Both China and New Zealand have devoted themselves to the maintenance of peace in the Asian-Pacific region and in the world. This is the political basis for developing friendly co-operation between the two countries. It can be expected that the good neighbourly relations between China and New Zealand will be further developed and will become a positive factor for peace in the Asian-Pacific region.

The Security of North-East Asia: Part I

PROFESSOR MASASHI NISHIHARA*

Basic problems of Japanese security
In May 1983, when Prime Minister Nakasone signed a statement at the Williamsburg Summit that Western security is 'indivisible and must be approached on a global basis', it was indicative of the change in Japanese security concerns – from regional to international or global. Three factors have actively contributed to the change: the fast pace of Soviet military deployment, now able to challenge the United States in some fields; the growth of Japan's own economic strength, now some 10% of the world's GNP; and Prime Minister Nakasone's leadership.[1]

In the past, Japan's military security concerns have been primarily regional. The Korean Peninsula, for instance, has been a vital interest. By contrast its non-military security concerns have been global; Japan has traded with practically all the regions of the world and depended upon foreign sources for the supply of vital goods such as oil, iron and rare metals. Yet in the last few years, the Japanese people have gradually become conscious that their military security concerns are of a global, not just a regional nature. Tokyo has been forced to see the link between SS-20 intermediate-range nuclear missiles (IRBM) deployed in Europe and in Asia because of their transportability: a US–Soviet agreement on the reduction of IRBM in Europe could result in the transfer of these missiles to Asia. An aggravated Middle East situation could disrupt the international economic system. President Reagan's Strategic Defense Initiative (SDI) has to be dealt with on the basis of allied cohesion and stable East–West relations. If Japanese technology is to make a significant contribution to research, Japan must think of its own responsibility for the security of the West.

This new awareness must still, of course, take into account some basic security problems which Japan faces. First its serious vulnerability as a resource-poor nation. In 1983, 82.2% of its energy and 30% of its food came from abroad, making the political stability of its supplier countries, most of them in the Third World, vital for Japan. All of its sources of nuclear energy which provides 8% of its total energy requirements, were foreign as well. It is also imperative that its long world-wide sea-lanes should remain safe, making a favourable maritime balance of power indispensable. Second, Japan's geographic proximity to the potential adversary, the Soviet Union, makes for military vulnerability. The air distance between Tokyo and Vladivostok is only about 600 miles (960 km). Hokkaido, closest to

Soviet territory, could easily be subject to Soviet attack. Third, Japan's domestic political constraints, symbolized by Article 9 of the Constitution and pacifist sentiment, limit the range of policy options such as the roles and missions and types of weapons of the Self-Defense Forces (SDF). Fourth, Asian apprehension about Japan's conventional build-up as a 'revival of Japanese militarism' serves as a restraint. The Japanese defence budget, just below 1% of GNP, was some $US 12.0 bn in 1984, about equivalent to the combined defence budgets of the ASEAN nations ($7.6 bn) plus South Korea ($4.5 bn).[2] Finally, the ties with the US are a vital source of security but also of fear, for too close an alliance may mean an unnecessary or unwilling involvement in US military activities.

How do these basic problems of Japan relate to its new awareness in terms of its military and non-military responses? This Paper attempts to identify and evaluate new military threats to Japan and responses to them.

New military threats
NORTH KOREA
Today, military threats in North-east Asia come from either the Soviet Union or North Korea or both. North Korean fire-power and armed forces have generally been considered to be stronger than those of South Korea, but a balance has nonetheless been maintained in various ways, notably by US military support for the South, strong Japanese and US economic ties with it, precariously normalized Sino-Soviet relations and friendly US-China relations. No external power sees another outbreak of armed conflict in the Korean Peninsula as in its interest, but despite some progress in a North-South dialogue, armed confrontation and tension continue there. For example, North Korea is known to maintain, just north of the demilitarized zone (DMZ), 80,000–100,000 commandos, the largest surprise-attack force in the world.[3] Three new elements have to be taken into account in assessing the threat from North Korea. First, the coupling of the high-growth South Korean economy with the succession issues in both Pyongyang and Seoul. Seventy-four-year-old President Kim Il Sung has been in power in the North for 38 years. He has apparently been preparing the ground for his son, Kim Chong-il, to succeed him, but he may not be able to leave 'a glorious and prosperous' North Korea for his son, because by the late 1980s the North's military strength may be overtaken by the South, with its fast growing economy and a GNP over five times as large.[4] In addition, the success of the Olympic Games scheduled to be held in Seoul in 1988 would enhance the South's international prestige at the expense of the North. Out of desperation President Kim Il Sung just might start armed conflict across the DMZ before or during the Olympics. The short-term stability of North-South Korean relations would depend partly upon whether Moscow decides to take part in

the Olympics. China is already committed, and if the Soviet Union should participate as well, it would no doubt press Pyongyang not to disrupt the Games through subversive activities or more open military operations.

The Soviet Union is currently strengthening military ties with the North. Since May 1985 it has supplied Pyongyang with some 25 MiG-23 fighter aircraft and obtained overflight rights in return. In August 1985 Soviet warships called at Wonsan, a large port facing the Sea of Japan, and a year later the North Korean Navy reciprocated by visiting Vladivostok. There is growing speculation that the Soviet Union has also aquired access to Nampo, a port near Pyongyang.

What is significant now is the apparently increased Soviet involvement in North Korea. This could imply that any conflict in the Peninsula might implicate the Soviet Union more directly than the Korean War of 1950 did, though conversely it could also mean that Moscow can exert more control over Pyongyang. Soviet-North Korean military ties could also suggest that the Soviet Union may use North Korea as a proxy against Japan and the US, which would quickly broaden any conflict in the region.

THE SOVIET UNION
Soviet military capabilities in Asia are formidable. The Japanese Defense White Paper each year emphasizes the alarming nature of the Soviet deployment of modern arms in Asia. The 1986 edition describes the Soviet Far East military presence as consisting in 1985, of 41 army divisions or 370,000 troops, 840 ships or 1,850,000 tons (835 ships or 1,780,000 tons in 1985) and 2,390 operational aircraft (2,200 in 1985), while SS-20 IRBM are now given as over 162 and *Backfire* bombers as over 85. The Pacific Fleet includes two aircraft carriers, 83 other principal surface combatants, 19 amphibious ships, 88 submarines, and other vessels.[5] Their naval bases at Vladivostok and Petropavlovsk are being enlarged, while those at Da Nang and Cam Ranh Bay in Vietnam are growing fast.

More specifically, where Japanese security is concerned, the Soviet Air Force has increased its flights near Japanese air space. Japanese interceptions (scrambles) of such flights went up from 305 in 1975 to 944 in 1984. The Soviet Union occupies the disputed Northern Territories off Hokkaido, where it deploys over one army division, about 40 MiG-23 fighters, some Mi-24 attack helicopters and ground-launched cruise missiles capable of carrying nuclear warheads.[6] In September 1985 Soviet forces conducted large-scale landing exercises on one of these islands, of a pattern which could be applicable to Hokkaido itself.[7] They involved the dispatch of three amphibious ships, including the *Ivan Rogov*, from Vladivostok through the Soya Strait to Sakhalin where the troops were embarked. *Backfire*, MiG-23 and MiG-27 aircraft participated in this exercise.

In addition to the increased Soviet-North Korean ties mentioned above, the Soviet-Vietnamese alliance, formed officially in November 1978, could also threaten Japanese security. The Soviet Union can do this by sponsoring subversive activities in the ASEAN region, thus weakening its economic viability and political stability, and by reinforcing its own military presence in Vietnam, which can challenge the US presence in the Philippines.

Soviet forces are now capable of conducting war against Japan on several scenarios, ranging from nuclear attack or blackmail to the armed occupation of Wakkanai, the northern tip of Hokkaido facing Sakhalin. According to the Defense Agency's estimates, the Soviet Union could allocate some eight divisions (five to six motor rifle, one airborne, and one naval infantry division) and four airborne brigades for an invasion of Japan, compared with just five divisions in 1976.[8] It is also estimated that if all landing ships were used, one and a half to two divisions could be landed in Japan in a short time.[9] Some Japanese officers consider that the USSR would seize part or the whole of Hokkaido in order to ensure safe sea passage between the Sea of Japan and the Sea of Okhotsk.[10] Soviet forces could also interdict Japanese sea-lanes in the Western Pacific, the South China Sea and the Indian Ocean.

However, despite the growing Soviet military strength in the Western Pacific, the general balance of power there still favours the US and its allies, Japan and South Korea. The maritime balance, for instance, is favourable to the US side, as the Pentagon admits.[11] A political coalition, though still loose, between America and China and between Japan and China isolates the Soviet Union, whose only friend is North Korea. Thus Soviet military power can perhaps be more effective for political intimidation in peacetime than for attack in war. Nevertheless, the fast pace of the Soviet build-up is alarming. Gorbachev's speech in Vladivostok in July 1986 seems to have been intended to end Soviet isolation and to claim its legitimacy as an Asian-Pacific power with its new military might.

Japanese military responses
In the face of these security threats, the Japanese government has made two forms of response, military and non-military. The development of these responses has shown that domestic political constraints on security policy are undergoing slow but notable change. The military responses that the government has made are of several kinds: increased defence expenditure; the purchase of more sophisticated weapons; more flexible interpretations of Article 9 of the Constitution to allow for a larger defence role; and closer defence co-operation with the US.

INCREASED DEFENCE EXPENDITURE
For 1982–6 the government has appropriated funds for the defence budget at an average annual increase of 6.9% nominal or 5.6% in real terms.[12] This percentage is higher than the 3.0% average annual rate

of increase of the total budget, and this special treatment for defence (at a time when the huge government debts have required tight budgets) has naturally caused heated debates in the Diet but been accepted in the end. There would have been much opposition ten years ago, but the Soviet threat and the perceived need to maintain good relations with Washington have contributed to the opposition being tamed.

However, the annual defence expenditure is still just below 1% of GNP, following the policy adopted in 1976. This has been a point of strong political controversy in the Diet. Yet even this political barrier seems to be beginning to erode; the new Minister of State for Defence, Kurihara Yuko, stated in July 1986, in face of little opposition criticism, that policy priority is now concerned with how to complete the 1986–90 defence modernization programme rather than with how to remain within 1% of GNP. The 1% ceiling is likely to be revised under the leadership of Nakasone, after his landslide electoral victory.

In August 1985 the Nakasone Government decided to appropriate for the 5-year 1986–90 programme ¥18,400 bn or ¥3,680 bn per annum. This annual spending would have been equivalent to $16.0 bn under the then ruling exchange rate of $1=¥230, but it now equals $23.7 bn at the current rate of $1=¥155. While the annual figure is still roughly 1% of GNP, when expressed in US dollars it looks quite impressive. It is larger than were the 1984 defence budgets of France ($20.1 bn), or West Germany ($20.4 bn) and only slightly smaller than that of Britain ($22.0 bn) – calculated at the exchange rates ruling at that time.[13] These European budgets have admittedly risen since, as have the currencies against the US dollar, but the sharp increase in the value of the yen confuses the arguments as to which of the US allies contributes most towards the burden of Western security.

MORE SOPHISTICATED WEAPONS

The Ground Self-Defense Force plans, for example, to strengthen the defence of Hokkaido by transferring some troops and tanks from other parts of the country and by deploying modern anti-tank helicopters. Its primary concern is to enhance readiness and sustainability. In July 1986 the three services undertook a large-scale joint exercise in which they transported 4,500 troops and 1,000 vehicles from Kyushu, the southern part of the country, to Hokkaido.[14]

In 1981 Prime Minister Suzuki stated that Japan would place its defence emphasis on air and naval power rather than on ground forces. To be able to defend long sea-lanes requires more sophisticated weapon systems. In 1982 the government decided to increase the number of P-3C anti-submarine patrol aircraft to be procured for the Maritime Self-Defense Force from 45 to 75, and then in 1985 to 100. Similarly, the number of F-15 interceptors to be procured for the Air Self-Defense Force was increased from 100 to 155 in 1982 and then to 187 in 1985.[15] It was also decided in 1982 to procure

Patriot surface-to-air missiles (SAM) to replace the obsolete *Nike*. E-2C early-warning aircraft are soon to be deployed and the government is considering the purchase of an over-the-horizon (OTH) radar to be installed perhaps in Iwojima, 780 miles (1,250 km) south of Tokyo. Airborne warning and control system (AWACS) aircraft may also be on the agenda in the near future.

RELAXATION OF CONSTITUTIONAL CONSTRAINTS
Article 9 of the 1946 Constitution renounces 'war ... as a means of settling international disputes', and does not recognize the right of belligerency. This Article has been a fundamental point of controversy in post-war Japanese politics. It has been interpreted variously. The original view of the government was that Japan should have no armed forces at all. The interpretation was then relaxed to mean that Japan might have forces, but only for 'individual self-defence', and not for 'collective self-defence'. The definition of individual self-defence then became and still is a matter of repeated parliamentary debate.[16] Successive governments of a conservative persuasion have attempted to introduce flexible interpretations, and Nakasone has widened the concept by accepting that the grey area between individual and collective self-defence should be included in it. Since he took office in late 1982, he has advocated, among other things, the constitutionality of Japanese naval forces helping to protect US naval forces operating outside the 12-mile territorial waters in wartime when these US forces were on the way to defend Japan, something considered unconstitutional in the past. This new interpretation widens the area of joint operations that Japanese forces can conduct with US forces, a significant step towards Japan acting like a normal ally of the United States.

CLOSER DEFENCE CO-OPERATION WITH US FORCES
Another important response to the Soviet military threat has been to build closer defence ties with US forces. In recent years, there has been an increasing number of joint exercises between the forces of the two countries. In 1985 there were eight joint naval exercises, related to minesweeping, anti-submarine warfare, surface operations and command post practices, and ten joint air defence, air combat and rescue exercises. The ground forces conducted six joint manoeuvres in that year, two in Hokkaido. Since 1980 Japan has also participated in the multinational *Rimpac* (Rim of the Pacific) naval exercises with the US, Canada, Australia and New Zealand (which was replaced by Britain in 1986).

Since 1978 officers of the two nations have been engaged in joint studies of how to work together in emergencies which threaten the security of Japan, its sea-lanes and South Korea. The Defense Agency has also increased its expenditure for the maintenance of US bases and some 46,000 US troops in Japan. In 1985 ¥277.5 bn or $1.8 bn ($1=¥155) was appropriated, representing about $39,000 per US serviceman in Japan.[17] Japan has also agreed to the US deployment of 40 to 50 F-16 fighters at Misawa, a base just south of Hokkaido, and made a financial contribution to the cost of the facilities there. This meets both Japanese and US interests in balancing Soviet air power in the North-west Pacific.

In 1983 the Nakasone Government agreed to transfer Japanese defence technology to America. Japan has a policy of tight control on arms exports, including defence technology, but the transfer of such technology to the US was treated as an exceptional case, justified under the Japan-US Mutual Defence Assistance Agreement of 1954. This was again designed to strengthen ties with the US. In September 1986 the government also decided that Japan should participate in SDI research, something not discussed further here for lack of space.[18]

Japanese non-military responses: the 'Comprehensive Security' approach

Along with the military responses, the Japanese government has various non-military ones, mainly economic and diplomatic. When Prime Minister Ohira introduced the concept of 'Comprehensive National Security' in 1979, the government explained that Japan's national security cannot be enhanced by defence efforts alone but that economic and diplomatic efforts were also needed. Japan has become more conscious of the impact of its economic power upon international relations. Japan would like to see China balancing the Soviet Union and to see South Korea functioning as a buffer state against North Korea. Its large yen loan to China ($1.3 bn for 1979–83 and $2.1 bn for 1984–90) and to South Korea ($1.8 bn for 1984–90) can be seen in this light.[19] There is no possibility in the foreseeable future, however, of a formal military alliance between Japan and South Korea or between Japan and China. Tokyo simply finds it politically most acceptable to seek close ties with them by non-military means.

Japan's basic concern is to help reduce tensions in the North-east Asian region and to help to maintain a favourable balance of power. The region has three areas of potential rupture: the Korean Peninsula, Sino-Taiwan relations and the Sino-Soviet border. The region has not reached the stage of detente where states such as the two Koreas, and China and Taiwan recognize each other diplomatically. Neither of the Koreas is recognized by the countries linked with their opponents. Japan maintains non-diplomatic contacts with North Korea and Taiwan despite complaints from South Korea and China, respectively, and tries to help reduce tensions between the two Koreas and between China and Taiwan by simply keeping communications channels open with all parties.

However, Taiwan and North Korea cannot be treated in the same way. Compared with Japanese relations with North Korea those with Taiwan are far closer, notably in the economic and tourism fields. The political stability of Taiwan and the fairly stable relations between Beijing and Taipei favour the security of Japan's southern sea-lanes. Japan considers its relations with North Korea as contributing to the stability of the Peninsula.

The absence of a clear demarcation line in North-east Asia between the US and Soviet spheres of influence makes any discussion of the regional balance of power very difficult. A major difficulty is China, which claims to be an independent power and yet has fairly close relations with the US, including military ones. Japan's interest is to ensure China's political stability and its friendly posture towards the West.

Similarly, Japan tries to establish stable, not friendly, relations with the Soviet Union. Japan assumes that it can hardly improve relations with the USSR because of historical distrust, the territorial disputes and differences of ideology, but it hopes that such impaired relations can be stabilized through economic and cultural contacts. The relations are, in fact, asymmetrical in that three Japanese Prime Ministers have visited Moscow in the post-war years, while no Soviet equivalent has ever been to Tokyo. Prime Minister Nakasone apparently wishes to improve relations by his invitation to General Secretary Gorbachev to visit Tokyo. The current diplomatic issue from Tokyo's point of view is the territorial dispute, whereas Moscow's apparent interests are to weaken Japan-US relations and to gain access to Japan's economic and technological strengths to develop Siberia. Japan's limited military capabilities can be supplemented by its non-military options, in such a way as to influence Siberian development in a direction which will not reinforce Soviet military power.

Japanese dilemmas
A significant new aspect of these Japanese responses, military and non-military, is that they have been made with a sense of contribution to Western, not just North-east Asian security. The 1981 Defense White Paper writes, for instance, that 'Japan's defense capability constitutes an important factor in establishing a relationship of trust between Japan and other free nations which share the same values and which are interdependent'.[20] But the question is whether or not the Tokyo government is making sufficient defence efforts as a member of the West. Japan faces a few dilemmas.

Japanese efforts to strengthen preparedness, sustainability, command, control, communications and intelligence, and a framework for closer working relations with US forces certainly contribute to Japanese security. And the overall balance of power in the Western Pacific appears still favourable to the United States, upon which Japan depends. But if there were multi-regional conflicts such as Europe, the Middle East and North-east Asia, in which US forces were to be engaged, Washington might not be able to mobilize sufficient forces in the Western Pacific. In addition, Soviet forces might concurrently assault parts of Hokkaido and let North Korea start a conflict at the DMZ, thus making demands on the US forces designated for the defence of Japan and South Korea. Under such circumstances, some 60 destroyers, 16 submarines and 350 operational aircraft that Japan possesses would not be sufficient to defend the country.

Japan will soon be able to take on a reasonable level of patrolling over the international straits around Japan and the 1,000-mile sea-lanes. With OTH radar it could also take on early-warning functions. But to defend the sea-lanes remains a highly difficult task, calling for a faster force build-up. The Japanese government is, however, always restrained here by domestic opposition, including opposition from several factions of the ruling party itself. This is the first dilemma.

If Japan cannot build up its capabilities fast enough, it must depend upon the US, as it has in the past. Nakasone's strategy is to please Washington by taking a positive posture on defence; and this has so far worked very well. Yet it would be risky for Japan to assume that the two countries fully share strategic interests. The US might, for instance, open a second front in the Western Pacific in order to divert Soviet forces from the European front. Japan would almost automatically be involved, against its will, in such a US strategy of horizontal escalation. The United States might like to mine the Soya Straits, for instance, against Japanese opposition, which Japan would not like to see happen. And SS-20 missiles deployed in Soviet Asia may be intermediate-range nuclear forces for Washington, but they are strategic forces for Tokyo, because they can destroy it. Here is a second dilemma.

So far Japan has been concerned primarily only with a conventional build-up and has avoided an important question of how this might be linked to nuclear warfare, if Japan were to follow the US doctrine of flexible response. That Japan should have no nuclear weapons fits the anti-nuclear sentiment among the Japanese people, but Japan pursues a highly sophisticated, if not contradictory, policy of expecting US nuclear protection but not allowing the United States to bring nuclear weapons into its territory. This policy, popularly symbolized by its 'three non-nuclear principles' (not possessing, not producing and not introducing nuclear weapons), has worked successfully in peacetime. But there is an absence of debate about how Japan should meet the SS-20 threats.[21] Tokyo has certainly expressed concern about the SS-20 in Asia on many occasions, but has stuck to the three non-nuclear principles.

SS-20 missiles targeted on Europe have led European NATO members to request the US to balance them by deploying cruise missiles and *Pershing* II in Europe. Those same Soviet missiles in Asia have had a different impact upon Japan: the matter has been left to the US, which has made no visible response so far other than to equip some US ships, and submarines in the Pacific with *Tomahawk* cruise missiles. A handful of Japanese defence specialists argue that the country should exercise a nuclear option,[22] while a few others maintain that Japan should relax the principle of 'not introducing' or not allowing the introduction of nuclear arms from outside, by openly permitting US nuclear-armed ships to enter Japanese territorial waters and make port calls in Japan.[23] (Even if Japan should relax this principle, this alone would not really strengthen the Japanese and US positions *vis-à-vis* the SS-20.) Most specialists, however, think that Japan should take no action nor panic on the SS-20 issue, because the position has not basically changed since the time when SS-4 missiles were deployed with the capacity to destroy Tokyo by a nuclear strike, the SS-20 have merely replaced them.[24]

Strategic debates about Japanese security as coupled with the US policy of extended deterrence and flexible response, have hardly begun in Japan, primarily due to the nuclear allergy. This is not to advocate a Japanese nuclear option in any form, but to stress the need to discuss theoretical ways in which Japan can ensure its security against limited and less limited nuclear wars. One such way might be the deployment of a theatre SDI which could destroy SS-20 in the boost phase. But given the time needed for the research and development of such a defence, an alternative option would be a faster conventional build-up by Japan, which would keep the nuclear threshold higher.[25] For the reasons mentioned earlier, this would be difficult. This is a third dilemma for Japan.

In the meantime, with changes in the Japanese posture, supportive of closer defence ties with the US forces, the Japan-US Security Treaty assumes new implications for global security. The two Pacific powers, whose combined economic might represents about one-third of the world total, can play a vital role in promoting comprehensive international security through economic and political activities as well as through the effective use of high technology. Japan's role, in this sense, has gone beyond North-east Asian security and begins to assume new implications for global security.

---

* Professor of International Relations, National Defense Academy. The views expressed here are entirely those of the writer and not of the Japan Defense Agency with which he is affiliated.

Notes

[1] New attitudes discernible, for instance, in Nakasone's Peace Problems Study Group (Chairman: Masataka Kosaka), *Kokusai kokka Nihon no soogoo anzen hoshoo seisaku* ([Report on] Comprehensive security policy for an internationalist nation, Japan), December 1984, pp. 1–3. See also Chalmers Johnson, 'Reflections on the Dilemmas of Japanese Defense', *Asian Survey*, May 1986, pp. 557–72.

[2] Calculated from the *The Military Balance 1985–1986*, (London: IISS, 1986)

[3] *Sankei Shimbun*, 5 November 1985. See also Larry A. Niksch, 'The Military Balance on the Korean Peninsula', *Korea and World Affairs*, Summer 1986, p. 261.

4 *Tooyoo Keizai Nippoo*, 15 August 1986. In 1984 South Korea's GNP was estimated at $81.1 bn, and that of North Korea at $14.7 bn. *The Military Balance 1985–1986* gives $83 bn for South Korea's GDP and $40 bn for North Korea. (*op. cit.* in note 2) pp. 126–7

5 Japan, Defense Agency, *Booei hakusho 1986* (Defense White Paper 1986), pp. 31–2; *The Military Balance 1985–1986*, p. 29

6 The last item was revealed by US Secretary of Defense, Caspar Weinberger, in a press conference in Tokyo. See *Sankei Shimbun*, 7 September 1985, morning edition.

7 *Sankei Shimbun*, 7 September 1985, morning edition.

8 *Sankei Shimbun*, 9 August 1985, morning edition.

9 *Ibid.*

10 Shigeki Nishimura, 'Soren: senzaiteki kyooi no jittai' (The Soviet Union: the real state of its potential threat), *Voice*, November 1985, pp. 84–93.

11 See, for instance, US Department of Defense, *Annual Report to the Congress, Fiscal Year 1987*, pp. 66–7.

12 Calculated from *Defense of Japan 1985* (Tokyo: The Japan Times, 1985), *Asahi nenkan 1986* (Asahi Almanac 1986), p.154; and *Sekai Shuuhoo*, August 12, 1986, p.72.

13 Based on the NATO definition of defence costs. See *The Military Balance, 1985-1986*, (*op. cit.* in note 2), pp. 40, 46 and 49.

14 *Asagumo Shimbun*, 10 July 1986.

15 Asagumo Shimbun Sha, *Booei handobokku 1986* (Handbook on Defense, 1986), p. 71.

16 Masashi Nishihara, 'Expanding Japan's Credible Defense Role', *International Security*, Winter 1983–4, pp. 180–205.

17 *Defense of Japan 1985*, p. 169.

18 For problems of Japanese participation in SDI research, see, for instance, Yasuto Fukushima, 'SDI to Nihon no sanka mondai' (SDI and problems of Japanese participation), *Sekai Shuuhoo*, 12 August 1986, pp. 12–17.

19 *Asian Security 1985*, (Tokyo: Research Institute for Peace and Security pp. 170–71.

20 *Defense of Japan 1981*, p. 120.

21 Tomohisa Sakanaka, 'Nihon no kaku senryaku ga towareru toki' (It's time that Japan's nuclear strategy was questioned), *Voice*, September 1985, pp. 232–43.

22 For views favouring a nuclear option for Japan, see, for instance, Ikutaro Shimizu, 'Nihon yo, kokka tare!' (Japan, be a state!), *Shokun*, July 1980, pp. 22–68; and Yatsuhiro Nakagawa, *Gendai kaku senryaku ron* (Contemporary nuclear strategies), *Hara Shoboo*, Tokyo, 1985, chapter 7.

23 For views favouring a slightly modified interpretation of the three non-nuclear principles, see, for instance, Masashi Nishihara, (*op. cit.*, in note 16), p. 198.

24 A typical view advocating no action against SS-20 may be found, for instance, in Ken'ichi Ito, 'SS-20 Kyokutoo haibi ni Nihon wa doo taioo subeki ka' (How should Japan cope with the SS-20 deployed in the Far East?), *Chuuoo Kooron*, special issue, July 1983, pp. 88–99.

25 Masataka Kosaka, 'Theater Nuclear Weapons and Japan's Defense Policy', in Richard Solomon and Masataka Kosaka, (eds) *The Soviet Far East Military Buildup: Nuclear Dilemmas and Asian Security*, (Dover, MA: Auburn House Publishing Co., 1986), pp.123–140.

The Security of North-East Asia: Part II

PROFESSOR KIM CHONGWHI

Looking at the East Asian situation in the past decade, some contradictory phenomena can be seen to have been emerging. First, apart from Kampuchea, there has been no major open conflict in the region since the Vietnam War, and the overall economic vitality has been very impressive. On the other hand, the military balance in North-east Asia, which ranks second only to Central Europe as the most heavily-armed area of the globe, has changed a great deal.

Until the late 1960s, the United States was the only global power with both the military capability and the political will to act accordingly, while the Soviet Union remained basically a regional power with its primary concern focused on Europe. Today the situation is significantly different.

This change is particularly true in North-east Asia, where a rapid Soviet military build-up has altered the regional power balance. Soviet ground forces in the Far East have increased dramatically from a mere 17 divisions in the 1960s and 31 divisions in 1976 to some 53 divisions now. The Soviet air force in the region now has some 2,400 combat aircraft, and its Pacific Fleet has rapidly grown from a coastal fleet to a blue water navy with 835 vessels. Today, one-quarter of its ground forces, one third of its naval strength, and one-quarter of its air forces are deployed in this region. The Soviet Union also has an Asia-oriented theatre nuclear force with more than 160 SS-20 intermediate-range ballistic missile (IRBM) launchers and over 85 *Backfire* bombers.

The Soviet military build-up in the region might have begun with the defensive objectives of protecting the border with China, deterring any attack on Soviet Far Eastern territory, and safeguarding the submarine-launched ballistic missile (SLBM) forces. However, the build-up has far exceeded its defensive need. Together with the establishment of a theatre-level command structure, the Soviet Union's formidable array of military forces has grown into a significant security threat to North-east Asia.

Today, the Soviet Union is a threat to China, Japan, South Korea and the American forces in the Pacific, with nuclear as well as conventional means. Secondly, Soviet forces can interdict the sea and air lines of communication of Japan, Korea and other Asian countries, and those of the United States to the region. Thirdly, Moscow has enhanced its ability to neutralize potential developments in US-China-Japan and US-Japan-Korea relations. Finally, the Soviet

Union is now capable of tying down the US forces in the Pacific and impeding their movement to the Middle East or Europe in a crisis.

Moreover, the Soviet military build-up in Asia and the Pacific is likely to remain a constant feature of the strategic environment throughout the coming years. In fact, there are many reasons for strengthening this capability even further, geopolitics being a critical one. The Soviet presence in this region and its status as a global power are inseparable from Moscow's strategic competition with Washington. The Soviet Union is determined to weaken the American alliance system, to contain China while improving its own relations with Beijing, and to project its own power and influence in this very important region.

Another factor is the Soviet economy. In the coming decades, Moscow will undoubtedly seek to develop Siberia, where a large proportion of its natural resources lie. Japan could provide capital and technology for Siberian development and the Asian-Pacific region could become an important market for its products. The third factor springs from certain fears and insecurities, some inherited from the past, some rooted in paranoia and others based on reality. For example, the Soviet Union fears a two-front war. There are also fears of an economically powerful and rearmed Japan and a huge, antagonistic, developed China.

The US has responded to Soviet policies by halting its military withdrawal from North-east Asia since 1978 and by gradually building up its deployed forces, particularly maritime. Although this has helped the US to maintain its naval superiority this US build-up will likely slow down in the coming years because of fiscal constraints. Moreover, exactly what form US defence strategy in the Pacific will take depends very much on contingencies in the Indian Ocean, since Washington has indicated that the Gulf region would be number two priority in wartime, Western Europe, of course, being number one.

It is also the case that the United States is becoming more convinced that its allies and friends in Asia will have to play a more significant role in deterrence and defence in the region. As the wealthiest and most technologically advanced nation in Asia, Japan has the capacity to help in the defence of the Pacific and both Japanese leaders and the public at large are now giving military issues more thought than before. Support for the US-Japan Security Treaty and for the gradual strengthening of the Self-Defense Forces has markedly increased.

The Japanese are certainly concerned about the growing Soviet military strength in North-east Asia – particularly the increase in Soviet naval power in the waters surrounding Japan and the Soviet military build-up in the disputed Northern Territories. Yet most people in Japan still doubt that the Soviet Union poses a direct and immediate danger, and are unwilling to spend much more to protect themselves against a threat which they regard as improbable. The trauma of defeat in World War II still exerts a powerful influence on Japanese thinking. There is marked reluctance to change a policy of 'economics above all' that has not only made Japan an economic superpower but has also successfully provided security at a very little cost.

Both the United States and China share a very important long-term interest in containing Soviet expansion in Asia. China needs Western help while it pursues its arduous process of economic modernization. It is clearly no match for the Soviet Union militarily and does not seem to wish to antagonize Moscow. China now seems to be more interested in establishing a better balance in its relations with the United States and the Soviet Union. The ability of America to interest China in greatly expanded security co-operation and participation in any direct anti-Soviet coalition therefore seems to be limited.

The Korean Peninsula
Another important security concern in the region is that there should be peace and stability in the Korean Peninsula. This problem is now examined in some detail.

Separated from Japan only by a narrow body of water and sharing a common border with the Soviet Union and China, Korea has historically been the arena of power struggles between the US, Russia, China and Japan. Since around the turn of the century, each of the four powers has intervened not less than twice in four major wars fought in or over Korea. Even today, the United States, the Soviet Union and China maintain treaties of alliance with South or North Korea, and Japan has repeatedly declared that the peace and stability of the Korean Peninsula is 'essential' for the security of Japan. If another war were to break out in Korea, the strategic importance of the Peninsula would quickly become self-evident because of the changes it would bring to the established order in North-east Asia and in the world: Soviet-American and Sino-American relations would be affected, as would Japan's security. And a war would of course be a tragedy for the Korean people.

The most serious threat to peace and security in Korea today is North Korea's intention to unify the Peninsula by force. Kim Il Sung frequently reiterates his right and intent to liberate the South. In December 1967, he declared that 'The northern half of the republic is a revolutionary base for accomplishing the cause of national liberation on a national scale – at all costs.' In 1975 he stated that 'if revolution takes place in South Korea, we as one and the same nation will not just look at it with folded arms but will strongly support the South Korean people . . . In this war, we will not only lose the military demarcation line but will gain the country's unification.' North Korean spokesmen have frequently asserted that the doctrine of peaceful coexistence can only apply between separate nations, whereas Korea is one nation with an illegitimate colonial regime occupying the South. As recently as March 1986, Kim declared that North Korea 'cannot afford to remain idle' while the 1988 Olympics take place in Seoul.

Since the Armistice Agreement of 1953 and more so since the early 1960s, North Korea has steadily built up its armed forces. Year after year, Pyongyang has spent some 24% of its GNP on its war machine – an abnormally high level by any standard, despite the resultant severe economic hardship for its people. As a result, North Korean military strength has surpassed that of the South in all important categories including the numbers of military personnel, army divisions, artillery pieces, tanks, combat aircraft, naval vessels and war reserves. (See Appendix on p. 22.) This is in spite of the fact that the South has a population twice as large as that of the North and an economic output five times greater.

North Korean forces are very much a derivative of those of their modern sponsor, the Soviet Union, with a few modifications for local conditions. The North Korean forces are therefore organized for pre-emptive surprise attack, massive artillery and missile fire support and high-speed mechanized warfare combined with commando operations. No doubt this accounts for the large increase in their armoured units and self-propelled artillery. By the end of 1985, their forces deployed in frontline areas had increased to 65% from the earlier level of 45%, as a result of which warning-time has decreased from several days to a matter of hours. North Korean special forces also continue to pose a serious problem for the South. Their 100,000-strong commando forces, the largest of their kind in the world, are equipped with 280 An-2 low-flying transports and now with 87 US-built helicopters, identical to those used by the South Korean forces. North Korea also has a formidable chemical warfare capability, with a stockpile estimated at 180 to 250 metric tons of chemical weapons, including mustard gas and nerve gas. Given the nature of the North Korean regime, South Korea fears that Pyongyang would not hesitate to use such weapons.

Taking advantage of its political system, which is capable of mounting a surprise attack, the military strategy of the North is presumably to seize Seoul by rapid combined regular and irregular operations. Korean reserve forces would be fully mobilized before US reinforcements could arrive. The North would have the initiative and the advantages inherent in being the attacker. This would lead it to attempt to sweep in the shortest possible time through the Seoul area, where as many as one-quarter of the population of the South resides. The fact that Seoul is only a mere 25 miles from the DMZ poses special problems for the South. Moreover, South Korea can be supplied only be sea or air, whereas the North has a land border with both the Soviet Union and China.

Since the North started its military build-up much earlier than did South Korea, it is anxious to seize an opportunity to invade the South before the weapons it now has become obsolete, and before the South can enhance its own military capabilities. In other words, the view in Seoul is that Pyongyang wants to employ its currently superior military strength to achieve its goal of unification by force before the end of this decade or the beginning of the 1990s, when the South-North military gap is expected to be conspicuously narrowed.

Successful deterrence and defence for South Korea primarily depends on its own defence posture and will serve to preserve its peace and freedom. However, outside factors are also very significant, notably the strategies of the USSR and China towards the Korean Peninsula. Soon after World War II, Soviet forces marched into the northern half of the Peninsula to establish a satellite state. However, the Chinese intervention in the Korean War set the stage for rivalry between the Soviet Union and China. Disappointed at Khrushchev's revisionist line, Kim Il Sung leaned towards China for a while, but this tilt soon changed when Brezhnev came into power. During the Cultural Revolution the ties between Pyongyang and Beijing worsened for a time, but changed for the better with the rise of Zhou Enlai and Deng Xiaoping.

Some outside observers might feel that both the Soviet Union and China, particularly China, will restrain North Korea from launching an all-out invasion of the South, and that they are capable of doing so. But the Sino-Soviet dispute has led to the independence of the Pyongyang regime, giving Kim Il Sung some latitude in action that he would not otherwise have achieved. His ability to act independently – in ways that neither of his allies might like – constitutes one of the prime dangers to peace in Korea. It should not be forgotten that North Korea is capable of fighting for a long period of time without external resupply (90 days), and that the Sino-Soviet dispute has also enhanced somewhat the North's ability to obtain military assistance from both sides. Of importance is the fact that once war began, the Soviet Union and China could not help but support the North.

Although Chinese and Soviet relations with North Korea can at present be said to be fluid, there are several strong indications of possible intimacy between the aggressive policy of the North and the expansionism of the Soviet Union. Although Tsarist Russia's ambition was set back by its defeat in the Russo-Japanese War, its interest in the Korean Peninsula started in the late nineteenth century when it began to look for a warm water port. Since World War II, the Soviet Union has seen North Korea as an important base for expanding its sphere of power, and in the last several years it has pursued the goal of improving relations with Pyongyang in order to complete the encirclement of China. It may also think that the seizure of the Korean Peninsula would be useful for accomplishing its goal of the 'Finlandization' of Japan. Further, as passage through the Korean Strait has become more important to the Soviet Pacific Fleet, Moscow's interest in the Korean Peninsula has grown.

In recent years, events have given support to Moscow's goals. First, Kim Il Sung, once disappointed with Khrushchev's revisionist policy now sees today's China as even more revisionist. More than likely

North Korea is becoming increasingly dissatisfied with the developments in China today, such as the downgrading of Mao, internal reforms, the modernization programme conducted with help from the West, and the reconciliation with the US and Japan. Then, to overcome major economic difficulties, Pyongyang is urgently seeking large-scale economic and technological aid, but China does not have the ability to meet its demands. Finally, the North is searching for newer and greater amounts of military equipment for a possible southward invasion, and Moscow is now meeting some of the North Korean needs with MiG-23 fighters and surface-to-air and precision-guided missiles.

Since Gorbachev's rise to power, the Soviet Union has intensified its efforts to cultivate ties with the North. In return for the provision of military equipment, Moscow has obtained overflight rights over North Korea, and Soviet aircraft now regularly fly reconnaissance missions along the DMZ and into the Yellow Sea. The Soviet Union also obtained permission for naval vessels to call at North Korean ports. In July 1986, the aircraft carrier *Minsk*, the Commander of the Pacific Fleet on board, led a flotilla into Wonsan, on the east coast of North Korea. Twelve Soviet MiG-23 fighters flew into Pyongyang for a friendship visit, led by the Commander of the Soviet Far Eastern Air Force. The Soviet-North Korean military links are bound to embolden Kim Il Sung in his schemes against the South.

The US is the South's most important ally and has certainly played a decisive role in deterrence and defence for South Korea. However, after the Vietnam War, the United States was caught up with the illusion of detente and appeared to take a relaxed attitude towards Moscow's expansionism, while pursuing military reductions. The policy of detente only encouraged the USSR in a series of expansionist steps from Angola to Afghanistan. Unilateral arms reduction by the US served to endanger the military balance between the two super-powers which is essential for deterrence.

As has already been noted, this became more serious in the Pacific region. The reduction of American military power was more apparent here, especially the plan for the withdrawal of US ground forces from Korea. Fortunately, however, following the Soviet invasion of Afghanistan and particularly since the inauguration of President Reagan, the United States has been enhancing its military strength and strongly pursuing a new policy of containment of the Soviet Union. The withdrawal from the Asian-Pacific region was stopped and the plans to withdraw troops from Korea abandoned. Today, US-South Korea security co-operation is on an extremely good footing.

Japan is the power which has probably the greatest stake in Korea and an outbreak of war there would be a great shock, with significant effects on Japanese domestic, foreign and defence policies. To put it bluntly, Japan benefits most from US-South Korean defence spending while itself concentrating on a policy of 'economics above all'.

However, some changes are taking place. The Japanese are beginning to recognize the Soviet military threat and are being pressed by the US administration to bear more of the defence burden. In contrast to the situation ten years ago, the public debate about the security of Japan is widening and public support for the SDF is on the rise. Japan's once hard-line aversion to military spending is softening, not only within the ruling Liberal-Democratic Party, but also in the opposition parties, such as the Democratic Socialist Party and the Komeito.

South Korea does not now oppose a gradual Japanese military build-up and an enlarged Japanese security role in the region, as it did in the past. At present, however, it is neither desirable nor possible for the South to have direct military ties with Japan, nor does it expect a direct Japanese military contribution in the event of hostilities on the Peninsula. What South Korea does wish, however, is that Japan should manifest its clear appreciation for and understanding of the security situation in Korea, and that it should improve its economic co-operation with Korea, especially in trade.

What South Korea plans to do in order to meet the challenges of a rapidly changing and difficult environment is, in this writer's view, to augment its all-round national security capability steadily, putting more emphasis on balance, flexibility and long-term perspectives.

The first priority is military strength. Koreans, perhaps more than anyone else, are well aware of the tragedy that war brings and why it must at all costs be avoided. Therefore credible deterrence of war, which lies principally in the Republic of Korea's own defence capability – currently inferior to that of the North – is being emphasized. The objective of the Force Improvement Plan (FIP) is to build an effective deterrence and defence capability. During the Second FIP period (1982–6), South Korea has spent approximately 6% of its GNP on defence. This is the equivalent of one-third of the national budget, a level of spending which is one of the highest among US allies. Taking the economy into account this defence effort is noteworthy.

Despite South Korea's plan for a continued high level of defence spending, it seems quite unlikely that a North-South balance will be achieved in the near future. North Korea's serious military build-up began in 1962, while the South's FIP was initiated only in 1974. This twelve-year gap, together with a system unique to North Korea (such as eight-year conscription), and the North's continuing military aid from the Soviet Union and China have made it difficult for the South to redress the existing wide military imbalance. However, if the South maintains its military expenditures at the current rate of 6% of GNP, it will be able to attain some 80% of the military strength of the North by the early 1990s, thus fulfilling the minimum defence requirement, even if the North continues to allocate 24% of its GNP to military spending. A rough equilibrium in South-North military strength would be achieved by the end of the 1990s.

Secondly, South Korea regards its military co-operation with the US as a key pillar of national security. It is the strong US security commitment and military presence which is helping to deter armed aggression by the North, and the US forces in Korea, with advanced aircraft, help to make up for some of the weakness of South Korean forces while they are being modernized. The Foreign Military Sales credits provided by the United States are also aiding South Korea to narrow the North's military lead. On the other hand, by maintaining the peace and security of the Peninsula, South Korea serves American interests in the region. In addition, it is offering as much as $1.2 billion a year, including funds for the Combined Defense Improvement Projects (CDIP), for the support of US troops in Korea.

The third area is that of economics. South and North also compete for the betterment of their people. Economic prosperity will provide a strong base for building and maintaining military capability, but also for a welfare society, which, in turn, will become a driving force to enable the political and social order to be stabilized and developed. In the early 1960s the two economies were not much different in size, but the dynamic economic growth of South Korea since then (the real growth in the first half of 1986 exceeded 10%) has now made its GNP five times that of the North. South Korea now sees this gap between the two economies continuing to widen and by the very early 1990s expects its GNP to be at least six times larger than that of the North.

The last priority concerns the relaxation of tensions and the eventual unification of the Peninsula. Despite the aggressive designs and constant provocations of the North, including the bombing incident in Rangoon in October 1983, South Korea has not abandoned its efforts to ease tensions and to bring about the eventual peaceful unification of the Peninsula. Although a dialogue between South and North will not necessarily lead to an immediate reduction of tensions, the South sees no hope at all of easing tensions without it. President Chun Doo Hwan has repeatedly proposed an epoch-making summit meeting between the North and South without any pre-conditions. Should it be difficult to hold such a meeting now, at least the South-North Red Cross Talks and Economic Talks suspended by Pyongyang should be resumed. In addition, South Korea is trying to develop contacts and exchanges with China, the Soviet Union and other Communist countries. Even though formal diplomatic cross-recognition may still be years away, it is the South Korean view that the process of 'cross-contacts' will inevitably accelerate.

Appendix
The Military Balance 1985

	South Korea	North Korea
Total Armed Forces (active)	598,000	838,000
Army		
Personnel	520,000	750,000
Tanks	1,200	3,425
Artillery pieces	3,100	4,650
Navy		
Personnel (including marines)	45,000	35,000
Submarines	0	20
Destroyers and Frigates	25	4
Other vessels	128	521
Air Force		
Personnel	33,000	53,000
Combat aircraft	451	800

SOURCE: The Military Balance, 1985-86 (London, IISS, 1985), pp. 126-8

Trade, Technology and Security: Implications for East Asia and the West: Part I

DR HANNS MAULL

Security and economics: some conceptual considerations
Any foray into the interstices of economics and security faces something of a paradox: talking about security and economics in one breath seems almost a contradiction in terms. While economics is about entrepreneurial risk-taking, security policies strive to reduce risks; economics is about dynamic change, about ever new, ever tenuous equilibria, while 'security' is often used almost as a synonym for 'stability' or at least for controlled change; in the economic realm, firms – often operating across national boundaries in informational markets – are the principal actors, in security matters, it is national governments. The two activities therefore tend to pull their interwoven strands apart. This difficulty might explain why the relationship between economics and security has not been explored conceptually in international relations theory with anything like the attention paid, for example, to the relationship between power and security.

Security may be defined as the absence of threats to a set of values that a people, a society, a nation consider basic and essential for their survival. Such threats can arise from the military power of other states and their desire to impose a different set of values. They may also stem from economic interaction with other states, as the Japanese concept of 'comprehensive security' implies – dependence on external supplies of resources and access to export markets in this view may potentially be as dangerous to a country as military weakness; economic interdependence will have to be managed in ways which eliminate or at least reduce insecurity.

But low politico-military security has important economic dimensions. As Figure 1 shows, there are two, the first related to the military strand of security policy, the second to the political realm. Strong defences require adequate economic inputs. In general terms, that means money, which in turn means a prospering economy. More specifically, however, it also concerns inputs of energy, resources, technology, capital and manpower required to maintain a military balance with a potential opponent. There is thus a broad spectrum of

Figure 1: Economic Dimensions of Security

	Politico-military security		*Economic security*
	Economic foundations of military strength/ military balance	Economic aspects of political relations	—
Related to			
	Capabilities	Intentions	Economic viability/ political legitimacy
At risk	Access to defence industry inputs	Access to important inputs to economy	Access to vital inputs to economy Functioning of the economic system
Sources of threat	Bottlenecks in inputs	Bottlenecks in inputs Access to markets blocked	External shocks Bottlenecks in vital inputs Access to vital markets blocked
Examples of problem areas	Availability of fuel supplies in military conflict Loss of technological edge in armaments	East–West economic relations: political implications Political implications of protectionism in North–South and West–West relations	Access to oil Access to critical minerals Access to food

economic issues which could be pursued further, focus here will be on only one: technology. The use of technological innovations generally enhances economic productivity. In the case of defence, productivity would be a rather Orwellian term for lethality or destructive power. The use of superior technologies can provide an additional margin of security. This presupposes, however, two things: the availability of innovative technologies and their effective translation into military power. The first is a question of the innovative strength of a nation's (and an alliance's) scientific establishment, the second requires good organization – in terms of procurement policies, for example.

There are several different, though not mutually exclusive ways to maintain or improve the technological edge with regard to Western security under conditions where – as is generally acknowledged – the West holds strong advantages in innovative dynamism. One is to enhance the advantage in innovative capacity; a second is to slow the transfer of technology to the adversary; a third consists of strengthening the processes of translating technological innovation into superior military power. While some of these issues will be pursued in greater depth below, it might be noted at this point that attention within the Western Alliance appears to have focused rather heavily on efforts to reduce the flow of advanced technology to the East. But while the Soviet Union is clearly inferior to the West in its innovative capacities, it seems to have done better in translating advanced technologies into weapons systems. This, at least, must be inferred from Pentagon estimates which show the United States leading the Soviet Union in most areas of advanced technologies (although admittedly seeing the USSR catching up in most of them) but with the Soviet Union level or even ahead in terms of the capabilities of many weapons systems.

The second economic dimension of security concerns the political implications of East–West economic relations. Trade and technology transfers between East and West can be, and have been, seen as providing not only the economic benefits normally associated with trade, but also political leverage and influence – in either direction: they might foster or, at least encourage, a general improvement in East–West relations, create incentives for constructive behaviour and even leverage on specific, though perhaps not on important issues in Soviet foreign policy. This viewpoint would support active policies of transfer of technology to Eastern Europe and even to the Soviet Union: too large a technological gap between the two halves of Europe would impede East–West economic relations in general and could result in serious economic and political crises within COMECON (Council for Mutual Economic Assistance) – something which might well dangerously heighten tensions between East and West.[1]

But East–West economic relations could also – as was argued by the Reagan Administration in the case of the European-Soviet gas pipeline deal – be seen as resulting in dangerous levels of Western dependence on Soviet supplies or Soviet markets, opening opportunities for Moscow to split the Western Alliance and to blackmail Europeans. East–West economic relations could thus in this view be used by the USSR to directly threaten Western security.

If judged by the rather stringent definition of security proposed above the relevance of East–West economic relations to security issues may, at least outside the realm of military or dual-use technologies, be quite limited. They have genuine significance only insofar as they would either significantly affect the likelihood of military conflict (eg, through changes in intention) or as their disruption would threaten economic prosperity to such a degree that political support for existing structures of security co-operation would be undermined. Neither appears to be the case at present.

The analysis of economic security issues properly speaking is concerned with threats which could seriously impair the functioning and well-being of national economies or, to put it more technically, change key economic parameters such as growth rates, levels of employment, inflation, or the external balance dramatically and quickly enough to undermine the economic foundations of existing political structures within and between states.[2]

The threat here is directed against economic prosperity in a fundamental sense, against economic viability. It would take the form of a severe economic depression, which in turn could well undermine the political legitimacy of existing democratic institutions and of established patterns of security co-operation.

Threats to economic security in this sense could come from a variety of directions; they might concern the availability and even the prices of key resources (the oil price revolutions of the 1970s certainly produced shocks to oil-importing economies of a magnitude that must be seen as a security issue),[3] the fluctuation of exchange rates, or access to export markets for manufactured goods. All these potential threats to economic security have one thing in common: they are related not only to actions by other states, but to their interaction in international 'regimes' or management structures of segments of the world economy. Later on this Paper will focus on one particular kind of potential threat: protectionism in manufactures and its possible effect on trilateral security.

The Alliance and technology transfer: the trouble with Janus
Janus, the Roman god, had two faces: a grim one, the face of war; and a benevolent face, that of peace. Issues in the interstices of security and economics often have the two faces of Janus; particularly so in the case of high technology. For high technology today not only plays a key role in determining the military balance between East and West; it is also an area of intense industrial and commercial rivalry between the states of Western Europe, Japan and North America.

The electronics industries (computers, software, office equipment, telecommunications etc.) in the non-Communist world alone in 1985 produced goods and services estimated at about $US 485 billion and thus accounted for 4.7% of Western world economic product. In the year 2000, this share is expected to reach 8%. Some 30% of total US exports in 1983 were accounted for by high-technology products; in this sector, the US economy was able to achieve a trade surplus of about $17 bn. High-technology industries in general, and the electronics industry in particular, are also generally seen as 'strategic' economic sectors: they will increasingly provide critical inputs to a broad range of economic activities. Little wonder then that they are thought to hold the key to future international competitiveness, which gives them crucial importance in terms of domestic economic and social prospects: high-technology industries are widely seen as providing the jobs of the future, as capable of absorbing new entrants into the job markets and perhaps also the millions of unemployed in mature industrial countries. In short, high-technology industries are generally seen as critically important for future economic prosperity, social peace and international standing.

The intense importance of high technology for those three areas of security, international competitiveness and prosperity has produced heavy government involvement in the sector. This has often implied complex and conflicting objectives: the imperatives of national security can obviously not always easily be reconciled with the desire to maximize commercial benefits from new technologies. Differences about what constitute security issues in East–West technology transfer, and about how best to deal with them have long been a source of friction within the North American-Western European-Japanese group. The growing speed of technological innovation, the spread of high-technology production among a widening group of countries, and the erosion of US leadership not only in high technology but also in the international regime governing East–West economic interaction have made the management of high-technology security problems all the more complicated. Yet while there has been considerable turmoil within the Alliance over those issues, the last two years have also brought significant progress in containing and even resolving the frictions.

One example of this has been the development of CoCom, the co-ordinating committee through which major NATO states and Japan try to control the transfer of sensitive technologies to Eastern Bloc countries. The structure of the organization has been strengthened (although the American initiative to have it formally institutionalized was turned down); a military advisory committee, the Security and Technology Experts' Meeting, has been set up to advise CoCom on the military significance of emerging technologies; and the CoCom list revision has been completed, with some 100 categories of goods and technologies now subjected to export controls through the national legislation of CoCom member states.[4]

The second area of friction within the Alliance has been over US national legislation to control high-technology exports. In principle, the US uses three different instruments to protect militarily relevant technologies: classification, control over publication of government-financed research, and export legislation such as the Export Administration Act – last amended in 1985 – and its specification in Export Administration Regulations.[5] There have been frictions within the Alliance over specific applications of all three instruments; the most dramatic example was probably the Soviet gas pipeline conflict between the US and several Western European nations, in which US sanctions against Western European companies involved in the pipeline deal were applied on the basis of the Export Administration Act. The 1985 Amendments to the Act, and the Regulations published in May 1986,[6] have not resolved the contentious issues such as the extraterritorial powers claimed by US legislation over the use and re-export of US technology by foreign firms or the question of the extent to which the very extensive US Militarily-Critical Technology List will be integrated into export control procedures involving non-American companies. Nevertheless, actual frictions have died down, with a growing willingness on both sides to find pragmatic solutions. This also applies to a third problem area, that of strengthening efforts to combat illegal forms of technology transfer to the East.

The present situation within the Alliance with regard to high-technology security issues is thus marked by a considerable degree of pragmatism and co-operation, which has certainly been helped by the limited commercial importance of East–West high-technology trade.[7] On the other hand, the structural causes of past frictions (different perceptions and interests between Alliance members, inherent tensions between security- and interdependence-oriented views of the problems, the continuing extraterritorial powers of US legislation) have not disappeared; there is therefore no reason to assume that tensions within the Alliance over East–West technology issues will not surface again. One trend which could in fact bring back those problems with a vengeance is the surge of military research and development (R&D) in the United States. This trend might conveniently, although somewhat misleadingly, be discussed under the heading of the Strategic Defense Initiative (SDI).

SDI

At the time of writing, the future of SDI is clouded by major uncertainties – technological, financial, strategic and political. The hypothesis that SDI could refocus Alliance concern about East–West and West–West technology transfers therefore rests on the assumptions that SDI research and development efforts will continue to grow substantially and that SDI would be expected to produce major civilian technological spin-off. Although the US Administration has cleverly underpinned its SDI programmes by mobilizing fascination with technological progress and science fiction and by appealing to American desires to become, once more, the West's unquestioned leader in technological and industrial prowess,[8] it is in fact far from clear whether SDI would produce the promised vast civilian spin-off. On past evidence from military and space R&D, it can be argued at least as plausibly that the major militarization of American R&D under way since 1980, will hamper rather than invigorate the innovative strength of the American economy.[9] Massive impulses for the US technological base from SDI thus cannot be taken for granted.

Assuming SDI proceeds apace, it would represent a rapidly growing part of US total R&D: allocations in fiscal year (FY) 1986 accounted for about 8% of total military R&D, and the Pentagon submission for FY 1987 (which, however, is unlikely to be met) demanded an increase by over 70%, to $4.8 bn or over 11% of total military R&D. Behind this, there has been the general reorientation of US military spending towards investment in new weapon systems, and particularly in R&D. If SDI is to succeed, it will need major technological advances in a wide range of areas; and it is basic innovations and dramatic improvements of this kind which would produce the greatest potential benefits for the civilian economies of trilateral countries. To the extent that SDI will be seen as creating major civilian technological spin-off, it will also appear as an effort of great significance for the future competitiveness and vigour of Western economies. This perception has certainly been dangled in front of the German and Japanese study commissions which visited the United States to prospect commercial opportunities, and has formed one important rationale for European and Japanese business participation in SDI. If, when and how these benefits would be made available to America's allies, could become highly contentious questions.

The problems which SDI might put into sharp relief are general in nature – ultimately, they relate to the growing importance of dual-use technologies for both civilian and military competitiveness, and to the tension between economics and security noted above. SDI will need a wide network of research institutions to succeed, it will have to mobilize the synergies of interdependence, both nationally and internationally. This implies a broad dissemination of information – through academic debate, conferences and publications, through technology transfers and links, through joint ventures and co-production. Yet this will sit uneasily with a bureaucracy (the Pentagon) with strong instincts towards secrecy and an inclination to give the protection of sensitive information, to slow the haemorrhage of technology towards the East, priority over additional impulses for the R&D process.[10] Restrictive tendencies could also be encouraged by considerations of international competitiveness – or at least there will be an inclination by allies to see technology transfer restrictions in this light – the Pentagon's R&D budget as a surreptitious industrial policy to regain unchallenged technological hegemony.[11]

THE POLITICAL DIMENSION

There is, however, another perspective on Western technology transfer to the East – related to the political dimension of military security. This perspective sees the transfer of technology to the East, and in particular to Eastern Europe, as an important precondition for maintaining and expanding economic co-operation between Eastern and Western countries. If Eastern countries were to fall back further in levels of technology, this would reduce their ability to absorb Western goods, and to earn the hard currency required to sustain economic links with the West. In Eastern Europe, this could severely aggravate existing economic problems, increase Eastern European dependence on the Soviet Union and potentially also produce risks of political tensions and instability within COMECON. This perspective is strongly held in West Germany, but can also be found in other Western European countries. It is based on social and cultural ties with the East which are qualitatively different from those of the US and Japan. Therein lurks another possible source of friction within the Western Alliance: as East–West relations move out of the period of stagnation in the years 1980 to 1985, the difference in regional approaches to economic relations with Eastern Europe (primarily security-oriented in the US; primarily commercial in Japan; and importantly, though not exclusively, political in Western Europe) might again produce strains and fissures.[12]

There are thus four areas where Western security could be adversely affected by efforts to control the flow of Western technology towards the East:

- First, technology transfer controls might seriously impede the dynamics of innovation and implementation of advanced technologies by constraining interaction between military and civilian R&D and diverting resources from the latter to the former.[13]
- Second, national security controls could also hamper technological link-ups among companies and research institutions within the Alliance. There are indications, for example, that some European firms are reluctant to get involved in technological co-operation which might be affected by national security controls.
- Third, political frictions over technology transfer controls and suspicions about a 'hidden agenda' of regaining technological and industrial hegemony could adversely affect security co-operation within the Alliance.
- Fourth, differences over the degree to which economic co-operation with, and hence technology transfer to, Eastern Europe will be desirable to support a climate of 'detente' and to strengthen Eastern Europe.

On the other hand, the transfer of militarily relevant technology to the Soviet Union clearly also constitutes a real security problem. The implication for Alliance policies on technology transfer is that there will be no easy and durable solutions: the trade-off between innovative dynamism and restrictions to maintain Western lead times in advanced technologies will have to be constantly fine-tuned. It seems unlikely that there can be more than a broad common agreement on principles among the Alliance members; specific cases involving the vast grey area of dual-use technologies are always likely to be contentious. It seems more realistic, therefore, to start from the assumption that differences of view will be normal rather than objectionable, and to focus on adequate mechanisms for conflict management, rather than to expend much effort and political capital on designing a common strategy. Second, the Alliance should pay more attention to technology application rather than to technology generation and transfer control: Soviet advantages appear to lie more in procurement than in acquisition of technology. And third, efforts should be made to make controls as cost-effective and simple as possible. This probably implies a drastic shortening of the US Militarily-Critical Technology List, which at present is very unwieldy.

Protectionism and security
The relationship between security and trade is frequently invoked, but rarely clarified. Growing protectionism is widely portrayed as a threat to the Western alliance system and hence to Western security; on the other hand, some industries suffering from import competition have also presented their problems as threats to national security. The massive Japanese trade surplus has frequently been linked by Americans outside the government to Japan's reluctance to spend sufficiently on defence, and there have been more or less blunt suggestions that the US should reconsider its security commitments to Japan if the bilateral trade imbalance were to continue. Fortunately, this has so far been mostly media rhetoric; the US government has, as will be argued below, kept those issue areas prudently apart, thus avoiding any linkage.

Still, it may be argued that protectionism undermines security – perhaps in a subtle, corrosive way. Could trade frictions not reach such a state that they would begin to destroy or at least seriously hamper security co-operation within the Western alliance system? It is a fact that protectionism has grown considerably since 1973. According to an analysis by OECD (the Organization for Economic Co-operation and Development), the share of restricted products in manufacturing imports rose between 1980 and 1983 alone from 6% to 13% for the US and from 11% to 15% for the European Community (EC). According to other sources, as a rule of thumb, one quarter of world trade is regulated today through quotas and non-tariff barriers, a further quarter by barter agreements in the broadest sense, and a third quarter is composed of intra-firm trade. While less than 1% of OECD automobile trade was affected by discriminatory restrictions in 1973, ten years later it had risen to nearly 50%. Add to this the long-standing tradition of protectionism in agriculture, which remains outside the focus of this Paper, but certainly also is a major source of friction in international relations. Protectionism thus clearly constitutes a growth industry. It will not go away – but neither is it likely to undermine the Alliance.

To start with supportive evidence for this qualified optimism, it has to be recognized that there is a difference between economic activity, economic relations, and politics.[14] To be sure, trade relations between Western Europe, Japan and the United States are bad, and have become worse; yet this has so far not prevented a substantial deepening of economic interdependence, nor has it seriously spilled over into 'high politics'. Detailed analyses of trade relations actually show, at least at present, a remarkable resilience of both economic relations and 'high politics' to the growing frictions in trade relations.[15] While this cannot be a guarantee for the future, there are good reasons for optimism:

- While the growth of protectionism has been dramatic, it has so far not prevented substantial increases in international trade flows, even in those sectors most affected.
- Intra-firm trade is still growing, and the internationalization of production appears to proceed apace, building more complex configurations of interest, which cut across traditional protectionist positions by giving domestic producers stakes in international trade.
- There have been a number of reactions to growing protectionism by firms affected. Strategies to counter such pressures have included direct investment abroad, a change in product composition, a shift of production into countries not (yet) affected by discriminatory restrictions, and into trade in intermediate goods. Trade imbalances have also triggered adjustment mechanisms such as exchange rate shifts; these will help to contain imbalances.
- Protectionism has been a blunt and largely ineffective instrument to prevent the loss of employment and is at the same time expensive to consumers.
- Last, but not least, protectionist measures run counter to wider economic and political objectives of those governments most concerned; the dangers inherent in a tumble into trade wars have been clearly perceived and have led to a new GATT (General Agreement on Tariffs and Trades) round.

The 'voluntary' Japanese agreement to limit shipments of cars to the US to 1.85 million units per year illustrates these points nicely. According to a study by the US International Trade Commission, in 1984 Japanese cars were sold at an estimated $1,300 above what would have been likely in the absence of the voluntary export restraints. The price of domestically-produced cars exceeded its theoretical level in the absence of trade restrictions by about $660. Profits of Japanese producers in the US market increased by at least 10%. The effect on employment has been estimated at 22,000 jobs saved in 1981–2 at a time when the recession in the industry led to a loss of more than ten times this number of jobs. General Motors, which wants to import small cars from its Japanese affiliates, Isuzu and Suzuki, came out against a continuation of the agreement in 1985; the restraints were lifted on 31 March 1985, to be replaced by a Japanese commitment to ship no more than 2.2 m units to the US market. The other American car firms have meanwhile also developed links with Japanese producers.

To sum up: protectionism in manufactures is unlikely to pose a threat to security relationships between industrialized countries. Restrictions on trade will not pose genuine economic security problems as long as the fundamental structure of the present regime for international trade remains intact – and this seems much more likely than is often assumed. There is also a very good chance that industrialized countries will be able to prevent trade frictions from spilling over corrosively into their security relationships and so avoid the indirect threat that economics could pose to the political underpinnings of security, if a modicum of good sense and policy management prevails. All this is not to deny the reality of protectionism: while mercantilist tendencies are on the rise in the US and Western Europe – witness the recent US-Japanese microchip agreement, which sets up a cosy oligopoly, ratifies dangerously 'reciprocal' notions such as agreed market shares for American producers in Japan, and includes a new, high-technology sector in politically regulated trade – so is economic interdependence, although not necessarily in traditional forms. The tension between liberalization and competing national economic objectives, between national autonomy and global interdependence, will probably continue to be managed in economically unorthodox and not necessarily completely efficient ways. But given sense and rationality there need not be dramatic deterioration of trade frictions. Nor does it seem likely that 'linkage politics' will seriously spill over from trade into security relationships.

But if protectionism thus seems unlikely to become a major threat to security co-operation between Japan, the US and Western Europe, it could well contribute to growing problems for their political and even security interests in the Third World. This seems at first glance contradictory: protectionism again has so far not seriously hampered the growth of interdependence along the North–South dimension – while, for example, the share of South Korean manufacturing exports to OECD countries affected by protectionist measures has gone up considerably, reaching a level of over 58% in 1982, those exports have continued to rise steeply. Moreover, even if they were to work more effectively, protectionist measures in themselves are unlikely to produce shocks of a severity sufficient to represent a destructive threat to developing economies. Yet there are reasons for concern:

- While protectionism in manufactures alone does not constitute a serious threat, its negative impact may be substantial, particularly on the second and third echelon of Less Developed Country (LDC) exporters. Moreover, this negative impact in some instances will compound the dramatic adjustment problems caused by falling commodity prices, exchange rate developments, high real interest rates and the debt service burden – problems which for some of those countries certainly represent threats to their economic security. UNCTAD (UN Commission for Trade and Development) estimates show that the decline in commodity prices in 1980–3 alone produced cumulative losses of about $28 bn for 48 commodity-exporting countries. This represents almost half the increase in their total indebtedness. The shocks to third-world economies thus did not only, or even primarily, originate from protectionism in manufactures – but protectionism could seriously hamper efforts to cope with the adjustment burden imposed by those shocks. A resolution of third-world debt problems will ultimately depend on an expansion of exports of manufactured goods to OECD.
- The web of interdependence seems to be in many instances profoundly less symmetrical, less beneficial than that between OECD countries. To take trade in manufactures as an example: according to UNCTAD, non-tariff barriers have disproportionately been directed against developing countries: 65% of their core exports of manufactures are now subjected to such barriers, against only 23% for trade between developed countries. This might cause resentment and frustration. Moreover, exporters in the Third World are heavily dependent on a few industrialized countries, and on the US in particular, for market access. The US in 1984 accounted for 57.5% of total OECD manufactures imports from LDC, the EC for 23.6%, Japan for 8%. The US alone absorbed nearly 80% of the increase of such imports between 1979 and 1984. Problems of market access can thus be expected to become more severe in the future, particularly for new exporters. As mercantilist tendencies in international trade policies are unlikely to dissipate, this will mean that questions of market access and transfer of technology will become subject to political bargaining processes; their outcomes will reflect the relative strength of the parties. This generally does not augur well for developing countries; moreover, it will probably accentuate differences within the Third World, with established Newly Industrializing Countries (NIC) and countries with special political importance (China, South Korea) doing relatively well to the detriment of others.

- Political structures within the Third World, and political alignment with Western countries, generally appear much less robust than within the West itself. Domestic political upheavals could be encouraged by socio-economic strains; those, in turn, could also imply dramatic changes in foreign policies and regional stability. Moreover, while key security interests of major industrialized countries are clearly complementary and underpinned by extensive ties and shared values, this is not always true of security arrangements between North and South. This again suggests that they could be renounced more easily.

In sum, the strains of economic adjustment appear to be more serious, and hence protectionism, as one (though not the most important) element in those strains, more dangerous for Western foreign-policy security interests in the Third World than in the case of intra-Western trade relations. Moreover, the robustness of political arrangements within third-world countries and their external linkages seems less certain. This implies that trade frictions over protectionism in manufactures could contribute to a corrosion of security relationships between the West and certain third-world countries – if only as one element in a whole matrix of economic pressures.

Implications for the West
As economic and security issues become more closely intertwined, and inherent tensions between those two realms therefore appear more prominently, the management of interdependence becomes more complicated. 'Comprehensive security' policies are certainly possible, but they involve a search, often difficult, for solutions which satisfy a wide range of different, and not always compatible, objectives and interests. Yet political processes dealing with such issues by and large have tended to follow established, compartmentalized tracks. This has advantages: it reduces risks of dangerous spill-overs between different issue areas and of gratuitous linkage politics. But it also poses problems. Where compartmentalization breaks down (as, for example, in CoCom), the establishment of new, integrative procedures and management structures can be painfully difficult, as not only CoCom but also the history of the Seven-Nation Summits demonstrate. Yet the challenges to policy integration are clearly on the rise, both with respect to technology and to trade in manufactures.

The source of those problems is the rapid advance of technology, which allows the evolution of ever deeper, constantly changing forms of interdependence between nations and societies. Those have produced a dramatic expansion of world trade into the 1970s, but also protectionist responses which have slowed down the speed of world economic integration through trade. There have also been other mercantilist reactions to growing interdependence – and this can be expected to continue, following in the tracks of technological changes and new patterns of economic interaction between societies. Yet although these mercantilist tendencies will certainly bend, channel and re-route the flow of interdependence, they are unlikely to alter the trend. Out of this stew of technological advances and mercantilist responses, of concerns over national security and autonomy and the pursuit of economic benefits, of a global corporate culture and the old-fashioned but dogged nation-state, will undoubtedly spring subtle shifts in relationships between the US, Japan and Western Europe – not in the sense of, say, a dramatic re-orientation of the US towards the Pacific but rather by way of a redistribution of resources, of attention, of the mix between co-operation and conflict. The implications of technological changes and deepening interdependence for North-South relations, on the other hand, might well be dramatic rather than subtle, if Western Europe, Japan and the US fail to develop policies which make the burden of adjustment for third-world countries manageable.

In preparing this Paper, and in particular the section on 'The Alliance and Technology Transfers', I benefited from an unpublished MA thesis by Kathrin Kleinjung on 'West-East Technology Transfer as a Problem of Transatlantic Relations', University of Munich, 1986. Special thanks are also due to colleagues at the Stiftung Wissenschaft und Politik in Ebenhausen and to various individuals in the German administration and in business organizations, who freely gave me their advice and time.

Notes

[1] This view is spelled out in Jürgen Nötzold, 'Technologie in den Ost-West-Beziehungen', in '*Aus Politik und Zeitgeschichte*', (supplement to the weekley newspaper *Das Parlament* 11 January 1986), pp. 15–25. It seems to be shared by West German Foreign Minister Hans-Dietrich Genscher.

[2] See my *Raw Materials, Energy and Western Security*, (London: Macmillan, 1984) Ch. 1. This is still not entirely satisfactory as it raises the question of what makes, and what threatens, the meta-stability of political structures. While it may not be possible to offer entirely satisfactory criteria for this, the basic idea is that revolutionary changes of the kind which occurred in the 1930s as a direct result of the Great Depression constitute 'insecurity'.

[3] The OECD estimated the quantifiable direct and indirect economic costs of the 1978/9 oil price explosion for the industrialized countries as a group at about $1,000 bn, or 5% and 8% of total GNP in 1980 and 1981, respectively. This calculation does not include the longer-term economic costs, nor the social and political damage wrought by this oil price shock. IEA, *World Energy Outlook* (Paris: OECD 1982), pp. 63.

[4] See David Buchan, '*Western Security and Economic Strategy Towards the East*' (London: IISS 1984), Adelphi Paper No. 192, pp. 23ff; *idem*, 'The West Plugs the High-Tech Drain', in *Financial Times*, 25 July 1984. The agreements reached on the revision of the list included most importantly and controversially the areas of computer hardware, software and telecommunications. The CoCom list itself is secret, its contents can, however, be deduced from national control lists, which are open. In the case of the Federal Republic, the CoCom list revisions were implemented in the 55th revision of the German export list in October 1985. As a consequence, the Bundesamt für gewerbliche Wirtschaft,

which deals with export licence applications, expects the annual number of applications to double from 70,000 to 140,000. See Wolfgang Hoffmann, 'Eine zweischneidige Waffe', in *Die Zeit*, 14 September 1984.

[5] See Werner Hein, 'Beschränkungen des internationalen Technologie-Transfers durch die USA', Washington, DC (mimeo) 1984; Hanns-Dieter Jacobsen, 'Fortgeschrittene Technologie in den Aussenbeziehungen der USA', in *Aussenpolitik*, No. 4/1985, pp. 400–12

[6] These regulations introduced the so-called 'gold card system', a general export licence granted to exporters of sensitive equipment and technologies considered reliable. The system essentially aims at simplifying licensing procedures by shifting the burden of supervision to the exporting companies, which are required to meet certain criteria to prevent the 'haemorrhaging' of critical technologies. See, *International Herald Tribune*, 18 June 1986.

[7] Total Western high-technology exports to the USSR in 1983 came to about $2.3 bn. Allen Lenz and Ken Stiltner, 'Quantification of Western Exports of High-Technology Products to Communist Countries Through 1983', Office of Trade and Investment Analysis, International Trade Administration, US Department of Commerce, (Washington, DC: USGPO 1985).

[8] Lieutenant-General Abrahamson, the Director of the SDI Office, has even suggested that SDI's technological spin-off could make the military programme 90% self-financed (*Washington Post*, 4 April 1985).

[9] For a summary of sceptical literature, see Reinhard Rode, 'Hochtechnologie: Ein Januskopf', in *Aus Politik und Zeitgeschichte*, (*op. cit.* in note 1), pp. 12 ff. See also *The Strategic Defense Initiative: Costs, Contracts and Consequences*, (New York: Council on Economic Priorities 1985), and *Süddeutsche Zeitung*, 9 April 1986, summarizing two recent German studies. A survey of past technology policies can be found in Kenneth Flamm, 'Technology Policy in International Perspective', in *Policies for Industrial Growth in a Competitive World*, prepared for the Subcommittee on Economic Goals and Inter-Governmental Policy, Joint Economic Committee, US Congress, (Washington, DC, USGPO 1984), pp. 23 ff.

[10] There has been a notable increase in attempted and actual restrictions imposed by the US government on academic exchanges and the publication of research findings over the last few years. This has caused concern within the academic community in the US, but also among Europeans. See Peter J.Gollon, 'SDI Funds Costly for Scientists', in *Bulletin of the Atomic Scientist*, January 1986, pp. 24 ff; Gary Putka, 'US Blocks Access of Foreign Scientists to High Technology', in *Wall Street Journal*, 25 January 1985; Hein. (*op. cit.* in note 5) A study team composed of members from the scientific community, industry and the Department of Defense analysed these issues and concluded that only in a very limited grey area were some restrictions to the free flow of academic research findings appropriate (National Academy of Sciences, Scientific Communication and National Security, Washington, DC 1982 (Corson Report)). According to one key member of the study group, the Reagan Administration has, however, practically ignored the findings of the report (Mitchell B. Wallerstein, 'Scientific Communication and National Security', in *Science*, 4 May 1984, pp. 460 ff).

[11] For European perceptions of this type, see Hein, (*op. cit.* in note 5); Jacobsen, (*op. cit.* in note 5); Gerd Junne, 'Das amerikanische Rüstungsprogramm: Ein Substitut für Industriepolitik', in *Leviathan*, No.13/1985, pp. 23–37. See also *Japan Times*, 1986, *Mainichi Daily News*, 22 September/12 August 1986.

[12] I am indebted to Jürgen Nötzold for this point. See also Nötzold, (*op. cit.* in note 1) It would be too simplistic to talk about one European view on this; there are differences not only in political circles but also among companies. The division of German high-technology companies in a group keenly interested in SDI participation and those rather hesitant to get involved may be a pointer to future strains between 'European' and 'global' orientations.

[13] One example of the problems of developing dual-use technologies under military R&D programmes in terms of their commercial utilization appears to be Very High Speed Integrated Circuits (VHSIC), where security controls have impeded rapid commercialization; conversely these problems may also have negative effects on R&D progress. See Hanns-D.Jacobsen, 'Die Technologiekontrollpolitik der Vereinigten Staaten und ihre Auswirkungen auf die West-West-Beziehungen', in *Europa Archiv*, No. 15/1986, 10 August 1986, pp. 443–50.

[14] See Edward J.Lincoln, 'US Japan Relations: Good or Terrible?' in SAIS Review, Winter/Spring 1984, pp. 31–44.

[15] *Ibid*. See also Albrecht Rothacker's study on European-Japanese trade frictions, *Economic Diplomacies between the European Community and Japan, 1959 – 1981*, (London: Gower 1983).

Trade, Technology and Security: Implications for East Asia and the West: Part II

PROFESSOR TAKASHI INOGUCHI

Introduction
Perhaps at no other time in history have trade, technology and security been intertwined more closely than they are today. A good illustration of this is provided by a recent Japan-US agreement on semiconductors.[1] For some considerable time Japan and the US have been competing very hard in this area, and Japan is clearly catching up. Responding to accusations by US semi-conductor producers that Japanese producers were dumping their products on the US market and to the demands for action under Article 301 of the US Trade Act, the US and Japan have recently agreed that the anti-dumping cases against the Japanese semi-conductor producers of the EPROM and 256K DRAM semi-conductors be suspended, provided that:

1) the Department of Commerce monitor all the quarterly statistics on Japan's production and sales of EPROM and 256K DRAM, and the Japanese government do the same on six other kinds of semi-conductors, including Japanese exports of semi-conductors to third countries; and

2) Japan set up an organization to expand its imports of semi-conductors from the US and other countries.

This is a familiar story of protection and managed trade. The agreement would have been impossible if the Japanese Ministry of International Trade and Industry (MITI) had not used its influence to persuade Japanese producers to comply. The Japanese government wanted the co-operation of the US government on such matters as the stabilization of the yen and protectionist legislation in Congress. The monitoring agreement covers not only Japanese parent companies but their overseas subsidiaries elsewhere in Asia, thus effectively precluding the possibility of shipping from there to the United States. Second, it reflects the race that is going on in one of the most important high-technology industries. The pricing agreement will bring higher profits to Japanese producers for the moment, but it will also sharpen the competitive edge that South Korean producers have in the market for standard mass-produced memories. Third, it is a manifestation of deep US concerns about national security, since semi-conductors are widely used in high precision, high performance weapons as well as in civilian applications. The US government is worried that, if US domestic producers become steadily less competitive and the US chip market is occupied largely by foreign-based producers, US defence equipment will have no alternative but to rely on them. The decline of the domestic industrial basis for manufacturing weapons is seen as a grave problem for US national security.[2]

The intimate relationship between trade, technology and security is worth close examination, especially in the context of East Asia, one of the most dynamic regions in the world. Three characteristics of East Asia make this region an excellent case for the study of the interactions between trade, technology and security. First, economic growth in East Asia is typically export-led; without smooth and large-scale trade flows, the East Asian economies cannot continue at their present levels of activity. Second, East Asia is continually seeking new and higher technologies; as a region it cannot compete without them because it is poor in resources. It is indicative of the importance attached to high technologies that the Japanese nickname for semi-conductors is 'the rice of industrial life'. Third, the countries of East Asia are invariably plagued by a deep sense of vulnerability that drives them to seek desperately for security, to the extent of subordinating other national aspirations and priorities to that search.

The purpose of this Paper is twofold: first, to show that trade and technology issues can often give rise to sensitive questions of security; and second, to argue that prudent and balanced management of trade, technology and security is increasingly necessary in this region, which is so full of energy and dynamism yet marred by a significant degree of uncertainty and unpredictability. The rest of the Paper will deal with some of these issues under the following headings: protectionism in manufacturing sectors; the decline in the prices of primary commodities; the pressure towards liberalization; the increasing costliness of technological innovation; and security-inspired technological protectionism. The primary concern is with Japan and to a lesser extent, the two Pacific Newly Industrializing Countries (NIC), South Korea and Taiwan, but also with China, the ASEAN countries and Australasia whenever it seems appropriate. This focus is justified because these three countries constitute a core component of the Western security system in East Asia and because they are the most dynamic countries in the region in terms of trade and technology.

Protectionism in manufacturing sectors

East Asia has its own rather heavy form of protectionism. A latecomer to industrialization normally has a wide array of regulations and protectionist policies designed to encourage indigenous industrialization. In order to obtain foreign currency reserves for the import of capital goods and technologies, agriculture (rice production) was heavily taxed in earlier periods,[3] but agriculture, especially rice and silk (which was one of the main primary export commodities) lost its competitive position as industrialization proceeded. This fact, together with high population density and poor natural resource endowment, has encouraged export-led industrialization that uses other markets of the world to the fullest extent to promote its own industrialization.

In those manufacturing sectors where the East Asian late-comers enjoy a competitive position – such as textiles, steel, chemicals and certain electronic products – they are very aggressive in penetrating the markets of less competitive countries. In those sectors where the late-comers do not have a competitive edge, including electronics, telecommunications, software and weapons, they try assiduously to protect their domestic market first. East Asia has enjoyed access to the huge US market for its exports for many years, but the US has been showing a steady decline in competitiveness in certain manufacturing sectors such as steel, chemicals, automobiles, textiles, machinery, and electric and electronic appliances. Protectionist measures are taken intermittently to provide emergency relief and time for adjustment. In 1984 US imports covered by special protection had a value of $US 68 billion, or 21% of total imports.[4] What matters is that many of the goods and services covered by US special protection are from East Asia. In more than half of the 31 cases examined in the volume by Hufbauer *et al.* on the topic, the suppliers affected by special protection were primarily East Asian. Such cases were textiles and apparel (three cases), specialty steels, ball bearings, colour television receivers, CB (citizens' band) radios, bolts, nuts and large iron and steel screws, automobiles (three cases), heavyweight motorcycles, ceramic articles, book manufacturing, rubber footware and canned tuna.

The intensification of trade disputes between East Asia and the US is not always politically explosive, let alone security-related. In most cases, it simply means that East Asia has become much more competitive in certain sectors while the US has become less so. However, it has longer-term security implications that cannot easily be dismissed. Since East Asia is dependent on trade flows to an unusual degree, what may be taken as 'improper' handling of East Asian countries by the US can provoke nationalistic reactions from them. It is reasonable to conclude that the recent flare-ups of Korean anti-Americanism took place against this background.[5] Though primarily directed against the South Korean government, the radical actions of students and workers seem increasingly to take on an anti-American character as well. Occupying US banks and cultural centres in Korea and committing suicide by self-immolation as a protest to the US and Korean governments are manifestations of the intensely political emotions of the Korean radicals. Nevertheless, the radicals aside, many Koreans seem to believe at the bottom of their hearts that South Korea, a front-line state which is shouldering heavy military burdens for the United States and the West in general, should be more or less exempt from US pressure over the regulation of exports of textiles and apparel, which is but a trifle compared with national security. This perception of the relationship that stresses its 'give-and-take' character could change the nature of alliance, with the erosion of what Koreans seem to believe is the 'take' side, namely the belief that the US should take a lenient and generous position on Korea's management of its economy and trade.

The US way of dealing with trade issues certainly seems to irritate some Koreans. On the one hand, the US encourages East Asians, as well as others, to become fully-fledged members of the free trade system, and requests (or even pushes) Korea to liberalize trade, to deregulate financial institutions and to raise the value of the won against the dollar so that Korea's trade surplus with the US will decrease. Yet this same US virtually imposes on Korea – at least Koreans seem to feel that way – its protectionist measures in textiles and other products without the courtesy of 'proper' consultations with the governments of countries known for the value which they place on face-saving measures and rituals.[6] Similar considerations apply to other East Asian countries but South Korea represents the most acute case, the one where trade and security are linked most closely, if not quite directly. Since trade is a linchpin for the survival and prosperity of the East Asian countries, it can be argued that the aggravation of trade disputes, left to themselves, could encourage these countries to reconsider their security arrangements seriously over the longer term.[7] This is a important point that should be stressed because the economic, technological and military capabilities of these countries are steadily increasing.

From the other side of the Pacific, what Americans see as the intransigence of these countries tends to reduce the willingness of the US to be ready to intervene effectively for their defence. Though public opinion about such willingness has been more or less stable for some years,[8] it is hardly necessary to state that in the longer term American public sentiment can be very volatile about its Asia policy. In other words, trade disputes have the potential to weaken the security ties across the Pacific substantially if they are not properly handled.

Decline of primary commodity prices
A recent study shows that throughout the world the amount of primary product required for a given unit of economic output has been shrinking by 1.25% a year since 1900.[9] Since the production of primary commodities has been increasing very rapidly as a result of the heavy use of chemical fertilisers, extensive mechanization and other advances in agriculture and mining, prices have been basically on the decline over a long period. In the mid-1980s, the prices of raw materials recorded their lowest levels since World War II in relation to the prices of manufactured goods and services, and according to

Peter Drucker this trend is not likely to be arrested for some time to come.[10] If that is the case, it is a grave matter for commodity-exporting countries. Half the exports of the Philippines, for example, are primary commodities.[11] It is thus no wonder that the Philippines, so heavily dependent on primary commodities for foreign exchange, has registered large current-account deficits, a problem further compounded by the borrowings from abroad for its industrialization efforts and the very high interest rates ruling during the first half of the 1980s in the US and other countries. Needless to say, there are many more factors in the economic stagnation of the Philippines than the collapse of commodity prices, but there is no doubt that this is one of the main causes. As in the Korean case, the decline in the prices of raw materials is not directly related to security, but exports of raw materials do carry great weight in the Philippine economy and provide a large amount of government revenue which can be used for achieving stability and fostering a sense of national purpose. Economic stagnation and political instability are almost inevitable when industrialization programmes do not progress faster and export earnings decline because of the collapse of primary commodities prices. Insurgency and instability obviously matter anyway, but the threat they pose to the two large and well-equipped US military bases in the Philippines concerns the security of the West in general.[12]

The decline of primary commodities trade affects not only the Philippines but also other resource-rich countries of the Asian-Pacific region, such as Malaysia, Indonesia, Australia and New Zealand. The general dissatisfaction of those countries with large industrial economies such as the EC, Japan and the US is clearly on the increase.[13] First, the industrial economies generally have a very high level of agricultural protection, which effectively prevents exporters of primary commodities from penetrating their markets. Among the East Asian countries, Japan, Korea and Taiwan have the tightest protection of rice prices in the world.[14] Second, a large proportion of agricultural trade now takes place among the industrial countries of the North rather than between them and the commodity-exporting countries of the South. The commodity-exporting countries are harmed by bilateral and multilateral agricultural deals largely engineered by the industrial countries of the North, whether between the US and the EC or between the US and Japan. For example, the bilateral deal for beef between the US and Japan has placed Australia at a disadvantage since lower-priced Australian beef could penetrate the Japanese market much more effectively, if that bilateral regulatory agreement did not exist.[15].

The prospect that the focus of the new round of GATT talks will include agriculture along with services, high technology and intellectual property does not excite most commodity-exporting countries, which were disappointed by the outcome of the Tokyo Round in agriculture.[16] There is general dissatisfaction on the part of raw material exporters with the closed European and Japanese agricultural markets, and with what seems to them to be the US attack on bilateral deals, using the US security leverage, which leaves them in an ever-worsening situation.[17] This widespread dissatisfaction is a powerful argument for devising a mechanism to ease the difficulties of commodity exporters in the region in the enlightened interest of the West.

Pressure towards liberalization
The Western Pacific has become one of the most dynamic regions in the world, and is increasingly linked with the no less dynamic North American region in terms of trade, technology and finance flows.[18] It is no wonder that many people in the Pacific region have come to think that they would derive much benefit from the demolition of the large barriers across borders to trade, technology transfer and finance. Since the US is the most powerful country in the region, its somewhat ambivalent strategy there merits special attention. The US needs access to an increasingly large and dynamic market in the Western Pacific, especially in those fields where the US performs excellently but the regional states may not be so competitive – namely, agriculture, services and high technology. In turn, the regional countries need access to the US market (and that of Japan) for their exports of manufactured products.

Against this background, the US has been following two tracks: multilateralism and bilateralism. The former is exhibited largely through the GATT trade talks and seeks the application of non-discriminatory free-trade principles, whereas the latter is manifested in bilateral negotiations towards free trade. What bothers some people in the Western Pacific is the tendency of the US to deal bilaterally with those regional countries where it can wield special influence in order to obtain concessions because of the security it provides.[19] Since liberalization is spearheaded by the US, a country which was once hegemonic but now somewhat resigned to being *primus inter pares*, though reasserting itself through reshaping international rules,[20] countries that feel pushed into liberalization often manifest various forms of nationalistic reaction. The problem is real for those late-comers who have long adhered to traditions – norms, rules and institutions – different from those of the early starters in Western Europe and North America. Japan and the Pacific NIC are such late-comers, broadly conceived. The question is whether these differences are manageable and how far the countries concerned can construct common rules.

One powerful argument for the necessity and desirability of such arrangements when there is severe conflict of interest has been put forward by Robert Keohane in a more general setting. He postulates that the US hegemony is over, and that co-ordination and co-operation with other states have become much more important than before in the maintenance of international rules and institutions for the provision of what are called 'international public goods' or the international arrangements for peace and prosperity.[21] Keohane's specific prescription is a 'tit-for-tat' strategy to induce co-operation in a situation resembling the prisoner's dilemma. That is to say, when two actors do not co-operate they produce the worst collective outcome, but the outcome is still the second best for a defector – but the worst for a co-operator – unless both co-operate, when they produce the best outcome. In order not to have the worst collective outcome in repeated rounds of the game, Keohane, following Robert Axelrod,[22] suggests that non-co-operation should be punished but co-operation be rewarded. This strategy is presented as that of a *primus inter pares* after hegemony; the US is still the greatest power, the one which takes the initiatives in an effort to exert its influence in reshaping international institutions towards common goals. Whether the 'tit-for-tat' strategy is productive, especially in relation to the nature of strategy and the domestic foundations that can sustain the strategy of (presumably rational) state managers, must be empirically examined.

In the setting of trans-Pacific frictions, what is often observed, at least from the viewpoint of the Pacific NIC and Japan, is that the US frequently resorts to request-cum-pressure, making full use of its security relationship with allies and partners in order to obtain further concessions from them in the forms of trade liberalization and financial deregulation.[23] Its strategy differs from one country to another: the most interesting case is perhaps that of South Korea where the US has accumulated large trade deficits and is now pressing for further and faster liberalization. A slightly different example is Taiwan, which has accumulated a large surplus with the US but has no security tie with it in the form of a security alliance. The US keeps pressing Taiwan for further trade liberalization, but in a somewhat milder fashion than with South Korea, although Taiwan does value the supply of weapons by Washington.

Of the three countries concerned, it is on Japan that the US perhaps exerts the strongest pressure for further trade liberalization. This seems to be based on the (largely justifiable) view that Japan should play a far larger role than it does at present in reshaping international rules and bearing the burdens of international management in co-operation with the US and other major countries.[24] Especially alarming to Japan's trade partners is its large current account surplus with them, including the US, the Pacific NIC and the members of ASEAN. For these countries, Japan represents the biggest problem among their trade issues. Their demands are basically threefold. First, that access to the Japanese market must be significantly increased. For that to happen, the various forms of regulation and protection applied by Japan in such matters as standards, distribution, employment and subsidies must be drastically reduced. Second, that the Japanese economy must be reframed to encourage much higher levels of consumption; this should include tax reforms and moderation of the over-dominant bureaucracy. Third, that Japan should be more generous in its international contributions in such matters as security and technology transfer. Though Japan is participating more widely in what is sometimes called 'the provision of international public goods', (for example, Official Development Assistance (ODA) and contributions to international organizations), it is a little harder to do this in the fields of security and technology. First, the pacifist-isolationist impulse has been a strong disincentive to wider government involvement in international security arrangements: military technological co-operation is restricted to Japan's ally, the United States. Second, being a more advanced late-comer, Japan has until recently been much more hesitant and less generous than the US about transferring technology to developing countries.

What bothers many Japanese is how the request-cum-pressure from the Americans is exerted. It is clear that many of the US demands are neither concerted nor co-ordinated within the United States. Rather, they are simply a manifestation of the pluralistic demands of the American political process. But from the Japanese viewpoint the US demands often give the impression that the US wants to transform Japan by twisting its arm. Since history has made it quite clear that Japan is more than capable of adapting to a new politico-economic environment, it is perhaps unnecessary to stress that its flexibility would largely cancel out any potentially destabilizing effects of such pressures on the local economy. The point here, however, is the impact over the longer term of these interactions of pressure and response, demand and acquiescence, as reported in the Japanese press, on the psychological attitude of the Japanese.[25] Confronted with the always irresistible forces of what the Japanese call 'internationalization', many of them seem to be reverting to the values of traditional morality, the work ethic and nationalism,[26] which may cause them to react unexpectedly to the three basic demands from abroad listed above.

What is more likely to become a perennial problem as Japan moves up the ladder of nations in economic, technological and military capabilities is that two opposing forces will emerge in Japanese society: internationalism and isolationism. The higher the perceived short-term costs of co-operating and co-ordinating policies with the rest of the world, the more powerful the impulse to 'go it alone'. Depending on this balance, the directions that Japan might take could vary significantly. This is why political upheavals, small or large, in countries adjoining the US are watched carefully in Japan. For instance, the US demand that Mexico scrap its nationalized industries, which form a linchpin of Mexico's ruling party, led to the resignation of its Finance Minister. In Canada, the Prime Minister's party has difficulty in pushing the 'go along with the US' policy in trade too far and too fast. South Korea's problems have already been discussed. For obvious reasons, these are developments that Japan cannot afford to overlook.

The increasing costliness of technological innovation
Technological innovation is always expensive for a forerunner. The costliness and uncertainties of technological advancement, coupled with the pervasiveness of technology in modern life, have made technology policy an area of very high priority for any government.[27] Furthermore, the fact that the US has been widely acknowledged as a leader in many high-technology areas places the rest of the world in the difficult position of looking up to and following the US, while at the same time exploring areas where it can achieve something itself, albeit with high costs and uncertainties.

Japan has become more keenly aware of this difficulty as it has reached technological frontiers in a number of areas. The percentage of total revenue spent on research and development (R&D) has risen steadily in many Japanese firms. The problem is that the US, which used to be very generous to followers like Japan in disseminating technological information, has become much less so because it realizes that it is being overtaken by some of these followers. Especially in the high-technology areas, the US seems determined to retain its superiority.[28] Two main arguments seem to be salient in US demands on Japan.[29] One concerns reciprocity; the other security. The reciprocity argument is that, despite recent Japanese technological achievements, Japan is niggardly about disseminating its own technological information to other countries, and that without reciprocity the US should deny Japan liberal access to American technology. The security argument is that Japan and some other countries are somewhat lax about making available some of the security-sensitive technologies to socialist countries, and so these technologies should not be given to Japan. The US also seems to feel that Japan is not as forthcoming as it would like in making Japanese technological information available to the US; thus the US Congress has recently passed a law intended to facilitate the translation of Japanese technological information into English.[30] There is a strong feeling in the US that, if the US is denied access to Japanese technological information, American universities and research institutions can legitimately stop the provision of such information to Japan. The reciprocity argument, of course, is often camouflaged by the security argument. In particular, the Act of 1985, which regulates exports of high-technology products and licences even to members of CoCom, effectively prohibits the dissemination of technologies even when they have been developed in US universities and research institutions under commissions from Japanese firms. The Act has recently been further revised to tighten the regulation, on the grounds that the Soviet Union obtains technological information from some Western countries.

The counter-argument (the liberal one) – that too much regulation of the dissemination of technological information will reduce the pace of US technological advance – is no less strong. The US government's regulation notwithstanding, US universities and research institutions have become increasingly dependent on collaboration with Japanese firms in financing research projects, as the US Federal Budget has become very tight. Against this practice not only security considerations but also concerns about competition are put forward; that is, that US-Japanese research collaboration facilitates the transfer of new technologies into manufacturing for Japanese firms, thus damaging US firms.

Japan's most likely course is to develop its two-track policy. One branch of this is to depart from the system of dependence on US research for technological information and to expand its niches on the technological frontiers autonomously, as far as it can; the other is to strengthen the Japan-US collaborative research system. Japan's choices in this respect will significantly affect the course it will take in terms of reframing its economy and restructuring its national security policy, and this is likely to be of great interest to the Western security system.

Security-inspired technological protectionism
The United States has intermittently manifested its strong protectionist impulse as many of its manufacturing sectors have become decreasingly competitive with Japan and some other countries. Pressure from these countries is such that as many as 200 protectionist bills have been tabled before Congress. In order to adhere to the overall principle of free trade, the President often accommodates some of the protectionist spirit in order to thwart protectionism. He vetoes outright protectionist bills while partially accommodating protectionist sentiments.[31]

One prominent example is the application of clause 232 of the Trade Enhancement Act, which purports to protect domestic industries for reasons of national security. Regulation of technology flows has become less effective since specialists have learned how to convert civil-use technology to military use without much difficulty. Given the inevitable diffusion of technology, the battle to move faster up the ladder of technological innovation is now fought much more fiercely. As domestic protectionist pressure mounts, its application has tended to widen. As far as Japan is concerned, the following five cases provide good illustrations:[32]

1) In February 1983 Kyoto Ceramics Inc. sold its subsidiary Dexel Inc. to Gould Inc. after it was advised to do so for security reasons;

2) In March 1983 President Reagan demanded voluntary export restraints on Japanese manufacturers of machinery until November 1986, when he was to make a decision on the application of clause 232 of the Trade Enhancement Act;

3) Mitsubishi Chemicals Inc. sold Optical Information Systems (a manufacturer of semi-conductors and laser instruments) to McDonnell Douglas Inc. at the request of the US Department of Defense (DOD) in December 1983;

4) Sumitomo Metallurgical Engineering, when purchasing Chase, Burns Inc., had to return the company's military division to Allegheny International at the 'request' of the Department of Defense in December 1983;

5) In September 1984 the Defense Department expressed concern about the purchase by Minnebear Inc. of New Hampshire Ballbearing Inc. and the matter is still in dispute.

There are four arguments relating to security-inspired technological protectionism. The first concerns security. In order to protect security-sensitive information, the argument runs, it is necessary to prevent firms that manufacture security-sensitive products from merging with, or being purchased by, foreign-based firms. If such mergers or purchases were allowed, security-sensitive products and technologies might be transferred to hostile foreign powers. This is actually the spirit of clause 232. The second concerns competition. In the US political system it is difficult to mobilize support without waving the banner of national security. Thus, even when it is simply a matter of reducing industrial and business competition, the national security argument can be used to justify prohibiting foreign firms from purchasing the manufacturers of security-sensitive products. The third is the technology argument. This claims that, even if dissemination of technological information and exports of sensitive products are forbidden, technology is bound to diffuse over the longer term because absolute geographical and communicational isolation does not exist. Even if isolation were possible, someone somewhere would probably come up with an idea leading to a technological break-through. In such a scenario, regulation might not matter too much either way. On balance, therefore, the negative effects of regulation on research achievements perhaps outweigh the positive ones in the longer run. The fourth argument is the liberal one, which goes as follows: under conditions where flows of trade and, by extension, flows of research communications are restricted, the global level of research advancement is likely to fall. Any hindrance to the freedom of research and communication is likely to produce goods that are less than satisfactory, and thus many countries will suffer from protectionism or autarchy in the longer run.

In the United States it is the first two arguments which have been strongly voiced recently, yet the technological imperatives also seem to be pushing in the direction of further collaboration with Japan. Japan therefore pursues, as noted earlier, a two-track policy: the autonomous development of technology side-by-side with close co-operative advancement with the US.

The decision about whether and how to participate in the US SDI research programme illustrates Japan's difficulties.[33] First, the Japanese government has had to take into account Japan's strongly pacifist bent, and the consequent legal and administrative commitments which constrain Japan's military and technological interaction with other countries. The first step towards participation in the programme through a governmental agreement has already been taken; in line with the Japan-US Mutual Defense Assistance Agreement of 1954, the November 1983 Weapons Technology Exchange of Notes on the Provision of Weapons Technology to the US and the December 1985 Exchange of Notes on Details of Implementation of the November 1983 Exchange of Notes were concluded. The Japanese government has disarmed criticism by using the 1954 Agreement with the US, and the two Exchanges-of-Notes have been concluded to adapt the Agreement to this particular case. Furthermore, the 1954 Agreement makes it easy to handle the implementation of the US demand for secrecy on certain matters, since it contains the appropriate clauses. Not surprisingly, it was only after the ruling Liberal Democratic Party's (LDP) resounding electoral victory on 6 July 1986 that the government announced (on 9 September 1986) its decision to participate in the programme through a formal agreement.[34]

Besides the problem of internal politics, the issue of technological costs and benefits must be considered. Many Japanese firms seem eager to be exposed to, and to benefit from, participation in parts of the SDI research programme, and the trend towards US-Japanese collaboration appears to be further enhanced by Japan's willingness to participate. It is true that there is some apprehension over how to use the resulting technology products, but many firms seem to have calculated that the benefits will be greater than the costs in the longer term. The SDI programme is seen – at least in the longer run – as opening up technological frontiers in many areas which will provide immense opportunities for Japanese industry. Government negotiations are under way about the problem of how to use the resulting technology products. It is yet to be seen, however, how successful the Japanese government will be in not accepting the formula contained in the agreement between the US and West Germany, in which Germany's use of the products is severely circumscribed.

The security issue is seen basically in terms of Japanese co-operation with and contribution to the US-led security of the West. It is true that the Japanese government is no less concerned with the US-Soviet military balance, with the potential instability brought about by enhanced competition in ballistic missile defence (BMD) between the two super-powers, and with the effects that SDI may have on the numbers of ballistic missiles now deployed. But the view seems to be widely held in Japan that the SDI programme will not create any immediate, tangible changes in the defence postures of the two super-powers or in the military balance. It is ironic that this view, coupled with the government's low-key and cautious attitude to the issue, has stifled any deepening of the discussion on Japan's participation in SDI research. The impact of BMD on Japanese security therefore, has been neither directly addressed nor widely discussed.

Four concerns seem to be common to America's allies. First, that US–Soviet competition over ballistic-missile offence and defence should not be allowed to increase military instability or the likelihood of a world war. Second, that US–Soviet competition should not work in the direction of subordinating considerations of national security to global security solely as perceived by the US government. Third, that US–Soviet competition should not exclude US allies from the benefits of technological diffusion and spill-over. Fourth, that US–Soviet competition should not be allowed to reduce the overall security of the West – including Japan. It seems that Japan and other East Asian countries are apprehensive about the general trend towards steady militarization in the region, but that most of them have not articulated their thoughts on BMD and the offensive stance that it may imply insofar as this affects their own security policies. China may be an exception to this observation. Being a nuclear power, China seems to be the most articulate about the SDI programme and its probable consequences for its own security.[35] Not unnaturally, China is alarmed by the prospect of Soviet BMD.

On the more immediate issue of balanced cuts in the Intermediate-range Nuclear Forces (INF) deployed in Europe and Asia by the US and the Soviet Union, both China and Japan are concerned that the US might not push the issue strongly enough with the Soviet Union, despite 'domestic political pressure, Soviet intransigence, and European insistence'.[36] Any US failure in this respect is likely to lead China to reconsider its strategy of using the US as a counterweight to the Soviet Union. It is also likely to affect the embryonic large-scale defence co-operation between the US and Japan. Japan has all along been less worried about Soviet INF than China, if only because of the belief that they are primarily targeted against China. Yet, if Japan becomes closely identified with US strategy, especially with its forward defence strategy, and if China distances itself further from the US, the Soviet Union might re-target some of its Asian INF from China to Japan. However, the new Soviet willingness to partake of what may be called Pacific economic dynamism with other Pacific countries, manifested in the Gorbachev speech at Vladivostok on 28 July 1986, might have some moderating effect on its policy towards Japan as well as China. South Korean developments should also be watched carefully in this regard. A recent publication of the 'Minutes of the Closed Hearings of a Subcommittee of the US House of Representatives' has shown that the US Air Force is planning to modernize nuclear munition stores in 26 US bases world-wide – including the US base at Kunsan, South Korea. This has brought a (somewhat disingenuous) statement from the South Korean government that it had not been informed of the plan. If it were implemented, it is perhaps possible that South Korea might reconsider its security policy.[37]

With respect to conventional weapons, the pacifist commitment of the Japanese government constrains the development of certain kinds of weapons. 'Offensive' weapons are not manufactured or imported and weapons manufactured by Japan cannot be exported. The government has even tended to discourage Japanese development of weapons. Thus half of the weapons of the Japanese Self-Defense Forces (SDF) are made in or licensed by the US. Yet the impulse towards autonomy in the production of weapons has not been negligible, especially in the production of fighter aircraft. Although the SDF at present has only one kind of indigenously-manufactured fighter, the F-1, the history of the development of the next ground-attack fighter, the FSX, is a manifestation of this impulse.[38] The final decision on the FSX appears to be that neither *Tornado* (built by three European countries), nor the F-18 (McDonnell Douglas), nor the F-16 (General Dynamics) satisfies the SDF. The three requirements the SDF sets for the FSX are that: *1)* a support fighter should have some air defence capability as well as a capability against ground and maritime targets; *2)* it should have two engines – for safety reasons; and *3)* it should have a radius of action of 450 nautical miles (nm) when loaded with four air-to-sea missiles. Needless to say, two unstated criteria, national pride and the desire to develop indigenous technology, seem to be of the utmost importance in the decision. Not surprisingly therefore, one hundred FSX fighter aircraft are to be manufactured by Mitsubishi Heavy Industries and other Japanese firms, with the participation of US engine manufacturers. The Japanese two-track policy on technology is evident here also.

Conclusion
Trade, technology and security are linked in the Pacific region, more so than some would like to think. They will remain linked because of East Asia's perennial sense of vulnerability and economic anxiety. Only if export-led growth, economies increasingly oriented towards high technology, and the restless search for security can be politically reconciled will the region remain stable. It is not clear that they can be reconciled satisfactorily for all parties because, as noted here, the elements of conflict undoubtedly exist and seem likely to remain unresolved. The problem is how to channel the region's undoubted energy in creative directions for the 'general good' of international security.

It could be argued that the East Asian countries, and more broadly the Western Pacific countries, have basically set the direction of their economic development, and that what remains for them is simply to achieve political maturity and the consolidation of democratic politics.[39] It is true that political issues have come to loom large in

East Asia, but it would be a mistake to think that the countries in the region have solved their economic problems for all time. Clearly they have not. Prudence and moderation are now needed more than ever, by all the actors across the Pacific, in dealing with these intricate issues.

I have benefited from helpful comments by Peter Drysdale and Nobuyasu Abe on an earlier draft of this Paper. Ellen Frost, Bernard Gordon, Lincoln Gordon, Ernest Guerri, François Heisbourg, Kenneth Hunt, Michael Intriligator, David Kelly, Joseph Nye, Yoshio Okawara, Robert O'Neill, Peter Polomka, James Richardson, William Schneider, John Wilkinson, Charles Wolf Jr, and many others made useful comments towards revision. Janet Healey has helped me to refine the manuscript. However, the responsibility for the views expressed is solely my own. The Paper was completed when I was a senior research fellow of the Australian-Japan Research Centre, Australian National University, July-September 1986.

Notes

[1] *Nihon Keizai Shimbun,* 4 July 1986, 1 and 2 August 1986, *Far Eastern Economic Review,* 17 July 1986, p. 52; *The Economist,* 15-18 July 1986, pp. 53-4. See also special issues on high technology and high-technology trade, respectively, in *The Economist,* 23-29 August 1986, special pages 1-20 and Issues in *Science and Technology.* vol. 2, no. 3 (Spring 1986), pp. 41-80.

[2] Winston William, 'Japanese Investment: A New Worry', *New York Times,* 6 May 1984, p. F1; *Electronic News,* 18 March 1986, p. 1, cited in Ellen L. Frost, *For Richer, For Poorer: Managing Money, Technology and People in US-Japanese Relations,* pre-publication manuscript for the Council on Foreign Relations, summer 1986. I am grateful to Ellen Frost for making this available.

[3] Kym Anderson and Yujiro Hayami, *The Political Economy of Agricultural Protection: East Asia in an International Perspective,* (Sydney: Allen & Unwin, 1986).

[4] Gary Clyde Hufbauer et al, *Trade Practice in the United States: 31 Case Studies,* (Washington, DC: Institute for International Economics, 1986), p. 21. On US competitiveness, see Robert Z. Lawrence, *Can America Compete?* (Washington, DC: The Brookings Institution, 1984).

[5] *Far Eastern Economic Review,* 10 July 1986, pp. 36-41: *Asahi Shimbun,* 11 June 1986.

[6] For 'Confucian propriety', see, for example, Lucian W. Pye, *Asian Power and Politics,* (Cambridge, MA.: Harvard University Press, 1985). In this connection, one telling event took place recently in Korea: shortly before the US Secretary of State visited Korea to meet the Korean Foreign Minister in early May 1986, the US Special Security Team brought sniffer dogs into the building in an attempt to detect explosives in the Foreign Minister's office and the VIP lift without the sufficient prior understanding of the Korean government. *Chungan Ilbo,* May 1986, cited in *Yomiuri Shimbun,* 31 May 1986.

[7] A similar view is found in Peter Polomka, *The Two Koreas: Catalyst for Conflict in East Asia?* Adelphi Paper 208, (London: IISS, 1986), p. 37.

[8] William Watts, *The United States and Japan: A Troubled Partnership,* (Cambridge, MA: Ballinger, 1984); *The United States and Asia: Changing Attitudes and Politics,* (Cambridge, MA: Lexington Books 1982).

[9] David Sapsford, *Real Primary Commodities Prices: An Analysis of Long-Run Movements,* IMF Internal Memorandum, 17 May 1986, cited in Peter Drucker, 'The Changed World

Economy', *Foreign Affairs*, vol. 64, no. 4 (Spring 1986), pp. 768-91

[10] *Ibid.*; World Bank, *World Development Report 1986*, Washington, DC: World Bank, 1986.

[11] World Bank, *World Bank Report 1986*, Washington, D.C.: World Bank, 1986.

[12] Research Institute for Peace and Security, *Asian Security 1985*, (Tokyo: RIPS, 1985).

[13] Peter Drysdale, 'Japan's US-Dependence Syndrome as seen from Australia', *Economics Today* (in Japanese), No. 1 (Spring 1986), pp. 96-103; and Drucker, (*op. cit.* in note 9).

[14] Anderson and Hayami, (*op. cit.* in note 3).

[15] Aurelia George, *The Politics of Australia–Japan Beef Trade: Current Issues*, Paper presented to the Australia, Asia and Agricultural Trade Issues Conference, Sydney, 18 June 1986.

[16] Gary Clyde Hufbauer and Jeffrey Schott, *Trading for Growth: The Next Round of Trade Negotiations*, (Cambridge, MA.: MIT Press for Institute for International Economics, 1985), pp. 47-53; Drysdale, (*op. cit.* in note 13).

[17] 'Farm Trade: Seeds of War', *Far Eastern Economic Review*, 11 September 1986, pp. 138-63.

[18] Hugh Patrick, 'The Burgeoning American Stake in the Pacific Region', in James W. Morley, (ed.), *The Pacific Basin: New Challenges for the United States* (New York: Academy of Political Science, 1986), pp. 59-75.

[19] See, for example, Drysdale, (*op. cit.* in note 13) although he does not include any discussion of security issues.

[20] Robert Keohane, *After Hegemony: Cooperation and Discord in the World Political Economy*, (Princeton, NJ: Princeton University Press, 1984). See also Robert O. Keohane and Joseph S. Nye, Jr., 'Two Cheers for Multilateralism,' *Foreign Policy*, No. 60 (Fall 1985), pp. 148-67; Andrew Mack, 'The Political Economy of Global Decline: America in the 1980s', *Australian Outlook*, vol. 40, no. 1 (April 1986), pp. 11-20; and Fred Halliday, *The Making of the New Cold War* (London: Verso, 1983).

[21] Keohane, (*op. cit.* in note 20).

[22] Robert Axelrod, *The Evolution of Cooperation* (New York: Basic Books, 1981). For a fuller examination of Axelrod's theory, see Christopher J. Makins, 'The Super-power's Dilemma: Negotiating in the Nuclear Age' in *Survival* July/August 1985, pp. 169-78.

[23] This question is addressed briefly in my *Perspectives toward the Twentieth-First Century with Special Reference to the Western Pacific*, Paper presented at the Annual Meeting of the International Studies Association, Anaheim, California, 26-9 March 1986.

[24] This and other related issues are more fully discussed in my 'Japan's Images and Options: Not a Challenger, But a Supporter', *Journal of Japanese Studies*, vol. 12, no. 1 (1986), pp. 95-119 and 'Conclusion: Japan Looking Ahead with Caution', in Takashi Inoguchi and Daniel Okimoto, (eds), *The Changing International Context*, vol. 2 of *The Political Economy of Japan*, Yasusuke Murakami and Hugh T. Patrick, (general eds.), (Stanford: Stanford University Press, forthcoming). On US-Japan economic issues, see C. Fred Bergsten and William R. Cline, *The United States Japan Economic Problem*, (Cambridge, MA: MIT Press for Institute for International Economics, 1985); Stephen Cohen, *Uneasy Partnership: Competition and Conflict in US-Japan Trade Disputes*, (Baltimore MD: Johns Hopkins University Press, 1985); Kiyohiko Fukushima, 'Japan's Real Trade Policy'. *Foreign Policy*, no. 59 (Summer 1985), pp. 22-39; Bernard Gordon, 'Truth in Trading', *Foreign Policy*, no. 61 (Winter 1985-6), pp. 94-108.

[25] See Ellen L. Frost, (*op. cit.* in note 2).

[26] Takashi Inoguchi, 'The Japanese Double Election of July 6, 1986', *Electoral Studies*, (forthcoming).

[27] Anne G. Keatley, (ed.), *Technological Frontiers and Foreign Relations*, (Washington, DC: National Academy Press, 1985).

[28] See Daniel Okimoto *et al*, (eds), *Competitive Edge: The Semiconductor Industry in the US and Japan*, (Stanford: Stanford University Press, 1984); and the two special issues in *The Economist* and *Issues in Science and Technology*, cited in note 1.

[29] *Nikkei Sangyo Shimbun*, 24, 25, 26 June 1986.

[30] *Nihon Keizai Shimbun* (evening edition), 24 June 1986.
[31] 'Routing Protectionism', *The Economist*, 9–15 August 1986, pp. 15–16.
[32] *Mainichi Shimbun*, 24 May 1986.
[33] On the SDI programme and issues related to it, see Office for Technology Assessment, *Strategic Defense Initiatives*, (Princeton NJ: Princeton University Press, 1986) and works listed therein. As for Japanese thinking, see for instance, *Tokyo Shimbun* (evening edition), 13 May 1986, *Nihon Keizai Shimbun*, 18 May 1986, *Asahi Shimbun* (evening edition), 1 May 1986. See also Daniel Sneider, 'Why does Japan avoid discussing its participation in the SDI Program in terms of its own security issues?' *Asahi Journal* (in Japanese), 25 July 1986, pp. 9–13.
[34] See, *The Asian Wall Street Journal*, 10 September 1986.
[35] Banning Garrett and Bonnie Glaser, 'Chinese Perspectives on the Strategic Defense Initiatives', *Problems of Communism*, March-April 1986, pp. 28–44.
[36] Banning Garrett and Bonnie Glaser, 'Asia's Stake in Moscow's Missiles', *Far Eastern Economic Review*, 24 July 1986, pp. 42–3.
[37] *Mainichi Shimbun*, 10 July 1986.
[38] *Asahi Shimbun* (evening edition), 6 June 1986.
[39] Richard Holbrooke, 'East Asia: The Next Challenge', *Foreign Affairs*, vol. 64, no. 4 (Spring 1986), pp. 732–51.

Prospects for Security Co-operation between East Asia and the West

AMBASSADOR YOSHIO OKAWARA

Any discussion of security co-operation between East Asia and the West is bound to be more speculative than practical at the present stage of the evolution of the concept of Western security. For, given the differences between East Asian and Atlantic (North American and West European) security which this Paper tries to underline, a practical basis for such co-operation hardly exists, if, indeed, it exists at all.

The fundamental question lies in the concept of Western security itself. This has been developed by the United States through consultations primarily with its European allies, or it certainly seems so to many in East Asia, despite the fact that the US fought both of its two major post-World War II wars (Korea and Vietnam) in Asia. US allies in East Asia, let alone many non-allied nations in the region, have regarded the concept as designed primarily to serve American or Euro-American interests more than their own. Many free-world nations in East Asia, allied or non-allied, know that they benefit from the American or 'Western' strategy to deter Soviet military interference, but, rightly or wrongly, have seen United States' strategy as more preoccupied with the security of North America and Western Europe than with their own. Despite the recent American and, to a lesser extent, Western European emphasis on the need for a global approach to Western security, countries in East Asia, with the exception of Japan and possibly South Korea, distinguish themselves from the so-called 'West'. Only within the last ten years has Japan come to act explicitly as a member of the West.

Looking towards the future, however, there appears to be a greater need for security co-operation between the countries of the Atlantic Alliance and the free-world nations in East Asia. The global expansion of Soviet military capability and the increased possibility of interaction between European and Asian security already underline the need for co-operation. The prospect that more East Asian nations will become 'industrialized democracies', if not specifically Western, suggests that co-operation might add to an element of convergence rather than divergence, between the traditional West and East Asia. This Paper tries to explore ways, if there are any, to seek such security co-operation.

Similarities
There are already similarities between the security circumstances of the NATO countries and those of certain East Asian nations: first, the Soviet Union is a primary source of military threat; second, alliance with the US is the mainstay of security; third, the regional stability of strategically important areas in the Third World is increasingly important; and fourth, public opinion has a great impact on the formation of security policies.

This is applicable particularly to Japan, and to Australia and New Zealand, which are inseparable from the security of East Asia. It also applies with some qualifications to South Korea, and to a lesser extent to the Philippines. It could also apply to a degree, to some non-allied countries in East Asia, particularly those of ASEAN.

The first point, that the Soviet Union is a *primary* source of threat to both the NATO countries and those in East Asia, is one of the major reasons why the need for a global approach to security has come to be emphasized among the Western industrialized democracies in which Japan is included. Such security concerns as the Soviet Union's invasion of Afghanistan and its deployment of SS-20 intermediate-range ballistic missiles (IRBM) have made it increasingly evident in recent years that the US and its allies in both Western Europe and East Asia share common interests. Moreover, given that the Soviet military build-up in East Asia in the past ten years appears to be designed to affect the global East–West military balance as well as the regional one, it has become increasingly important for all Western nations, whether or not in East Asia, to be concerned with this.

With regard to the second point, alliance relationships with the United States, a growing American tendency to demand that its allies should bear a greater share of the burden of international security has been making the management of alliance politics a matter of common concern to US allies in both Western Europe and East Asia. Moreover, while political solidarity between the US and its allies becomes vital in coping with such questions as arms control and the transfer of high technology to the USSR, yet the problems involved in these areas are also working to awaken US allies in Western Europe and East Asia to interests which they might possibly share in their relations with the United States.

Third, the question of regional stability in the Third World has become a matter of common concern to the industrialized nations of the Atlantic Alliance and East Asia, as the growing interdependence, political and economic, between various parts of the world has become plain. The increased impact which third-world conflicts could have on global security has given this greater emphasis, the Arab-Israeli wars and the Iran-Iraq war being cases in point.

The political and economic stability of the countries in East Asia is also important to Western security. The political stability of the Philippines is vital for the functioning of the American deterrent capability in the Western Pacific, which has significant implications for the protection of Western interests in the Indian Ocean and the Gulf. It is also obvious that ASEAN is important for the West as a whole. The economic difficulties of these nations, if not properly attended to by the Western industrialized democracies would provide a welcome opportunity to the Soviet Union for political, if not military, advances into the region. Western nations should similarly be alert to the recent Soviet moves in the South Pacific.

With regard to the fourth point noted above, public opinion, it hardly needs stressing that one of the most important common tasks is to respond to public fear and anxiety about nuclear weapons and about US, let alone Soviet, nuclear strategy. Modern communications and mass media allow such public concerns to spread between nations faster and more directly than ever before.

Differences
Despite all these similarities, there are some marked differences between the security conditions of the NATO countries and those of the free-world nations in East Asia.

The first is that there is a variety of threat perceptions in East Asia, which derive from different local circumstances. The existence of China particularly distinguishes East Asian security concerns from those of the Atlantic allies. Of course, the North American and Western European nations and many in East Asia share the common interest that China should maintain its independent foreign policy, particularly in its relations with the Soviet Union. But the implications of China for the regional military balance are more direct, and therefore more complex, in East Asia than in Western Europe. It should be noted here that for many in Asia such an eventuality, for example, a direct military conflict between the Soviet Union and China that might involve other neighbouring countries, is a source of serious concern. And the enhancement of Chinese military strength, with a possibility that this might pose a regional military threat, is a subject of anxious attention, particularly for countries in South-east Asia. It needs to be underlined in this regard that the Western industrialized nations should not take for granted the present Chinese posture towards the West. China pursues its independent foreign policy not only in its relations with the USSR but also in its approach towards the West. Efforts to keep China favourably disposed to the West therefore need to be sustained.

The second difference relates to alliance relationships with the US, which vary between Western Europe and East Asia. Most of the countries in Western Europe are in NATO, while only a few in East Asia are allied with the United States. In East Asia, to maintain close co-operation with non-allied free-world nations, such as many in ASEAN, is most important for Western security. However, all the American alliance systems functioning in East Asia – except for ANZUS in its original form – are bilateral ones. Furthermore, the pattern of alliance relations is also different. The relationships between Western Europe and Canada and America are based on historical, social and cultural bonds, whereas the alliances with the US in East Asia are set against varying political, economic, cultural and historical backgrounds. This results in differing patterns of alliance politics.

Most fundamentally, military strategy differs. While NATO needs American nuclear weapons as well as American ground forces to make up for a Western European weakness in relation to the Warsaw Pact in conventional forces, the alliance systems in East Asia, except in the case of South Korea, are not faced with such an obvious conventional imbalance, at least not so far. This is largely because the Pacific Ocean is the setting for the US military presence. The function of American nuclear forces is therefore far less conspicuous in East Asia.

South Korea alone is faced with a Communist adversary across the border, as is Western Europe. The presence of US armed forces there is vitally important for the security of South Korea, backed by the essential presence of US naval and air power in the Far East and the Western Pacific. The US-Japan and US-Philippines security arrangements are important for the effective functioning of American deterrence in the region, although their importance is of course far more extensive than this.

A third marked distinction between the security of East Asia and that of the NATO countries is the vital problem of regional domestic stability. Many countries in East Asia are still at the developing stage and remain fragile politically as well as economically. They are vulnerable to interference from outside. To ensure domestic stability is thus a premise for the security of the countries in East Asia. Although many of them in recent years have made dynamic economic progress, their economic and political structures are as yet weak and they are now facing an economic slow down.

Concerning public opinion, there is little need to explain the differences of interests and preoccupations between Western European and East Asian publics, let alone the differences between US public opinion and those of its allies. To complicate matters further, the level of mutual understanding between the publics of Western Europe and East Asia remains, broadly speaking, low, despite a growing awareness among experts and professionals of the need to improve it. It is particularly worrying here that mutual recrimination between the Western European countries and Japan is rising over trade and economic issues.

The differences noted above are the major ones affecting the security of NATO and East Asia, as seen from a Japanese perspective. There are no doubt many other differences which should be taken into consideration if security co-operation between countries in NATO and in East Asia is to be sought. A conclusion that could possibly be drawn from these observations is that security co-operation between the free-world countries in the Atlantic Alliance and East Asia will not readily be forthcoming.

Japan's security policy
Japan stands unique among East Asian nations. Depending heavily upon the alliance with the US for its security, Japan's security policy has an overtone of being a member of the Western Alliance in a broader context of the word. First, Japan has been intensifying its efforts to strengthen its Self-Defense Forces (SDF), with a particular emphasis on air and naval capability. Although the operational responsibility of the SDF is strictly confined to the defence of Japanese territory and sea-lanes, strengthening the SDF's capability would help the United States allocate its resources to other areas so as to enhance the security of the region and, as a result, that of the West as a whole.

Secondly, Japan has also been intensifying its efforts to enhance the effectiveness of the Japan-US security arrangements. These efforts are in broad policy areas such as providing 120 facilities for the US forces; sharing part of the financial costs for the presence of US forces in Japan and facilitating the so-called 'home-porting' of a US aircraft carrier. The defence co-operation between the SDF and the US forces, which has been progressing rapidly in recent years, is serving the mutual interest in implementing better the security arrangements between the two countries.

As a third aspect of its security efforts, Japan conducts diplomatic activities aiming at the political and economic stability of the countries in the region. One such example is Japan's efforts to strengthen its political as well as economic support for South Korea. Japan was one of the first countries to extend support for the economic reconstruction of the Philippines. It is also the biggest donor to Thailand, which has been much troubled by the Vietnamese invasion of Kampuchea. The political and economic support of the ASEAN countries has been one of the major preoccupations of Japanese foreign policy. All these efforts are aimed at contributing to the peace and stability of East Asia. In the same vein, Japan extended financial support to Pakistan, Turkey, Egypt and Central American-Caribbean countries from the viewpoint of helping countries which are strategically important for regional stability. Japan's diplomatic efforts also include activities aiming at creating an environment which would facilitate a settlement of the Kampuchean question and the Iran-Iraq war.

Fourthly, Japan, with an increased awareness of the need to act as a member of the Western industrialized democracies, became a positive participant in the concerted Western efforts on such issues as the Soviet invasion of Afghanistan and the Poland crisis. Japan supported NATO's position on INF at the Williamsburg Summit. It is from the same viewpoint that Japan started to participate in the process of consultations within the Western Alliance over arms control.

To act in international politics as a member of what might be called, in a broader context of the word, the Western Alliance, is now an important dimension of Japan's security policy.

Security co-operation
Yet, it is unrealistic to seek direct co-operation between NATO and the Japan-US security arrangements.

A more realistic approach to co-operative relationships between the NATO countries and Japan would be by way of closer consultations over questions of mutual concern. In this respect, it is a very welcome trend that the economic summits now pay attention to political and security questions. It is also encouraging to see that the bilateral consultations on security questions between Western European countries and Japan have increased at all levels, in addition to the already close US-Japan consultations. It is desirable that those consultations should help the countries concerned to understand each other's policy and thereby help to work out mutually productive co-operation in the spirit of partnership.

There is a timely subject for such consultations: how to co-ordinate policy towards the new Soviet approach towards Asia. The Soviet Union appears to have decided to re-emphasize its interests in East Asia, and the Gorbachev speech at Vladivostok in July 1986 was no doubt a part of this. Given the prospect that Soviet initiatives aiming at increasing influence in East Asia would have significant implications for Western security in the world as a whole, it is high time for the NATO countries and Japan to seek even closer co-operation in working out Western responses to these initiatives. One important such Western response is, of course, the efforts of the US and its allies to intensify defence efforts. To co-ordinate diplomatic responses is also vital. This is particularly true for Japan, which is seemingly one of the prime targets of the new Soviet policy towards East Asia.

Because of the characteristics of East Asia described earlier, the efforts to secure the political and economic stability of the countries in the region are important to Western security. For these nations are vulnerable to Soviet political, if not military interference. The North American and the Western European countries have already been exerting efforts with regard to the strategically important regions of Africa, the Middle East, South-west Asia and Latin America, and Japan has taken part in these concerted actions. In the same spirit, it is important to add the issue of regional stability in East Asia to the common agenda for Western security.

Looking towards the future, it is important for the Western nations, including Japan, to try to expand policy co-operation in the security field to include other East Asian nations, allied or non-allied. In the light of the importance of many non-allied nations in East Asia for Western security, it is too narrow to confine such co-operation to the one framed solely by the present alliance systems.

Such an attempt would obviously involve many difficulties. Yet, a combination of efforts designed for mutual benefit could be tried with the hope of improving the conditions surrounding relations between Western and many East Asian nations. It is plausible to expect in this regard that countries in East Asia might possibly come to seek closer co-operation with the Western industrialized democracies when they see Soviet attempts to increase its influence in East Asia. The prospect that not a few countries in this region are bound to become industrialized democracies could also work to create a favourable environment for closer co-operation between Western countries and those in East Asia.

A few approaches to this end are conceivable. First, the free-world countries in North America, Western Europe and East Asia could increase bilateral as well as multilateral opportunities to discuss security questions. They could also organize more systematic exchanges of information through a network of bilateral channels. Such information should include security policies and the analysis of international security conditions, particularly the assessment of threat. This is important to facilitate policy consultations.

Secondly, joint research and studies as well as dialogues on policy issues should be further strengthened at the private level among these nations. Needless to say, non-governmental dialogues could be much freer and therefore more creative in exploring avenues for security co-operation.

Thirdly, it is advisable to establish a forum for dialogue among the members of the legislatures of the free-world countries in North America, Western Europe and East Asia on security issues. It is encouraging to see that Japanese and Australian members have been attending the sessions of the North Atlantic Assembly for the past several years.

Dialogues among the elected officials of the countries concerned are important in order to reflect varying public security perceptions of the countries involved in debates exploring mutual security co-operation. Needless to say, public support is indispensable for any such co-operation. It is particularly so because in recent years the public opinion of democratic nations is the very target at which Soviet diplomatic strategy has been aiming.

These approaches would be painstakingly slow and they would in no way assure any positive result. After all, security co-operation has proved to be a difficult task even among the Western industrialized democracies, particularly in the absence of a common security perception. To expect any immediate result from these approaches would therefore be too ambitious. But dialogues along the lines described above would at least help the countries involved to understand each others' security perceptions as well as the different security conditions in which they find themselves. This could be the first step in the direction of seeking common ground for security co-operation, if there is any, between the West and the free-world nations in East Asia.

Comment on Ambassador Okawara's Speech

PROFESSOR JOSEPH S. NYE, JR

Ambassador Okawara has given us a highly intelligent speech, as one would expect from such a distinguished Japanese diplomat. It was also a creative and innovative speech. It was a remarkable sign of how far the Japanese debate on security issues has advanced in the last decade.

Nonetheless, there are many details of Ambassador Okawara's proposal that remain to be worked out. For example, what will be the role of the developing nations in the region? What will the European role be in Asian security issues? A realist would expect multilateral co-operation in the Asian-Pacific area to remain limited. The basic reality to security in the region remains the central role of the United States, and most consultations will remain bilateral between the US and other countries in the region. While an informal multilateral process is to be welcomed, it is also important to ask what will be the substance of either bilateral or multilateral co-operation in the region.

Let me suggest how security co-operation in East Asia looks to at least one American. I shall start with the basic reality of the balance of power. The Soviet geostrategic position in the centre of the Eurasian land mass has strong effects on the balance of power in both Europe and Asia. After 1947, the United States defined its interests in terms of close relations with the industrialized peripheries adjoining the Soviet Union and which felt threatened by it. Those alliances remain central to the balance of power and to US security today. But there are important geopolitical differences between the security problems at the Asian and the European peripheries. In Europe, the military balance is a land balance along relatively clearly demarcated lines and with a fair degree of domestic stability in the countries involved. The critical problems are how to maintain a consensus on defence which allows democratically elected governments to produce the resources necessary to maintain a balance along those clearly demarcated lines.

In Asia, the balance of power is more flexible. In a sense, it is more like the nineteenth-century balance of power in Europe with a more changeable and flexible diplomacy than one finds in Europe today. This gives rise to four substantive components of an Asian-Pacific security strategy. First, it is important to remember the complexity of the balance. Not only does this mean keeping in mind that different countries feel different threats from different directions, but also that economic and military power are related in a more complex way. In a sense, East Asia is an area in which there are three military super-powers and two economic super-powers, with the United States being the only country which is included in both. I agree with Henry Kissinger that it would be foolish to press Japan into a major military role which might give rise to fears which would have a destabilizing effect on the region, and I also agree that Japan must find ways to use its economic power to play a more important indirect role in the security of the region. Both the US and Japan must think of ways to manage their economic relationship so as not to jeopardize the security relationship. That includes an awareness that protectionism in Europe and Japan may be extremely damaging to sensitive areas such as the Philippines and Korea, as well as in a direct bilateral relationship. The US must be more aware of the ways in which actions such as its sale of subsidized wheat can hurt important allies such as Australia.

A second dimension of an Asian security strategy is its heavy reliance on naval power. Earlier in this Conference, Henry Kissinger questioned why the US should hold to the view that it is unwise to have troops on the continental land mass of Asia. I am surprised that he forgot the Nixon Doctrine which he helped to author. The answer to the puzzle is that strategy must always balance interests with resources. This was the crucial flaw in America's Asian strategy in the 1960s. Interests were defined so broadly that it was impossible to maintain domestic support that would provide resources commensurate with an expansive definition of containment in Asia. It is ironic that Americans defined interests in terms of a 'domino theory' and stopping Communism on the Asian continent. Rather than dominoes, we should have thought in terms of checkers (perhaps Chinese checkers) and realized that the ancient adage 'the enemy of my enemy is my friend' could produce an internal balance within Asian Communism. What we find in East Asia today is a far more stable security situation than when the US had troops on the land mass of Asia. Naval and air power will have to remain the major American components of an East Asian security strategy.

A third dimension is to remember that there are two exceptions to this rule: Korea and the Philippines. For both historical and strategic reasons, the American position in Korea and the Philippines remains crucial. Both of these developing countries are potential sources of instability in the larger security equation, but both have seen encouraging developments in recent years. It is critical for the US and Japan to co-operate in the development of multilateral support in underwriting stabilizing economic and political change in both countries.

Finally, the fourth substantive component or dimension of an Asian-Pacific security strategy is to remember to maintain the underlying strategic balance, but also to refrain from proposals which may look attractive at first glance, but be difficult in terms of maintaining the American naval presence. In particular, I refer to the ways in which nuclear-free zones in the Pacific area might be formulated. As the author of the book *Nuclear Ethics*,[1] perhaps I can be permitted to warn against proposals that sometimes look noble in intention but might have destabilizing consequences.

In short, we should welcome Ambassador Okawara's suggestion about an informal multilateral process of security consultation in the Asian-Pacific region, but we should also remember the substance that these consultations must deal with. From an American point of view, consultations which are aimed at producing a stable security situation in East Asia must deal with each of the four dimensions I have mentioned.

Note

[1] Joseph S. Nye Jr, *Nuclear Ethics* (New York: The Free Press/London: Collier Macmillan, 1986).

Comment on Ambassador Okawara's Speech

DR JOHAN JØRGEN HOLST

Ambassador Okawara has done a very fine job in delineating some of the salient similarities and differences between the security order in the North Atlantic and Asian-Pacific areas. I have no quarrels with his analysis or general prescriptions, but I want to elaborate on a few perspectives and observations.

Viable alliances are needed in order to protect the interests of free nations in both areas. Management of alliance relations is a difficult task. It involves the management of complexity and diversity in both areas, even if those of the Asian-Pacific region exceed those of the Atlantic Community. Differences are bound to emerge in the relation between the dominant power, the United States, and its allies in either region. Such differences must be contained within a framework of common interests. They must be handled as differences among sovereign nations, not as conflicts with client states. The imperial impulse of resorting to punishment and sanctions will but sour relations and entrench the differences. Enlightened leadership – and there is no substitute for American leadership – should observe certain basic rules of management of which I want to emphasize four:

1) Do not insist on imposing uniformity and clarity on an alliance relationship where diversity and ambiguity are endemic and indeed provide a wherewithal for diplomatic flexibility;

2) Delimit and fractionate the differences rather than convert the handling of specific controversies into general examples;

3) Do not let the best outcome become the enemy of a good one;

4) Establish and adhere to recognizable priorities.

The Soviet Union constitutes the heartland power which produces the major military threat linking the security orders in Europe and Asia. The nations inhabiting the Eurasian land mass have no alternative to sharing a continent with the Soviet Union. Therefore containment and co-operation with the Soviet Union must be part of any long-term strategy for peace on the continent. The balance of power must be maintained, as must a balance of incentives designed to induce co-operative behaviour and mutual restraint in the use of military force. Mutual vulnerability constitutes a condition imposed by history and technology. Nuclear weapons forge a common destiny through the bonds of interdependence.

The lines are drawn more clearly in Europe than in Asia. The Eurasian heartland power constitutes the overriding challenge to regional security in Europe and is perceived in those terms. Although it should be kept in mind that the Greek-Turkish conflict over Cyprus and the suppressed cleavages of ethnicity in Eastern Europe are contained within the general system of East–West relations in Europe. The security order in the Asian-Pacific region, by contrast, harbours many regional conflicts beyond that of the East–West confrontation as well as several examples of internal strife and social instability.

Inevitably the interrelation of the two regions will come to the fore in connection with attempts to negotiate arms-control agreements. The regional versus the global perspective, fears of transferring pressures from one front to the other will emerge, exacerbated by the negotiating need to separate and break down issues in order to provide a basis for agreement. The SS-20 missile problem in the INF context is a case in point. Here, as well, the rules for alliance management apply. European and Asian differences may grow if, for instance, the position of certain Asian countries be perceived in Western Europe as blocking a zero-zero INF agreement in Europe or if such an agreement be viewed in Asia as having been bought at Asian expense. The need for a global perspective does not imply a need for an identical construction for each region. Orchestrating provisions for reductions, freezes and non-circumvention is the order of the negotiating day.

In the course of our Conference I have been struck by the many similarities between the security challenges in North-west Europe and North-east Asia. In both areas the Soviet navy and its operational requirements for unimpeded access to the high seas are at the core of the security problems of the littoral states. In both areas confusion about the new US maritime strategy for dealing with the challenges has given rise to anxiety and concern. To some extent this is due to the kind of exuberant oversell which often emerges in the American political culture, particularly in the context of fighting for money. In part it is due to a confusion of operational tactics with grand strategy. The maritime strategy is designed to orchestrate the naval means for forward defence of vital sea lines of communication and the exposed territories of allies. But the confusion and anxiety produced by insensitive presentation demonstrate the need to align the formulation of overall strategy with the fine web of political commitments and restraints in the regions where it is to be applied. It demonstrates as well the difficulties which arise when the major guarantor of allied security develops and presents basic strategy doctrine outside the framework of alliance.

The concerns which have been expressed at this Conference for the implications of a policy of horizontal escalation are related to the limits of interdependence, to the need to deal with challenges in their own terms and settings rather than in terms of some abstract notion of a global chess-board. It reflects the need to develop tailored strategies rather than general responses, and it reflects the profusion of misleading rhetoric which permeates so much of the public debate on strategy.

Industrial democracies face the need to devise strategies which are socially acceptable in addition to being militarily effective. The requirements of deterrence must be tempered by the need for reassurance. Sometimes difficult trade-offs have to be made, and differences are bound to arise as to how to weigh the competing considerations. In no context is this more important than with regard to nuclear-weapons policy. The unfortunate conflict which arose between New Zealand and the US over port visits and nuclear weapons provides ample illustration of the potential turbulence involved. Again we confront the need to manage diversity and ambiguity, to align the posture of the flag states of neither confirming nor denying the presence of nuclear weapons on warships with a port state posture of neither verifying nor ignoring such presence. Delicate alignments must be tailored to specific circumstances while recognizing the power of precedence.

Within a general framework of alliance solidarity, diversity rather than uniformity has been the norm in NATO with regard to the involvement and role of the Western European allies of the United States in nuclear deterrence. Norway, Denmark, Iceland, Spain and Portugal do not permit the stationing or stockpiling of nuclear weapons on their territories. Some Asian and Pacific nations, most notably Japan, observe similar self-denying ordnances. Reliance on nuclear weapons, particularly on early use, is higher and more pronounced in Western Europe than in the Asian-Pacific region.

It is at the core of some of the Asian concerns about the danger of horizontal escalation. However, the winds of change are blowing in the direction of reduced reliance on nuclear weapons in Europe. Such change would facilitate strategic co-ordination and political co-operation between Western Europe and East Asia. Their common security would stand to gain from a major reduction in the arsenals and roles of nuclear weapons in the postures of the alliances concerned.

Concluding Remarks

DR ROBERT O'NEILL

These concluding remarks are addressed to three topics: what are the key factors shaping Western and East Asian security interests, separately and jointly; what are the principal problems that should concern policy-makers and public opinion in our various countries in the coming years; and what should we do to meet them?

That we held this Conference at all is a clear recognition that the West, the old, traditional West of the Atlantic Alliance, and the East (or what before the electronic and jet era was the Far East), have security interests of growing commonality. We would not have raised the necessary money and invested effort over three years of preparations to discuss how little they have in common. We of this Institute know that nothing stays the same for long and we have all been impressed particularly (not only in the past four days) by the dynamic nature of our subject. Not everything is moving in the same direction. We have learned of divergence of security interests as well as of convergence. A Japan which relieves the United States of some of its Western Pacific burden through rearmament may receive approval in Europe but not necessarily in East Asia. But change is under way and the fact that we can all see it so clearly on the surface suggests that even greater change is taking place beneath the surface.

The factors of change
These processes of change have been sustained by five principal factors. Military force in World War II redefined the basic structure of political and military power in both the West and East Asia, yielding the familiar lines of confrontation in Europe and extending the US embrace in the Pacific to include Japan. But since 1945, with the notable exceptions of the Korean and Vietnamese conflicts, military power in the West and East Asia has served more to inhibit change in the international order than to promote it. Borders are more or less frozen. States do not disappear, devoured by others.

Social forces set loose before, during and after World War II led to the dissolution of the colonial empires in Asia and elsewhere, revolution in China, civil war in Korea, protracted upheaval and finally a revolution of a kind in Vietnam (an old, genuine revolution in the North imposing itself on a reluctant South), the Cultural Revolution in China, the new era of reform there since the fall of the Gang of Four, and democratization, first in Japan, then spreading to other states of North-east and South-east Asia, such as the Philippines and South Korea. In the West we have seen few social upheavals except the era of protest of the late 1960s, but the changes, we all know, have been steady and significant in their effect.

But let us look for a moment at the nature of this dynamic. Are we likely to see more revolutions in Asia on the grand and not so grand scale of the past forty years? I doubt it. Rather, as national societies develop they are learning to accommodate the changes induced by societal forces without shattering or collapsing. Thus, while these forces are producing different, sometimes strikingly different, changes within individual states, they appear less potent as factors producing sudden or dramatic international change.

In the case of economic factors this is obviously not so. Economic change is affecting dramatically the relative standing of states in our purview at this meeting, and the rates of change, while difficult to predict, show no sign of moderation. This is also true of the effect of technological factors. When they are aligned with appropriate economic and social factors (not to mention military), as in the case of Japan, the result is profound, so profound that it is difficult to define let alone to evaluate with precision.

The fifth factor that I wish to emphasize is change in the nature of the international system. This change has taken place in so many different ways: politically, through the working of global and regional bodies; militarily, through alliances, assistance treaties and agreed limitations on forces; economically, through trade and financial movements and agreements, multilateral and bilateral; technologically, through the communications and data-processing revolution; and structurally, through the emergence of new states and their active participation in shaping the directions of international policies. The net effect is to promote all kinds of linkages, enhancing the collective power of those whom they embrace *vis-à-vis* those who remain outside. But linkage has its negative side too, as we all know from debates about international debts and the imbalances of trade flows. While it is difficult to forecast revolutionary change in the nature of the international system, in that global anarchy will surely continue, trends towards reduction of that anarchy are under way both within and between the states of the West and East Asia.

Thus as factors promoting change, we should be most cognizant of economic and technological forces, including those of military technology, with international systemic then social and finally military factors in subordinate positions.

From what we know of the ways in which these factors operate, it is clear that there is a general convergence of security interests between the West and East Asia, but not necessarily a convergence of the ways in which these interests are served. While the Soviet Union remains largely outside the Western economic system there seems little likelihood of significant convergence of its security interests with the West. Its limited technological engagement with the West further decreases this probability.

The problems
But for the West and East Asia, the linkage between security, trade and technology is, as we know, a nest of problems. If it is correct to hold that economic and technological factors will be the most powerful promoters of international change, at least in the next generation, we face a major challenge in framing policies to utilize them without destroying the fabric of national and international security. Of course there will continue to be many other serious problems to plague those who have to shape military, social and international co-operative policies, but we know more about how to tackle them and thereby strengthen security. In the more consequential economic and technological fields, we are much more in the dark.

This problem was clearly revealed by the debates in Committee 6 (on Trade, Technology and Security). Despite greeting the topic so enthusiastically that the Committee congratulated the Institute on selecting it for examination, there was little agreement on how these three are linked and how the linkages operate. The situation was complicated further by the different levels of linkage involved: security is the province of governments while trade is more the province of non-state actors. Technology involves them both but usually not together.

It seems fair to posit a positive linkage between economic growth and security, but there is no necessary connection. Is South Korea more secure in 1986 than in 1956? It is much stronger, but its developed economy is more dependent on the highly vulnerable Seoul conurbation than earlier. Its more prosperous, better-educated population is less amenable to regimentation. Its economy and domestic politics are more sensitive to international market conditions. States of South-east Asia, such as the Philippines, Thailand and Indonesia, with a narrow range of exports but rising public expectations, are even more sensitive to world market conditions.

Yet when one looks at the more developed economies of the US, Japan and Western Europe it is clear that the linkage between economic development and security can be made overwhelmingly positive in its effect. If South Korea and the ASEAN states can move smoothly through another decade of economic and political development, they will be in a less sensitive condition. For this to happen they will need some special relief from the effects of the protectionism which more robust states may apply, principally with each other in mind.

The Committee also noted the damaging effect of protectionism on alliance cohesion. It was bad enough in the cases of relations between the stronger powers but quite severe in the more asymmetric alliances such as ANZUS and that between the US and South Korea. While the growth of anti-American feeling is difficult for the Soviet Union to exploit directly, it flows readily into motivation for declaring non-nuclear zones, banning naval port calls and closing bases. A new dimension was added to the burden-sharing debate by calls for the more protectionist states to pay more for the defence of their allies whose prospects they were damaging. The response, I might say, was a deafening silence.

The growing sensitivity of technology transfers to the requirements of security policy further complicate the security–trade–technology nexus. The security-motivated transfer restrictions applied by the United States were seen partly as commercially-oriented by allies in both Europe and the Asian-Pacific region. Technological co-operation with the SDI programme was criticized by several as likely to confer such economic benefits on the United States that it was virtually a piece of American commercial policy. This interpretation was hotly disputed by an American participant: after all, who was paying for the SDI research? But the weight of European and Pacific criticism was such as to suggest that allied co-operation in the programme would remain a highly contentious item on the agenda of public debate in the co-operating states.

If technology transfer to allies becomes increasingly restricted on security grounds, whether justified or not, economic growth in the states discriminated against will suffer, resentment will grow and prospects for wider sharing of the defence burden will be further diminished. While there is nothing new about this as far as the Atlantic debate is concerned, it is interesting to note this new form of commonality between Western Europe and the Asian-Pacific allies of the United States. Not all complaints were directed in that quarter, however: Japan was also the object of much criticism for unwillingness to share technology. The security consequences of anti-Japanese feeling abroad, however, are somewhat less than those of anti-Americanism.

The second problem is, of course, the threat posed by the Soviet Union. The consensus of both Plenary and Committee debates is that the Soviet Union is not about to make major policy changes or significant concessions on any of the principal regional issues, particularly those relating to Japan and China. Distrust of the Soviet Union has been in no wise allayed by Mr Gorbachev's Vladivostok speech. His call for an Asian security conference is seen widely as a propaganda device. The general view of Gorbachev to date is one of scepticism about his style and rejection of his overtures. He looks to be too much of a tactical exploiter of opportunities to command Western and East Asian confidence, offering the prospect of a significantly different relationship with the Soviet Union. We were reminded to view his charm offensive against the background of the continuing Soviet military build-up in Eastern Siberia in order to see what was really going on in his mind. He surely must realize that this build-up substantially undermines his diplomacy towards China and Japan, so what is he on about?

Those who debated Soviet policy agreed that economic problems severely disadvantaged the USSR in terms of being able to ride the currents which had brought so much strength to Western Europe and Japan in recent years. The differential effect of the forces of economic and technological change brought comfort to hawks and doves alike. To the former, the Soviet Union should be left isolated to stew (or not to stew) in its own juice. To the latter these are strong grounds for opposing Western crash programmes to build military strength and for seeking reduction of tensions.

Whether we are justified in taking such a dismissive view of the longer-term prospects of the Soviet economy is worth pause for thought – not a long pause perhaps, but if we are wrong in our judgment, we face some unpleasant consequences in terms of the military effort that Western and East Asian states will have to sustain for many years to come. Given that our own economic outlook is not all that bright, and that national electorates are unlikely to become less selfish, the burden-sharing debates would be endless and increasingly acrimonious. Do we not sometimes indulge in some wishful thinking about the Soviet economy? The consensus arouses suspicions.

Nonetheless, with international markets dictating harsh terms to flagging economies and likely to become more severe in the next century as competition increases, the Soviet position is increasingly a difficult one. If Gorbachev is seriously interested in improving economic strength, he is likely to direct investment priorities more to favour European USSR than Siberia. Indeed indications already show that after his recent return from Siberia, this process has been set in motion. Hence the economic importance of Siberia may wane.

Whether Soviet military strength in Siberia offers credible options for limited operations aimed at spoiling China's economic growth was the subject of debate in Committee 2b. The Kissinger-Haass thesis encountered more opposition than support: the escalation risks and costs of such operations were seen to be too great for cautious Kremlin policy-makers to accept. Just what these escalation risks might be, given the current very limited nature of Sino-American military co-operation, is far from clear. The Chinese also are sceptical about such escalation and are doing their best to ensure that they can handle a moderate Soviet incursion by themselves, but it will take time.

Thus far these factors raise common problems for the West and East Asia. The contrast between the integrated NATO capacity to resist Soviet aggression and the fragmented defence structure of East Asia and the Western Pacific suggests that the Soviet Union may see more opportunities to exploit military power, in peace as well as in war, in the east. Having been blocked in Europe and the Middle East the Soviet Union has an incentive to apply pressure and exploit divisions in and around the Pacific. A proposal to return to Japan two of the four Northern Territories could cause intense debate there, especially if it was linked with a favourable economic deal for Japan in Siberia. The USSR may make some marginal gains at the expense of the United States and its allies by exploiting anti-nuclear sentiment in Australia, New Zealand and the South Pacific generally.

The unwillingness of America's East Asian and Pacific allies to accept a 'flexible response' strategy, in which 'first use' might be made of nuclear weapons, offers another contrast between Western European and East Asian interests and policies. The difference is unlikely to disappear. Also unlikely to disappear is the Asian concern that Europe will support a zero-zero solution to the INF problem in Europe only. Thus, while the general growth of the Soviet military threat is consolidating interests between the West and East Asia, the special nature of the security problems of each area reveals substantial and continuing divergences that the USSR may be able to utilize.

There are other types of security problem for the West and East Asia to consider: regional conflicts such as Korea and Kampuchea and national instabilities, such as those of the Philippines. Security in East and South-east Asia remains sensitive to internal forces, religious, ethnic and socio-economic. Given the politically counter-productive nature of direct Western intervention in these situations, and European reluctance to accept commitments outside the NATO area, there seems to be in a negative sense another convergence of security interests between East Asia and the West. In dealing with internal problems self-help is usually not only the best but also the only remedy available.

Approaches towards solutions
The role of the United States remains central to the security of both Europe and East Asia. Growing pressures on the US budget and political reluctance to accept as much of the joint defence burden as before give both sets of allies much to think about regarding their own policies. Whether they do much of this thinking together remains to be seen, if as Committee 1a noted, Europeans try to control the agenda by imposing their own analytical framework on Asian security problems in real life, just as they did in the Committee discussions.

Perhaps the same criticism could be made of the US response to anti-nuclear sentiment in New Zealand, and in the South Pacific at large. In its firm reaction to the Lange Government's policies the Reagan Administration was thinking more of the way it would deal with a recalcitrant NATO state than responding to a very different debate in one which lies several thousands of miles away from the Soviet Union and perceives very little by way of threat. US alliance management techniques in Europe and the Pacific were criticized as lacking in sensitivity and discrimination between the differing security needs of various allies. Perhaps this demonstrates that allies should not be encouraged to compare notes on their leader, but it is too late for such thoughts. What needs to be kept in mind by all concerned is that stresses and strains in one alliance system tend to be repeated soon afterwards in another. Solutions to such problems need to be considered jointly rather than in isolation if they are not to reappear.

In both Committees concern was expressed that American doctrines for response to a crisis were tending to become destabilizing. A particular object of criticism was the maritime strategy associated with Secretary Lehman, which was perceived in some allied states in the Pacific as escalatory. Irrespective of the truth of the criticism, it has gained sufficient currency to require corrective action by the Reagan Administration.

Allied governments, for their part, have to acknowledge a need to explain alliance policies more clearly to their own people so that unwarranted criticisms are rebutted or pre-empted before they gain currency. To do this often requires allied policy-makers and their advisers to study the constraints acting on their American counterparts more closely than they do. Allied security depends, in the Pacific as in Europe, on US access and facilities. All too often throwaway criticisms expressed by US or allied participants in the debate in one region are taken seriously in another. A little more travel and contact between legislators, officials and opinion leaders of the various alliance systems would, as Ambassador Okawara suggested, greatly reduce the scope for misunderstanding and foolishness demonstrated so often by clever people who make up their minds too early on the basis of a one-sided review of the evidence. The forward structure of the United States in the Pacific, in Japan and the Philippines, together with facilities in Australia and the right to make port calls by nuclear-armed and nuclear-propelled warships, are vital to the maintenance of the existing favourable balance of power. But restraint and sensitivity on all sides will be necessary if they are to remain available.

The issue of burden-sharing between the US and Japan was taken up in Committee 1b in the form of a Japanese-sponsored Marshall Plan for the Pacific, East and South-east Asia and even the Gulf States. While a more positive Japanese approach to the issue of foreign aid in recent years was noted, a revolution in attitudes would have to occur before this notion becomes credible. Not so fantastic is the prospect of modest expansion of the Japanese programme, which would surely remove any temptation for Pacific micro-states to make deals with the Soviet Union.

The view of China's future contribution to peace and international security in Asia and the Pacific that emerged in the discussions of Committee 3 was marked by strong optimism regarding economic development and qualified optimism regarding the management of political and military disputes. In the coming decade China's policies are likely to be marked by continuity. The difficulties of economic reform at home and conflict in North and South-east Asia will set limits to what might be achieved, but progress will continue. The uncertainties that were recognized did not dim either the sense of confidence about the future or the belief in gradual progress towards economic reform in China and peace in the region.

These uncertainties flow principally from Soviet support for North Korea's military modernization, Soviet activities in South-east Asia, their threat to sea lines of communication and the difficulties in accommodating the competing results achieved by the many states of the region striving for rapid economic growth, within the constraints of current international institutions and market conditions. Concern was also expressed about the consequences of China's economic success for the smaller competing economies of the region: Taiwan, South Korea and the ASEAN states.

China's contribution to peace and security was seen in its position on the sidelines, desperately needing and seeking peace and economic relations with all countries, a China turned more inward by the requirements of economic reform and development and, paradoxically, a China contributing to peace by proposing conditions for settling conflicts in the region that few analysts expect to be met.

This Committee was remarkable, in the view of one consummate connoisseur of international conferences as 'a *truly* salient discourse on regional issues'. Participants from Taiwan, China, Japan, the United States, India and Korea sought to understand each others' policy options in a way not previously encountered. Of particular value was the access provided to Chinese views which only rarely can be explored with experts who know how these assessments are made:

– The Soviet Union is the *only* military threat to China.
– China cannot negotiate under military threat.
– The proposed Soviet withdrawals are meaningless.
– Gorbachev's Vladivostok speech had aroused some interest, but judgment was suspended pending Soviet action.
– China is confident that North Korea will not start another war and that its dependence on the Soviet Union will remain limited.
– China was generally optimistic about its own future and that of the region, including its relations with Japan.

The discussions of Committee 4 on the role of Japan and the Korean problem were to some extent schizophrenic, or at least paradoxical. For in the face of an alarming increase in the military threat to and within the region, there was only calm confidence expressed, while in the context of unparalleled prosperity there was considerable uncertainty and concern over interstate competition and even international stability. Only on the second day of discussion was the link drawn between these two paradoxes, a link that runs through Washington; if it is the US nuclear umbrella that ensures confidence in an increasingly precarious military context, it is the US trade and budget deficits that threaten to disrupt the domestic and interstate fabric of the region. Most paradoxical of all, as already stated, this link has not been the subject of extensive analysis, often leaving the Committee groping for concepts and frames of intellectual reference to integrate economic and military issues. This deficiency may arise in part from an understandable Asian concern lest a too-strict scrutiny of US intentions actually precipitate disharmony as has been the case in Europe: but just as surely it arises from a poverty of intellectual effort to unite these different areas.

In considering the military situation, attention was drawn to the increasing Soviet willingness to arm North Korea with more sophisticated hardware and to reduce restraints. This development coincides with a waning of North Korean military superiority, threatening to close in the next 5–6 years, any final opportunity for the North to unify the Peninsula by force. Tensions could be high during that period. A Japanese participant also drew attention to these same developments, noting that the Soviet force structure was no longer Eurocentric. In the case of Japan, little prospect was seen that it would or could increase defence expenditure sharply or alter its adherence to the principles of non-nuclear policy. Somehow the putative contradiction between the non-introduction of nuclear weapons and extended deterrence which bedevilled ANZUS seems likely to survive with careful management. A slow change in Japanese attitudes towards defence spending, a slight reinterpretation of legal texts – these were all that was thought possible or necessary. To some extent, this confidence arose from the fact that the threat was overstated in some quarters. The Soviet build-up was directed at the United States and China. This confidence was also a measure of the strength of the US commitment and the skilful work of Prime Minister Nakasone to enhance US-Japanese co-ordination.

In the debate on economic security issues there was little optimism. The spectre of protectionism loomed large. In assessing the results of the East Asian economic miracle which had tended to discredit the Soviet Union and induce the market revolution in China, disturbing consequences were seen, pitting the US, Korea and Japan against each other and against the under-developed world. Economic power was seen as the source of both strength and vulnerability, because the economic dynamism of Asia requires open, stable markets. But no positive steps were prescribed for resolving the dilemmas of protectionism. Despite the efforts of those who urged an integrated approach to security and economic issues, they had no analytical tools to hand to make this possible. The Committee's debate provides further emphasis that more work on such integration is badly needed.

Finally, let me offer some thoughts from Committee 5, which examined the changing nature of warfare in East Asia. It was a rich debate led by the two authors who shared the perspectives of young officers on opposing sides in the Korean War, of mid-career officers during the period of rising concern about a Sino-American confrontation arising out of changes in South-east Asia, and of general officers during the Vietnam War. Their different starting points led to strikingly similar conclusions on the importance of human factors, such as morale and popular support in a conflict, and the quality and determination of the mind behind the weapon. It could not be denied, however, that the weapon was becoming more important, and the era of mass peasant armies was over.

The spread of new military technology was seen as affecting the political utility of both standing forces and military operations. The greater destructiveness and cost of modern conflict tended to limit its occurrence. Intense conventional war was becoming less important as an instrument of policy. This trend was not seen with regard to modern low-intensity operations, such as continue on the Sino-Vietnamese border, in the Korean Peninsula and in many parts of the world beyond this region.

These trends complicate the task of those who have to design and operate forces. How to achieve political and political-military objectives is more open to debate than how to achieve military goals. Military experience is not of such commanding importance in conferring the necessary capabilities to know how to reach such goals. While the contribution of the military professional remains of fundamental importance, the contributions of the political-strategic analyst are increasingly necessary if governments are to receive value for their defence expenditures. We need to do more to develop such analysts in many parts of the world.

The growing costs and risks associated with the use of military force in the Asian-Pacific environment pose special conceptual problems: how to graft the logic and language of European defence strategy onto the strikingly different stem of Asian military logic. This task, while seen as necessary, was clearly very difficult, but a determined start had been made in China. It seems reasonable to expect that the interaction of the two schools will not be all in one direction. Western military specialists should watch the process to learn technical lessons. Western political leaders should study it because its success or failure will affect regional and global balances.

In conclusion, after making a detailed review of the Committee reports which I cannot fully embody in these remarks, I am impressed by the new ground opened in the debates of this Conference. Such a conference was clearly due, although perhaps not overdue. A key component has been the willingness of our Asian participants to enter debate on issues usually the exclusive province of Westerners. This readiness probably did not exist even a few years ago. As one of our Chinese participants observed to me, 'This is the beginning of a beginning – not the end of a beginning'.

Ambassador Okawara's proposals for action suggest that this judgment is correct. We cannot be sure of what we are beginning, but we can say at least that it is a much wider debate and, hopefully, a more interesting one than some of the transatlantic exchanges which, as Henry Kissinger remarked, tend to be so tediously repetitious. I hope that this Conference will set its mark on the work of the Institute for many a year to come.

Index

Abrahamson, Lieutenant-General 195 n8
Abrams, General Creighton 67,72 n36
academic research findings, US restriction 195 n10
adversarial relationship, Soviet Union, with major East Asian powers 134
aerial tankers 43
Afghanistan 14,37,42,79,85,86,87, 89,90,108,115,116,120,127,129, 135 n18,139,157,177,215,218
Africa 219
agricultural production, China 137
agriculture
    mechanization 200
    protectionism 190,201
    taxation 198-9
aid, Soviet Union 109
air attacks, Vietnam 65,66
air defence, extended 29
air forces
    Soviet Union 9,10,172-3
    US, in Pacific 43
air power
    Korean War 63
    Soviet 84
    US 222
Air Self-Defense Force, Japan 165
Airborne brigade, South Vietnam 61
airborne warning and control system aircraft 43,166
aircraft carriers 68-9,105 n16, 129
Alaska 49 n3
Aleutian Archipelago 45,49 n3
Aliyev, G.A. 128
All-Asia Forum 37,38,96,133
Allegheny International 207
alliance relations
    managing 224,225
    patterns of 216-7
allies, United States 215
American Tunaboat Association 59
amphibious assaults, Korean War 63,64
amphibious exercises, Soviet/Vietnamese 104 n2

Amur River islands 115
An-2 low-flying transports 175
Anderson, Kym 211 n3,212 n14
Andropov, Yu.V. 90,100
anti-dumping cases 197
anti-submarine warfare aircraft, Soviet 129
anti-submarine warfare cruisers 10
anti-tank helicopters 165
ANZAC Pact 57
ANZUS 30,48,50,54-6,59 n1,126, 216,229-30,235
ANZUS Treaty 21,35,46,88,133
Aquino, Corazon 57,88,135 n17
Aquino Government 34
Arab-Israeli wars 215
Arkhipov, I.V. 89,134 n17
armed forces
    Australia 56
    South Korea 60
    South Vietnam 60-1
Armistice Agreement, Korea 175
armoured units, North Korea 175
arms agreements, US-Soviet 118
arms control 215
    consultations 218
    East Asia 30,38-9
arms reduction 101
ARVN 60-1,65,67,70 n5,71 n29
ASEAN 17,126,127,139,164,216
    defence effort 35
    defence expenditure 162
    development 231
    Gorbachev policy towards 89, 95,101
    importance for West 216
    Indochina policy 32,37,146
    nuclear-free zone 97,106 n26
    relations with China 159
    relations with Japan 203
    relations with Soviet Union 120,132-3
    relations with US 53-4,110
    security 215
    success 30
    US-Japanese competition in 141
Asia, perceptions of security 1-2
Asian Collective Security Plan 37,133
Asian Security concept 96-8,102
Asian Security Conference 96,230
Atlantic Alliance 19,29,30,214

237

Australia 19,43,44,48,97,98,110,
  124,149,201,220,222,231
    defence efforts 35
    perception of Soviet threat 20
    relations with China 160
    relations with US 55-6
    security 215
    security links 21,30,50
    Soviet trade 128
    US installations 56,58,59
    Vietnam War 62
Australian Labor Party 56
automobile industry,
  protectionism 190
avionics packages, sales to China
  144
AWACS 43,164
Axelrod, Robert 203,212 n22

B-29 Superfortress bomber 71 n20
B-52 bombers 43,68,71 n30,134 n14
Backfire bombers 21,85,172
Badger bombers 22,129
Bahrain 43
balance of power
    East Asia/Pacific 126-9,221
    Western Pacific 168
ballistic missile defence, US-
  Soviet competition 208-9
ballistic missile submarines,
  Soviet 124
Bangladesh 48
barter trade
    agreements 189
    Soviet Union 104 n11,117
Bear G strike aircraft 132
Bear naval intelligence
  collectors 132
Bear reconnaisance and ASW
  aircraft 129
Bell, Coral 23,28 n3,50
Ben Hai River 71 n26
Bergsten, C. Fred 212 n24
Bering Strait 123
Bernstein, Alvin H. 134 n12
Bertram, Christoph 24,28 n1,28 n7
Bien Hoa 71 n28
bilateral agreements
    agricultural prices 201
    defence 50-1
bilateral alliances, US-East Asia
  216
bilateral security treaties 21
Brezhnev Doctrine 4

Brezhnev, L.I. 37,85,93,95,130,
  139,140
Britain 30,55,91,100,101,136
Buchan, David 194 n4
Buchanan, USS 59 n1
Buddhist Revolt, Vietnam War 62-
  3,70 n12
budget deficit, US 234
budgetary restraints, US 48-9
buffer states, Europe 24
Bundesamt fur gewerbliche
  Wirtschaft 194 n4
bureaucracy, Soviet 103,107
Bureyev, M. 154 n7

Cam Ranh Bay 21,22,45,59,72 n33,
  85,93,104 n2,127,130,139
Cambodia 61,67,68,70 n10,72 n36
  see also Kampuchea
Canada 30,217
Caribbean countries 218
cars, export restraints, Japan
  190-1
Carter Adminstration 9
Carter, President Jimmy 11
casualties, Korean and Vietnam
  Wars 72 n41
Cedar Falls 66
Central America 218
Central Highlands, Vietnam 65,67
Chase, Burns Inc. 207
chemical fertilizers 200
chemical warfare capability,
  North Korea 175
Chen Yi 64
Chernenko, K.U. 90,93
Chian 108
Chichkanov, V.P. 122 n2
China 1,19,45,61,68,100,105 n21,
  105 n24,111,156,216,227,234
    ASEAN attitudes to 53,54
    bordering Soviet Union 107-8
    contribution to regional
      security 235-6
    and East Asia 31,37-8,77,136-7
    economic development 125,137-8
    Gorbachev policy towards 90-2,
      102,103
    Japanese loans 167
    Korean War 66,70,75,76-7,181
    modernization 4,5,10,13,14,32,
      33,53,140,150,152-3,177
    as nuclear power 39,209
    nuclear weapons 123

238

China (continued)
  perceptions of security 4-6
  relations with ASEAN 159
  relations with Japan 14,15,
    140,141-5,158
  relations with newly
    industrializing countries
    148-50
  relations with North Korea
    176-7
  relations with regional
    communist powers 145-8
  relations with South Pacific
    countries 160
  relations with Soviet Union
    25,86-7,110,111,114-17,122,
    131,138-41,157
  relations with Taiwan 20
  relations with USA 10,11,46,
    81,87,140,141-2,156-7,174
  relations with Vietnam 110,
    158-9
  role in East Asian security 80
  security issues 37-8
  Soviet fears of 180
  Soviet military build-up
    against 84,99,106 n31,115,
    124,129,135 n18,172,230
  Soviet policy towards 95,97,
    126
Chinese People's Volunteers 158
Christmas Island 56
Chun Doo Hwan, President 33,34,
  88,179
civilian spin-off, SDI 187
Clark Field Air Force Base,
  Philippines 43,46,57,87,93
Cline, William R. 212 n24
Cockburn Sound 58
CoCom 144,154 n16,187-8,193,194
  n4,205
Cocos Island 56
Cohen, Stephen 212 n24
colonialism 76,78,227
Combined Defense Improvement
  Projects 179
COMECON 131,183,188
command structures, Korean and
  Vietnam wars 61-3
commando forces, North Korea 175
commodity prices, fall 192,200-2
Communism, containing 77
Communist movements, Asia 109
Communist parties, Philippines
  98,125

competitiveness, East Asia 199
Comprehensive National Security
  (Japan) 169-70
comprehensive security 181,193
computers 194 n4
confidence-building measures 25-
  6,105 n25,133
Confucian propriety 211 n6
Congress Party, India 121
constitutional change, South
  Korea, prospects 33-4
constitutional constraints,
  Japanese defence 164,168
consumption levels, Japan 203-4
conventional forces, Western
  Europe imbalance 217
conventional war 236
conventional weapons, Japan 210
corps areas, South Vietnam 62-3,
  72 n4
Corson Report 195 n10
costs, technological innovation
  205-6
Council on Economic Priorities,
  US 195 n9
Council for Mutual Economic
  Assistance 131,183
counter-insurgency theory 68
Crowe, Admiral William 135 n19
cruise missiles 171
Cuba 56,131
Cultural Revolution 176,227
current account surplus, Japan
  203
Cyprus 225

Da Nang 21,65,71 n29,85,127
decision-making, ideological
  factors 77
defence agreements, USA 43
defence capability, South Korea
  185
defence co-operation, Japan-US
  168-9,218
defence expenditure 17
  Japan 36,162,174-5,235
  North Korea 175
defence technology, Japan,
  transfer to US 167
Defense White Paper, 1981, Japan
  168
Defense White Paper 1986, Japan
  171 n5

239

demilitarized zone
  Korea 168,175,177
  Vietnam 66,71 n26
democracy, South Korea, prospects 33-4,88
democratization, East Asia 227
Democrats 49
demonstrations, anti-Japanese, China 143
Deng Xiaoping 15,54,115,136,137, 142,150,151,153 n3,153 n5,154 n14,154 n27,176
Denmark 226
Department of Commerce, US 197
Department of Defense, US 48,207
detente 30,177
deterrence 22,23,26-7
developed countries, manufactured imports 192
development, Siberia 173
Dexel Inc. 206
Dibb, Paul 123
Dibb Report, Australian armed forces 56
Diego Garcia 43,45
Diem, Ngo Dinh 62,65
Dien Bien Phu 67,71 n26
diplomacy
  Soviet Union 13,86,130,230
  wars 75
diplomatic activities, Japan 218
distances, Indo-Pacific region 45-6
Dixie Station 72 n33
domestic concerns, Soviet Union 108
domestic policy, Soviet Union 121
domino theory 77,222
Dong Hoi 65
DRAM 197
Drucker, Peter 201,211 n9,212 n13
Drysdale, Peter 212 n13,212 n16, 212 n19
dual-use technologies 187,196 n13
dumping 197

E-3 AWACS 43
East Asia
  alliance with US 216-17
  compared with Western Europe 29-31
  divided states 25-6
  economic development 79-80, 210-11

East Asia (continued)
  economic relations 34-5
  geostrategic location 76-7
  Gorbachev policy towards 102-5
  military balance 35-7
  non-nuclear policies 23
  security 20-1,30-1,221-3
  stability 9-13,215-16,217,219
  US allies 214
  US-Soviet tensions 151-2
  wars 73-82,235
East Germany 20
East-West strategic balance 30
Easter Offensive, Vietnam 67,72 n39,72 n40
Eastern Europe, technology transfer 185-6,188-9
economic aid
  Japan 33,36,218
  US-Philippines 34
  Vietnam 128
economic boom, Taiwan 150
economic development
  China 125,127-8
  East Asia 12-13,79-80,155,210-11,2228
economic dimensions, security 181-4
economic factors, relocation of US bases 47
economic growth
  East Asia 234
  export-led 198
  links with security 229
  South Korea 179
economic influence, Soviet, East Asia/Pacific 127-8
economic interdependence 81,191, 192,193
economic policy, Soviet Union 111-13
economic position, Soviet Union, in Asia 108-9
economic problems
  South Pacific 47-8
  Soviet Union 230-1
economic relations
  China/NICs 148-9
  East Asia 34-5
  Sino-Soviet 140
  US-Japan 222
economic security, East Asia 31, 235
economic slowdown, United States 88

240

economic stability, East Asia 217,218
economic superpowers, East Asia 222
economy, Soviet Union 173
Egypt 36,43,218
Eighth US Army in Korea 63
Eisenhower, President Dwight D. 65
electronics industry 185
energy imports, Japan 161
energy resources, Siberia 124
EPROM 197
escalation, horizontal 26-7
ethnic minorities, Soviet Union 108
European Community 29,191,201
EUSAK 63
evacuation, Saigon 68
Exchanges of Notes, weapons technology, Japan/US 208
expenditure, SDI 187
Export Administration Act 186
Export Administration Regulations 186
export growth, East Asia 34-5
export licences 195 n6
   high technology 207
export processing zones 149
export restraints, cars, Japan 190-1
export-led growth 198
export-led industrialization 199
exports
   high technology
      to Soviet Union 195 n7
      US 186
   Japan-US 17
   primary commodities, Philippines 201
   South Korea 191-2
   voluntary restraints 206

F-1 fighters 210
F-15 interceptors 165
F-16 fighters 167,210
F-18 fighters 210
F-86 Sabre jets 71 n20
Far East Air Forces, US 70 n15
Far East Strategic Theatre, Soviet 124,125-6
Far East Theatre of Military Operations, USSR 84,124
Fencer 9

Fifth Air Force, US 63
financial role, Japan 16-17
I Corps, ARVN 67
1st Cavalry Division 70 n13
1st Marine Division, US 64
fishing agreements, Pacific Islands/Soviet Union 48,88
fishing fleet, Soviet 128
fishing limits 128
Five Principles of Peaceful Co-existence 157
Five-Power Defence Arrangements 3-,21,55-6
Flamm, Kenneth 195 n9
flexible response 169,231-2
Flogger fighters 9,129
Foley, Admiral S.R. 44-5,49 n2
food imports, Japan 161
Force Improvement Plan, South Korea 178
foreign aid
   Japan 218,233
   US 48
Foreign and Commonwealth Office 134 n16
Foreign Military Sales credits 179
foreign policy, China 136-7,216
foreign policy bureaucracy, Soviet 103
foreign trade, China 137
forward offensive strategy (Lehman doctrine) 49 n4,209
four modernizations 73,153 n3,156
Fourth Field Army, Chinese 71 n18
FPDA 21
France 69,91,100,101,165
   nuclear tests 38,55,57
Free World Military Forces 62,66
French Indochina 65
Frost, Ellen L. 211 n2,212 n25
FSX ground-attack fighters 210
Fukushima, Kiyohiko 212 n24
Fukushima, Yasuto 171 n18

Gaddis, John 28 n10
Game Warden 66
Gandhi, Rajiv 96
Gang of Four 227
Garrett, Banning 213 n35,213 n36
gas pipeline, European Soviet 183-4,186
GATT 111,190,201
Gelman, Harry 28 n4,40 n5,83,104 n3,106 n28,122 n7,128

General Dynamics 210
General Motors 191
Geneva Accords 71 n26
Genscher, Hans-Dietrich 194 n1
geographical factors, warfare 77-9
geography
    Indo-Pacific region 45-7
    Korea 61
    South Vietnam 61
geopolitical demands, China 89-90
geopolitical environment, Soviet Union 107-8
geopolitical expansion, Soviet 139
George, Aurelia 212 n15
geostrategic location, East Asia 76-7
Glaser, Bonnie 213 n35,213 n36
Goh Keng Swee 149
gold card system, export licences 195 n6
Gollon, Peter J. 195 n10
Gorbachev, Mikhail 4,7,83-4,85, 87,89-98,100,101,102-3,104 n10, 105 n19,107,110,111,114,115,118, 122,130,131,133-4,139,140,141, 152,157,164,168,177,209,219,230, 231,234
Gordon, Bernard 212 n24
Gould Inc. 206
gradual escalation 76
Great Britain *see* Britain
Gromyko, A.A. 90,100,118,130
ground forces
    balanced reductions 89,92
    proposed withdrawal from South Korea 177
    Soviet 9,128,172
ground operations, Vietnam 66
Ground Self-Defense Force, Japan 165
GTVD 124
Gu Yuanyang 154 n25
Guam 23,43,45,46,53,123,124,129, 134 n14
Guam Doctrine 51,56
guerilla warfare 74,78
guerillas, Philippines 93,120
guided missiles 74
Gulf of Siam 61
Gulf states 30
Gulf of Tonkin 61

Halliday, Fred 212 n20
Hanoi 72 n40,76
hardware, computers 194 n4
Hastings 66
Hawaii 44,45,124,129
Hayami, Yujiro 211 n3,212 n14
Hein, Werner 195 n11,195 n5
helicopter operations, Vietnam 66
helicopters 71 n23,74,129,165,175
Helsinki Accord 20
high technology 17
    East Asia 198
    exports to Soviet Union 195 n7
    information transfer 205-6
    international competition 184-5
    trade surplus, US 185
Ho Chi Minh Trail 66
Ho Dam 154 n23
Hoffmann, Wolfgang 195 n4
Hokkaido 161-2,164,165,166,167, 168
Holbrooke, Richard 104 n8,213 n39
Holst, Johan J. 224
Hong Kong 19,30,38,136,149,150, 151,152
horizontal escalation 26-7,225, 226
Howard, Michael 28 n5,78
Hu Yaobang 104 n114
Huan Xiang 106 n29
Hue 72 n36
Hufbauer, Gary C. 199,211 n4,212 n16
Hunt, Kenneth 31

ICBMs, silos, Siberia 124
Iceland 226
Iceland summit 101
ideological factors, decision-making 77
imports
    US-East Asia 35
    US-Japan 53
Inchon landing 73
independence movements, national 76
India 42,86,102,105 n20,108
    relations with Soviet Union 110,120-1
India-Pakistan War 104 n6
Indian Ocean 30,36,41,46,110,129, 130,164,173

Indochina 31,37,90,126,127,128, 146
Indochina Wars 73,75
  see also Vietnam War
Indonesia 12,16,32,38,41,54,56, 135 n17,201
  economic insecurity 229
  relations with US 58
  Soviet policy 92,127,133
industrial production, China 137
industrial world, China's links with 116
industrialization 198,199
industrialized countries, effects of oil price rise 194 n3
industry, Soviet, modernization 102
INF 14,38,92,97,105 n24,106 n29, 106 n31,218,227,232
  balanced cuts 209
  political effects 98-102
information transfer, technology 205-6
innovation, technological 183
Inoguchi, Takashi 40 n3,197,212 n23,212 n24,212 n26
insurgency, Philippines 42,57,152
intercontintental ballistic missiles, silos, Siberia 124
intermediate-range ballistic missiles 10,22,85,161,172,215
international competition, high technology 184-5
International Energy Agency 194 n3
international system, changing 228
International Trade Commission, US 190
intra-firm trade 190
investment, in China 142
Iran 41,120
Iran-Iraq war 215,218
IRBM 172,215
Irkutsk Air Army 88
Isuzu 191
Ito, Ken'ichi 171 n24
Iwojima 173

Jacobsen, Hanns-Dieter 195 n11, 195 n5,196 n13
Japan 1,23,30,32,46,48,69,91,103, 106 n31,129,135 n13,154 n16,202, 214,236

Japan (continued)
  aid 33,36,218,233
  ASEAN attitudes to 53-4
  bilateral security agreements 31
  car exports to US 190-1
  conventional weapons 210
  defence expenditure 17,18,36, 235
  as economic super-power 173-4
  export growth 34-5
  Gorbachev policy towards 90
  high technology 184,205-6
  imports from LDCs 192
  INF issue 100,209
  international co-operation 203-4,219-20
  intervention in Korea 174
  military co-operation with US 105 n21,125,166
  protectionism 201
  rearmament 227
  relations with China 14,15, 136,137,140,141-5,147,153
  relations with South Korea 33-4
  relations with Soviet Union 84,85,89,110,117-19,122,127, 131,168
  relations with US 16-18,52-3, 123,162
  relations with Western Europe 6,20,101,110,147
  relocation of US bases 46
  role in future crisis 45
  SDI participation 38,187,208-9
  security 11-12,17,39,42,161-2, 164-8,215,218-19,234
  Soviet technology transfer from 111,112
  Soviet threat 172,230
  Soviet trade 102,104 n10,128
  stake in Korea 177-8
  trade relations 190
  trade surplus 31,189
  US bases 166
Japan Defense Agency 164,166,171 n5
Japan Peace Treaty 50
Japan-US Mutual Defense Assistance Agreement 167,208
Japan-US security arrangements 218,219
Japan-US Security Treaty 170

243

Japanese Archipelago 22
Jenkins Bill 35
jet aircraft 74
Johnson, Chalmers 170 n1
Johnson, President L.B. 65,67,70 n2,71 n31
Joint General Staff, South Vietnam 61,62
Junne, Gerd 195 n11

KAL 007 11
Kamchatka Peninsula 18
Kampuchea 102,127
    ASEAN policy 32
    Chinese aid 146
    Soviet Policy 14,37,116,132, 139
    Vietnam settlement terms 97, 105 n17
    Vietnamese invasion 73,75,78, 81,85,86,94,218
    Vietnamese occupation 135 n18, 158-9
    war 89,155,174
    withdrawal of Vietnamese troops 131
    see also Cambodia
Kapitsa, M. 91,98,105 n17,135 n17
Kazakhstan 115
KC-10 aerial tankers 43
KC-135 aerial tankers 43
Keatley, Anne G. 212 n27
Kemp, Geoffrey 41
Keohane, Robert 202,203,212 n20, 212 n21
Khe Sanh 66,67,72 n36
Kiev-class aircraft carriers 10, 22,129
Kim Chong-il 95,147
Kim Chongwi 172
Kim Il Sung 93-6,119,132,145,147, 148,174,176,177
Kiribati 48,56,93
Kirov-class battle cruisers 129
Kissinger, Henry 1,10,222
Kissinger-Haas thesis 231
Kommunist 125
Korea 232
    geography 70 n7
    prospect of war 41,58,151-2
Korea Strait 129
Korean Air Lines 11
Korean Peninsula 31,40 n2,79,96, 104,105 n21,119,146,236

Korean Peninsula (continued)
    military balance 179
    military confrontation 155,158
    security 174-9
    as security issue 32-4
    unification 94,95,235
Korean War 16,41,44,50,54-5,73-5, 76,214,229,234
    compared with Vietnam War 68-9
    geographical factors 77-9
    US casualties 72 n41
    US command structures and leadership 61-3
Kosaka, Masataka 9,28 n6,37,122 n4,169 n1,171 n25
Kovalenko, Ivan 90,103
Krushchev, N.S. 86,111,117,130, 176
Kunsan 209
Ky, Nguyen Cao 62
Kyoto Ceramics Inc. 206
Kyushu 165

labour force, Philippines 46
labour movement, Philippines 120
Lam Son 719 72 n38
Lange, David 21,47,55
Lange Government 51
Laos 61,66,67,68,70 n10,72 n33, 72 n38,102,127,132
Latin America 219
Lawrence, Robert Z. 211 n4
Le Duan 128
Lee Kuan Yew 12,35,54
legislation, US, high technology exports 186
Lehman Doctrine 58-9,233
Lehman, John 49 n4,59
Leninism 109
Lenz, Allen 195 n7
Less Developed Countries 192
Li Peng 131,142
Liberal-Democratic Party, Japan 52,178,208
liberalization, trade 202-5
Libya 56,93
licences, high technology exports 205
limited war 74,75
Lin Piao 64,71 n21
Lincoln, Edward J. 196 n14
Linebacker 72 n40
Linebacker II 72 n40

lines of communication 44
    Soviet threat 172,233
logistics, US, in Pacific 44
long-range ballistic missiles 27
long-range reconnaisance aircraft 22
low-intensity operations 236
Lukacs, John 122 n1

M/IRBM 85
MacArthur, General of the Army Douglas 61-2,63-4,72 n36,74,77
Macau, future of 38
McDonnell Douglas Inc. 207,210
Mack, Andrew 212 n20
McNamara, Robert, S. 71 n31
Makins, Christopher J. 212 n22
Malaysia 16,20,21,25,30,54,55-6, 130,133,135 n17,159,199
Malaysian Communist Party 54
Manchuria 124
Manila Treaty 21,50
manufactured imports, developed countries 192
manufacturing industry, protectionism 198-200
Mao Ze-dong 74,116,137,177
Marcos, President Ferdinand 57, 87-8,93,120
Marcos regime 34
Marine brigade, South Vietnam 61
maritime strategy, US 225,232-3
market socialism 111,112
Market Time 66
markets, access to 202,203
Marxism 109
Maull, Hanns 181,194 n2
mechanization, agriculture 200
Mekong River 70 n10
mercantilism 191,192,193-4
merchant ships, Soviet 128
Mexico 204
microchip agreement, US-Japanese 191
Micronesia 110
Middle East 14,30,161,219
MiG-15 interceptors 71 n20
MiG-23 fighters 22,94,105 n20, 129,132,179
MiG-27 9
Militarily-Critical Technology List 186,189
militarization, Northern Territories 84,85,86

military aid
    Soviet-North Korea 94
    US-South Korea 33-4
    Vietnam 128
military applications, semiconductors 198
Military Assistance Advisory Group, Saigon 65,71 n26
Military Assistance Command, Vietnam 65,70 n11
military balance
    East Asia 22,35-6,216
    Korean Peninsula 180
    North-East Asia 172-3
    US-Soviet 208-9
    Western Europe 221
military build-up
    Eastern Siberia 230,231
    North Korea 151,175-6
    Soviet Union 21-3,26,73,83-5, 114,131,172-3
military capacity
    South Korea 94-5
    Soviet Union 9-10
military co-operation 45
    South Korea-US 179
    US/Japan 168-9
military committments, Pacific 31-2
military competition, US-Soviet 144,151
military confrontation
    Korean Peninsula 155,158
    Soviet Union-China 105 n15
military establishment, Soviet 107
military exercises, Soviet 129
military expenditure
    Japan 53,178
    South Korea 178
military forces
    South Korea 12-13
    United States 123
military leadership, Korean and Vietnam wars 61-3
military power
    Soviet Union 14,126-7,128-31, 139
    United States 110
military presence, United States, Pacific 44-5,152,217
military research and development 186-8,196 n13
military responses, Japan, to security threats 164-7

245

military security 181-3
military situation, Asian-Pacific region 155-6
military strategy, NATO-East Asian differences 217
military strength, super-powers 78-9,221-2
military superpowers, East Asia 221-2
military technology 228,236
military threat, Soviet Union 45, 116,214,215,224,234
mineral resources, Siberia 124
Ministry of International Trade and Industry 17,197
Minnebear Inc. 207
Minsk aircraft carrier 94,177
Misawa 167
MITI 17,197
Mitsubishi Chemicals Inc. 207
Mitsubishi Heavy Industries 210
modernization, China 4,5,10,13, 15,32,33,53,140,150,152-3,177
Mongolia 19,24,37,85,86,89,92, 102,104 n6,109,115,116,120,124, 126,127,128,131,134 n17,157
   troop reductions 115
monitoring, semiconductor production and sales 197
Moynihan, Senator 144
Mujaheddin 115
multilateral agreements, agricultural prices 201
multilateral security consultations 220,223
Mururoa 55,57
Muslim countries 14
Mutual Defence Assistance Agreement, Japan-US 167

Nakagawa, Yatsuhiro 178 n22
Nakasone Government 165
Nakasone, Yasuhiro 1,3,15,36,118, 161,166,168,169,170 n1,235
National Academy of Sciences, US 195 n10
national independence movements 76,78
national interest, perceptions of 121
nationalism, Asia 109
nationalized industries, Mexico 204

NATO 20,23,24,30,34,36,41,50,97, 99,100,106 n25,154 n16,171 n13, 185,215,216,218,226
natural gas project, Sakhalin 118
natural resources, lack of, Japan 161
Naval Aviation, Soviet 85
naval blockade, Korea 63
naval build-up, Soviet 84-5
naval exercises
   Japan-US 166
   Soviet/Vietnamese 104 n2
naval forces
   Korean and Vietnam wars 69
   NATO 36
   Soviet Union 9-10
   US, in Pacific 43-4
naval operations, Vietnam 66
naval power, US 222
naval strategy, US 51
negotiation, wars 75
New Economic Policy, China 116
New Hampshire Ballbearings Inc. 207
New People's Army, Philippines 120
New Zealand 14,19,21,23,30,35,41, 44,48,50,133,145,201,231,232
   non-nuclear policy 38-9,47,51, 59 n1,88,97,98,106 n24,226
   relations with China 160
   relations with US 54-6
   security 215
   Soviet trade 128
New Zealand Labour Party 55,56
newly industrializing countries 112,192,202
   relations with China 148-50
   relations with Japan 203
Ngo Dinh Diem 57
Niagara 67
Niksch, Larry A. 170 n3
Nimitz-class carriers 22
9th Marine Expeditionary Brigade, US 65
Nishihara, Masashi 25-6,28 n8, 161,171 n16,171 n23
Nishimura, Shigeki 171 n10
Nitze-Kvitsinsky Walk in the Woods formula 106 n30
Nixon Doctrine 222
Nixon, President Richard 11,67, 72 n36,72 n40
No Man's Land, Korea 71 n24

non-tariff barriers 189
North Atlantic Assembly 227
North Korea 7, 13, 16, 19, 20, 24, 25, 31, 32, 33, 42, 86, 97, 102, 105 >20, 105 n23,108,109,115, 117,124,128,134 n17,139,145,158, 164
North Korea
  armed forces 44
  attitudes to China 176-7
  Gorbachev policy towards 93-6
  invasion of South Korea 61,63
  military build-up 151,175-6, 233
  military threat 58-9
  relations with China 146-8
  relations with Japan 167-8
  relations with Soviet Union 119,126,132,147-8,235
  terrain and climate 77-8
  unification aims 174
North Korean Peoples' Army 63
North Vietnam 68
North-east Asia 19
North-west Cape, US installations 56,60
Northern Territories 89,90,131, 231
  militarization 84,85,86
Norway 226
Notzold, Jurgen 194 n1,195 n12
nuclear balance 26
nuclear capability, Soviet Union 22,98-102
nuclear deterrence, Soviet 85
nuclear energy, sources 161
nuclear free zones 47-8,56,97,98, 106 n26,106 n27,222-3,231
nuclear munition stores, modernization 209
nuclear strategy
  public concern 216
  United States 22
nuclear tests, France 38,55,57
nuclear weapons 38-9,224,226
    China 123
    Japan 169-70,171 n22
    US Navy 47
Nurrungar, US installations 56
Nye, Joseph S., Jr. 212 n20,221, 223 n1

OECD 189,190,191,192,194 n3
Office for Technology Assessment 213 n33
Official Development Assistance 204
Ogarkov, Marshal N. 125
Ohira, 167
oil, dependence on 30
oil price rise, economics costs 194 n3
oil supplies, security 41,42,45, 47
Okawara, Yoshio 214,221,223,224, 233,236
Okimoto, Daniel 212 n28
Olympic Games, Seoul, 1988 95, 152,174
Oman 43
O'Neill, Robert 227
operations
  Cedar Falls 66
  Game Warden 66
  Hastings 66
  Linebacker 72 n40
  Linebacker II 72 n40
  Market Time 66
  Niagara 67
  Prairie 66
  Rolling Thunder 65
  Sea Dragon 66
  Strangle 71 n25
  Tiger Hound 66
Optical Information Systems 207
Organization of African Unity 29
Organization for Economic Co-operation and Development 191, 193,194,196 n3
over-the-horizon radar 166,169

P-3C anti-submarine patrol aircraft 165
Pacific 36
  military commitments 30-1
Pacific Basin Economic Council 21
Pacific Economic Co-operation Conference 21
Pacific Fleet, Soviet 126,129, 172,176
Pacific Islands 19,50,88,97,126, 127
  Gorbachev policy towards 93
  relations with Soviet Union 56-7,128,132-3

Pacific power, US as 69
Pacific sea lanes, patrolling,
  Japan 169
pacification, Vietnam 66,67,72
  n34
Pakistan 36,42,86,103,120,218
Palau island 46
Papua New Guinea 56
Park Chung Hee, President 12
party relations
  China-Eastern Europe 104 n12
  China-Soviet Union 91
Patrick, Hugh 212 n18
Patriot surface-to-air missiles
  166
Peace Accords, Vietnam War 67
Peace Problems Study group 170 n1
Pearl Harbor 41,70 n1
peasant armies 235
PECC 21
Pei Monong 154 n9,154 n25
Peng Teh-huai 71 n21,71 n22
People's Liberation Army 94
Pershing II 169
Persian Gulf 36,41,42,45,47,173
Philippine Treaty 43
Philippines 2,16,20,25,31,45,50,
  53,54,104,113,135 n17,222,227,232
  insurgency 42,57,152
  Japanese aid 218
  political stability 87-8,133,
    215-16,222
  primary commodity exports 201
  relations with China 159
  relations with Soviet Union
    93,120
  relations with US 57
  role in future crisis 45
  security 34,215
  US bases 35,43,46-7,48,49,98,
    105 n19,123,124,172
Pine Gap, US installations 56
Pleiku 65,72 n28
Poland 218
political change, South Korea 14,
  16,33-4,57-8,96
political confrontation,
  East/West 29
political dimensions, technology
  transfer 188-9
political effects, INF 98-102
political factors, relocation of
  US bases 46-8
political influence, Soviet, in
  East Asia 109,127

political security 185-6
political stability
  East Asia 152,218,219
  Third World 215-16
political structure, South
  Vietnam 61
political succession, China, post-
  Deng 136
political trends, Soviet Union
  113-14
Pollack, Jonathan 122 n6,136
Polomka, Peter 211 n7
Popular Forces, South Vietnam 70
  n6
Portugal 226
Prairie 66
primary commodities, prices 35,
  200-2
prisoner's dilemma 203
protectionism 31,34,35,152,193,
  222,229-30,235
  agriculture 201
  manufacturing industry 198-200
  and security 189-200
  technological 206-10
  US 88,105 n18,197
public opinion, security policies
  216
Pusan Perimeter 70 n14
Putka, Gary 195 n10
Pye, Lucian W. 211 n6
Pyongyang 64,69

Qui Nhon 65
quotas, trade 194

railway project, Sino-Soviet 115
Rakhmanin, Oleg 103
Rangoon, bombing incident 95,179
raw material resources, Siberia
  124
raw materials, prices 200-1
Reagan Administration 54-5,58,
  183,195 n10,233
Reagan, President Ronald 9,49,52,
  91-2,101,177,206
rearmament, Japan 6,227
reassurance 27,222-3
reconaissance 27
Regional Forces, South Vietnam
  70 n6
Reischauer, Edwin 52
Republic of Korea Treaty 43

248

research and development
   Japan 205
   military 186-8,196 n13
research findings, US
  restrictions 195 n10
Research Institute for Peace and
  Security 212 n12
revolutions, Asia 228
Reykjavik Summit 38,106 n31
Ridgway, Lieutenant General
  Matthew B. 64,74
Rimpac naval exercises 166
riverine operations, Vietnam 66
Rode, Reinhard 195 n9
Rolling Thunder 65
Ross, Edward 154 n17
Rothbacker, Albrecht 196 n15
Rowen, Henry 26,28 n9
Royal Navy 63
Russia 176
Russo-Japanese War 176
Ryabov, 135 n17

Sa Benwang 154 n18
SA-3 surface-to-air missiles 94,
  105 n20
Sabre jets 71 n20
Saigon 67,68,69,71 n28,72 n36
Sakanaka, Tomohisha 171 n21
Sakhalin 164
Sakhalin natural gas project 118
SAM 99,166
Sapsford, David 211 n9
Sato, Seizaburo 19,122 n3
Saudi Arabia 43
Scalapino, Robert A. 107,122 n3
Schott, Jeffrey 212 n16
SDI 17,27,37,38,101,171 n18,186-8,195 n12,195 n8,230
   Japanese participation 208-9
Sea Dragon 66
Sea of Japan 59,61,164
Sea of Okhotsk 17,23,59,84,85,
  104 n1,118,164
sea lanes, patrolling, Japan 169
SEATO 50
security
   convergence of interests 228
   East Asia 221-3
   economic relations and 34-5,
    181-4
   Japan 161-2,164-8,204
   Korean Peninsula 174-9
   links with economic growth 229

security (continued)
   protectionism and 189-93
   Siberia 125-6
   technological protectionism
    206-10
   technology transfer 185-6
security co-operation 26-7
   East Asia-Atlantic Alliance
    214
   Japan-NATO 219-20
Security Council, United Nations
  63
security interests
   East Asia 20-1
   Western Europe 20
security policies
   Japan 218-19
   South Korea 209-10
   Soviet Union 114
security relationship, US-Japan
  222
security role, Japan 17
Security and Technology Experts'
  Meeting 185
Segal, Gerald 122 n5
Self-Defense Forces, Japan 36,
  162,165-6,173,178,210,218
semiconductors, Japan-US
  agreement 197
Seoul 63,69,71 n16,175,229
Seven-Nation Summits 193
Seventh Fleet 70 n11,110
Sharp, Admiral Ulysses S. Grant
  62
Shevardnadze, E.A. 37,90,118,131,
  132,134 n17
Shimizu, Ikutaro 171 n22
Siberia 21,92,102,104 n10,104 n5,
  122 n2,123-5
   development 112,131,173
   economic importance 231
   security 125-6
   Soviet forces 84
Simmons, Brigadier-General Edwin
  60
Simon, Denis Fred 154 n15
Singapore 12,21,30,54,55-6,128
   relations with China 148,149,
    159
Sino-Japanese Treaty of Peace and
  Friendship 158
SLBM 84,104 n1,172
Sneider, Daniel 213 n33
Sneider, Richard L. 40 n1

249

software, computers 194 n4
Solomon, Richard 28 n6,122 n4
Solovyov, S.M. 123
Somalia 43
South China Sea 22,46,61,70 n9,
   70 n11,72 n33,129,164
South Korea 7,19,20,23,25,40 n2,
   41,86,97,105 n21,105 n23,123,166,
   214,222,227,234
   confrontation with North Korea
      20,31,42,162
   defence 44,60,94-5,162,178,179
   domestic stability 222
   economic development 12-13,179
   exports 191-2
   Japanese aid 167,218
   political change 14,16,33-4,
      57-8,96
   pressure for trade
      liberalization 203
   protectionism 201
   reactions to protectionism
      199-200,203
   relations with China 146,148-
      50
   relations with US 50,88,110,
      127,164
   security 11-12,39,209-10,215,
      217,229
   Soviet policy 119
   Soviet threat 172
   US military support 32-3
   Vietnam War 62
South Pacific 231,232
   Gorbachev policy towards 92-3
   nuclear tests 38
   nuclear-free zones 106 n27
   US role 47-8
South Vietnam 57,68
   armed forces 60-1,65,67,70 n5,
      71 n29
   collapse 51
   war in 65-8
South-east Asia 19,47
   Gorbachev policy towards 92-3
South-west Asia 219
Soviet aid, Vietnam 131
Soviet Central Asia 128
Soviet Far East 172
Soviet forces, Chinese border
   104 n6
Soviet Irkutsk Air Army 85
Soviet Naval Squadron 129

Soviet navy
   access to high seas 227
   build-up 90,98
Soviet Pacific Fleet 9-10,21-2,
   126,129,172,176
Soviet Union 20,35,51,68,97,152,
   189,195 n7,221
   Asian policy 20-1,37,40 n5,
      108-11,119-21,126-30,155,219
   and Asian security 1,7-8
   diplomacy 13,86,130
   economy 111-13,173,230-1
   geostrategic position 17,20,
      107-8,221
   intervention in Korea 174
   military build-up 9-10,21-3,
      26,73,83-5,114,131,172-3
   military power 14
   military presence in Pacific
      41
   military threat 45,214,215,224
   nuclear capability 98-102
   prospects in region 130-3
   proximity to Japan 161-2
   relations with China 86-7,114-
      17,138-41
   relations with East Asian
      countries 24-5
   relations with India 110
   relations with Japan 122-4,175
   relations with North Korea 93-
      6,119,126,132,147-8,176,233,
      235
   relations with Pacific Islands
      56-7
   security policies 114
   support for Vietnam 86,119-20,
      128,131-2,164
   technology transfer to 189
   threat to Japan 166
   threat to USA 42
   Vietnamese bases 21,22,45,59,
      85,93,104 n2,127,129-30,134
      n14,139
   Western European attitudes
      towards 30
Soya Straits 17,169
Spain 226
special economic zones 149
SS-4 missiles 170
SS-20 missiles 2,10,21,22,38,85,
   86,90,92,99-101,104 n4,104 n5,
   105 n16,106 n29,106 n30,106 n31,
   118,161,169,170,171 n24,172,215,
   225

250

SSBN 84,104 n1
Stalin, J.V. 130
Stalinist economic order 115
Stephan, John J. 122 n2
Stiltner, Ken 195 n7
Strangle 71 n25
strategic arms limitation
  agreement 114
strategic balance, East-West 30
strategic bases, Philippines 35
strategic confrontation,
  East/West 29
Strategic Defense Initiative 17,
  27,37,38,101,161,171 n18,188-90,
  195 n8,208,213 n33,230
strategic factors, relocation of
  US bases 46
strategic weapons, Vietnam war
  68-70
strategy, US, in Pacific 44-5
students, Chinese, US
  universities 144
Su-24 9
Subic Bay Base 46,57,87,93
submarine-launched ballistic
  missiles 23,171
submarines, Soviet 22,59,129,134
  n11
Suez Canal 130
Suharto, President 12
Sumitomo Metallurgical
  Engineering 207
Sun Tzu 81
Superfortress bomber 71 n20
superpowers 76,78-9,80,221-2
  relations with China 138-45
surface-to-air missiles 94,166
surveillance 27
Suslov, 140
Suzuki 191
Suzuki, (Prime Minister) 52,165
Syngman Rhee, President 16,62,63

tactical air power
  Soviet 84
  US 69
tactical zones, ARVN 70 n4,70 n5
Taiwan 19,20,26,31,37,43,127,144,
  149,151,152,234
  economic boom 150
  pressure for trade
    liberalization 203
  protectionism 201
  relations with Japan 167-8

Taiwan (continued)
  relocation of US bases 46
  security problems 39
  settlement of issue 156-7
  trade with China 148
Taiwan Strait 79
Tan Eng Bok, Georges 104 n2
Task Force 77 63,72 n33
Tchepone 72 n38
technical assistance, Soviet, to
  China 141
technological development,
  Chinese industry 142
technological innovation, costs
  205-6
technological protectionism 206-
  10
technology
  effect on warfare 79,80
  promoting change 228
  security and 183,197-8
technology transfer 183,184-9
  Japan-Soviet Union 111,112
  Japanese contribution 204
  restriction 230
  Soviet Union 215
  to China 142,143-4,154 n14
telecommunications 194 n4
X Corps, US Army 63,64
territorial issues, East Asia 25-
  6
terrorism 49
Tet offensive 67
textile imports, US 35
Thailand 20,31,32,42,43,50,70
  n10,86,105 n17,105 n18,133,135
  n17
  economic insecurity 229
  Japanese aid 218
  relations with China 159
  US ally 53
Thi, General Nguyen Chanh 70 n12
Thich Tri Quang 70 n12
Thieu, Nguyen Van 62,67
Third World 138,144,194
  effects of protectionism 191-3
  political stability 215-16
38th Parallel 63,64
Three Non-Nuclear Principles 52,
  169
Tiger Hound 66
Tokyo 161
Tokyo Round 201
Tomahawk cruise missiles 169

251

Tonkin Gulf Resolution 60,70 n2
Tornado fighters 210
trade
    China-Japan 158
    China-Soviet Union 91
    liberalization 202-5
    and security 197-8
    Soviet, with East Asia 102,128
trade agreement, Sino-Soviet 141
trade balance
    East Asia-West 34-5
    Japan 31,189
    US 18,185,234
trade deficit, China, with Japan 142-3
trade disputes, East Asia-US 199-200
Trade Enhancement Act 206
trade wars 190
trading partners, Japan 203
Trans-Siberian Railway 105 n15, 126
troop reductions, Mongolia 115
Truman, President Harry S. 60,62, 63,64,65,70 n3
Tsarist Russia 176
TU-16 *Badger* 129,132
TU-95 *Bear* 129,132
Tumen River 70 n7
tuna fishing, Pacific Islands 88, 92
tunnel warfare 74
Turkey 218
TVD, Soviet 84,124
24th Division, US 63,70 n13
25th Division, US 70 n13
256K DRAM 197

unification, Korea 174,179
United Nations, forces in Korea 61,71 n17
United Nations Commission for Trade and Development 192
United Nations Security Council 63
United States 1,14,17,29,30,103, 115,122,138,164,234
    allies, East Asia/Pacific 50-9,127,215
    criticisms of 232-3
    economic slowdown 91
    end of hegemony 195-6
    high technology 184,185,186, 205-6

United States (continued)
    imports from LDCs 192
    interests in Asia 2-3,42-3,155
    intervention in Korea 174
    involvement in Asia 3-4
    Japanese car imports 190-1
    Kampuchea policy 32
    Korean policy 32-3
    military committments in Pacific 30-1,35-6,43-4,152
    nuclear strategy 22
    Pacific strategy 44-5
    policy directions 48-9
    political influence in Asia 87-9
    pressure for trade liberalization 203-5
    protectionism 34,35,189,199-200,201
    relations with China 10,11,79, 87,136,140,141-5,174
    relations with Philippines 34
    relationship with East Asia 21
    relationship with Japan 6,16-18
    South Korean ally 177
    technological protectionism 206-10
    trade relations 190
US Air Force 43,66,209
US Department of Defense 134 n2, 171 n11
US Far East Air Forces 70 n15
US Marines 71 n29,71 n30
US Navy 43-4,84-5
    nuclear weapons 47
US Pacific Fleet 45,49 n1
US Seventh Fleet 63
US Special Security Team 211 n6
US troops, withdrawal from South Korea 11,12
US-Japan security arrangements 217
US-Japan Security Treaty 17,43, 173
US-Philippines security arrangements 217
US-Soviet arms agreements 118

Van Fleet, General James 64
Vanuatu 56,93
Viet Cong 62,65-6,71 n28,72 n34
Vietnam 1,9,11,14,20,21,22,24,25, 31,32,37,42,102,104 n6,108,109-10,114,116,126,127,134,136

Vietnam (continued)
  ASEAN attitudes to 54
  and future of Kampuchea 145-6
  geography 70 n9
  invasion of Kampuchea 73,75,
    78,79,81,85,86,94,218
  occupation of Kampuchea 31,42,
    135 n18,139,158-9
  proposed Kampuchea settlement
    97,105 n17
  relations with China 110,146,
    158-9
  revolution 227
  Soviet bases 21,22,45,59,85,
    93,104 n2,127,129-30,135 n14,
    139
  Soviet support 89,119-20,128,
    131-2,164
  terrain and climate 77-8
  war in Kampuchea 89
Vietnam War 41,44,50,65-8,76,177,
  214,227,235
  compared with Korean War 68-9
  geographical factors 77-8
  US casualties 72 n41
  US command structures and
    leadership 61-3
  see also Indochina Wars
Vietnamization 67,72 n36,72 n37
Vladivostok 161
VSTOL aircraft 22

Wake Island 64
Wakkanai 164
Walk in the Woods formula 106 n30
Walker, Lieutenant General Walton
  63,64
Wallace, Mike 153 n5
Wallerstein, Mitchell B. 195 n10
Wanandi, Jusuf 122 n3
warfare, effects of technology
  79,80
wars, East Asia 73-82,235
Warsaw Pact 20,23,24,217
water management projects, Sino-
  Soviet 115
Watkins, Admiral 59
Watts, William 211 n8
weapons, acquisition, Japan 165-6
weapons systems, Soviet 183
Weapons Technology Exchange of
  Notes, Japan/US 208
Wei Yangshen 154 n25
Weinberger, Caspar 36,171 n6

West Germany 20,27,36,119,188,
  196 n4
  defence budget 165
  SDI participation 187,208
Western Australia 45
  relocation of US bases 46-7
Western Europe 19,138,217
  compared with East Asia 29-31
  high technology competition
    184
  imports from LDCs 192
  NATO membership 216
  security 20,29-31,101,225
  trade relations 190
Western Pacific 164
Westmoreland, General William 62,
  67,70 n11,71 n31,72 n36
Whiting, Allen S. 122 n2
William, Winston 211 n2
Williamsburg Summit 101,161,218
Wolf, Charles, Jr 153 n2
Wonsan 94
World Bank 212 n10,212 n11
world order, post-World War II 76

Xie Wenqing 154 n26
Xinjiang 115

Yakovlev, Aleksander 103
Yalta summit 76
Yalu River 70 n7,71 n25
Yankee Station 72 n33
Yao Wenbin 155
Yellow Sea 61,177
yen, stabilization 197
Yuko, Kurihara 165

Zhang Jingyi 73
Zhao Ziyang 153 n1,153 n6,154
  n19,154 n24
Zheng Tuobin 143,154 n13
Zhou Enlai 10,176

253